THE
PASSION
TRANSLATION

THE BOOKS OF

JOSHUA,
JUDGES,
and
RUTH

courage to conquer

BroadStreet
P U B L I S H I N G

A NOTE TO READERS

It would be impossible to calculate how many lives have been changed forever by the power of the Bible, the living Word of God! My own life was transformed because I believed the message contained in Scripture about Jesus, the Savior.

To hold the Bible dear to your heart is the sacred obsession of every true follower of Jesus. Yet to go even further and truly understand the Bible is how we gain light and truth to live by. Did you catch the word *understand*? People everywhere say the same thing: "I want to understand God's Word, not just read it."

Thankfully, as English speakers, we have a plethora of Bible translations, commentaries, study guides, devotionals, churches, and Bible teachers to assist us. Our hearts crave to know God—not just to know about him, but to know him as intimately as we possibly can in this life. This is what makes Bible translations so valuable, because each one will hopefully lead us into new discoveries of God's character. I believe God is committed to giving us truth in a package we can understand and apply, so I thank God for every translation of God's Word that we have.

God's Word does not change, but over time languages definitely do, thus the need for updated and revised translations of the Bible. Translations give us the words God spoke through his servants, but words can be poor containers for revelation because they leak! Meaning is influenced by culture, background, and many other details. Just imagine how differently the Hebrew authors of the Old Testament saw the world three thousand years ago from the way we see it today!

Even within one language and culture, meanings of words change from one generation to the next. For example, many contemporary Bible readers would be quite surprised to find that unicorns are mentioned nine times in the King James Version (KJV). Here's one instance in Isaiah 34:7: "And the unicorns shall come down with them, and the bullocks with the bulls; and their land shall be soaked with blood, and their dust made fat with fatness." This isn't a result of poor translation, but rather an example of how our culture, language, and understanding of the world has shifted over the past few centuries. So, it is important that we have a modern English text of the Bible that releases revelation and truth into our hearts. The Passion Translation (TPT) is committed to bringing forth the potency of God's Word in relevant, contemporary vocabulary that doesn't distract from its meaning or distort it in any way. So many people have told us that they are falling in love with the Bible again as they read TPT.

We often hear the statement, "I just want a word-for-word translation that doesn't mess it up or insert a bias." That's a noble desire. But a word-for-word translation would be nearly unreadable. It is simply impossible to translate one Hebrew word for one English word. Hebrew is built from triliteral consonant roots. Biblical Hebrew had no vowels or punctuation. And Koine Greek, although wonderfully articulate, cannot always be conveyed in English by a word-for-word translation. For example, a literal word-for-word translation of the Greek in Matthew 1:18 would be something like this: "Of the but Jesus Christ the birth thus was. Being betrothed the mother of him, Mary, to Joseph, before or to come together them she was found in belly having from Spirit Holy."

Even the KJV, which many believe to be a very literal translation, renders this verse: "Now the birth of Jesus Christ was on this wise: When as his mother Mary was espoused to Joseph, before they came together, she was found with child of the Holy Ghost."

This comparison makes the KJV look like a paraphrase next to a strictly literal translation! To some degree, every Bible translator is forced to move words around in a sentence to convey with meaning the thought of the verse. There is no such thing as a truly literal translation of the Bible, for there is not an equivalent language that perfectly conveys the meaning of the biblical text. Is it really possible to have a highly accurate and highly readable English Bible? We certainly hope so! It is so important that God's Word is living in our hearts, ringing in our ears, and burning in our souls. Transferring God's revelation from Hebrew and Greek into English is an art, not merely a linguistic science. Thus, we need all the accurate translations we can find. If a verse or passage in one translation seems confusing, it is good to do a side-by-side comparison with another version.

It is difficult to say which translation is the "best." "Best" is often in the eyes of the reader and is determined by how important differing factors are to different people. However, the "best" translation, in my thinking, is the one that makes the Word of God clear and accurate, no matter how many words it takes to express it.

That's the aim of The Passion Translation: to bring God's eternal truth into a highly readable heart-level expression that causes truth and love to jump out of the text and lodge inside our hearts. A desire to remain accurate to the text and a desire to communicate God's heart of passion for his people are the two driving forces behind TPT. So for those new to Bible reading, we hope TPT will excite and illuminate. For scholars and Bible students, we hope TPT will bring the joys of new discoveries from the text and prompt deeper consideration of what God has spoken to his people. We all have so much more to learn and discover about God in his holy Word!

You will notice at times we've italicized certain words or phrases. These portions are not in the original Hebrew, Greek, or Aramaic manuscripts but are implied from the context. We've made these implications explicit for the sake of narrative clarity and to better convey the meaning of God's Word. This is a common practice by mainstream translations.

We've also chosen to translate certain names in their original Hebrew or Greek forms to better convey their cultural meaning and significance. For instance, some translations of the Bible have substituted James for Jacob and Jude for Judah. Both Greek and Aramaic manuscripts leave these Hebrew names in their original forms. Therefore, this translation uses those cultural names.

The purpose of The Passion Translation is to reintroduce the passion and fire of the Bible to the English reader. It doesn't merely convey the literal meaning of words. It expresses God's passion for people and his world by translating the original, life-changing message of God's Word for modern readers.

We pray this version of God's Word will kindle in you a burning desire to know the heart of God, while leaving an impact on the church for years to come.

Please visit **ThePassionTranslation.com** for more information.

Brian Simmons and the translation team

ABOUT THE TRANSLATOR

Dr. Brian Simmons is known as a passionate lover of God. After a dramatic conversion to Christ, Brian knew that God was calling him to go to the unreached people of the world and present the gospel of God's grace to all who would listen. With his wife, Candice, and their three children, he spent nearly eight years in the tropical rain forest of the Darien Province of Panama as a church planter, translator, and consultant. Having been trained in linguistics and Bible translation principles, Brian assisted in the Paya-Kuna New Testament translation project, and after their ministry in the jungle, Brian was instrumental in planting a thriving church in New England (U.S.). He is the lead translator for The Passion Translation Project and travels full time as a speaker and Bible teacher. He has been happily married to Candice since 1971 and boasts regularly of his three children and nine grandchildren.

Follow The Passion Translation at:

Facebook.com/passiontranslation

Twitter.com/tPtBible

Instagram.com/passiontranslation

For more information about the translation project please visit:

ThePassionTranslation.com

THE PASSION TRANSLATION

THE BOOK OF

JOSHUA

a new beginning

BroadStreet
PUBLISHING

JOSHUA

Introduction

AT A GLANCE

Author: Traditionally Joshua
Audience: Originally Israel, but this theological history speaks to everyone
Date: 1451–1426 BC
Type of Literature: Theological history
Major Themes: Land of promise, covenant and obedience, typology of Christ, and conquest and God's character
Outline:
Entering the Land — 1:1–5:12
Conquering the Land — 5:13–12:24
Dividing the Land — 13:1–22:34
Farewell and Burial in the Land — 23:1–24:33

ABOUT JOSHUA

A new beginning stretches out before us! When we read the book of Joshua, we learn the ways of God: how he moves us forward, how we triumph over our enemies, and how we do the impossible. Joshua, a former slave in Egypt, became the leader of God's people after the death of Moses. A generational transfer took place as a younger generation rose with fresh vision, a bold faith, and renewed passion to possess all that God had given them. All this and more is contained in the sacred book you have in your hand, the book of Joshua.

Joshua is the hinge of Israel's history. The wilderness wandering was now over as the promised land was before them. The manna ceased, the Jordan was behind them, a new leader rose, and a new beginning opened up for the people of God. Walled cities and fierce enemies are no match for the living God. But it would still require a faith-filled people to move in and possess what God had given to them.

As the sixth book of the Bible, Joshua begins the section of Israel's history. Bundled together, Joshua through Esther make up the biblical, inspired history of the Jewish people. Our Jewish brothers and sisters call this section of the Bible (Joshua, Judges, Samuel, Kings) the "Former Prophets." Since this section of the Bible can be considered prophecy, Joshua prophesies to the church today (see 1 Cor. 10:11), giving us instruction for how to live before God. The truths of Joshua are as much for today as the teachings of Paul or Peter. These Former Prophets lay out in front of us the secrets of victory.

The title Former Prophets demonstrates the prophetic nature of God's dealing with his people and also the nations. It is the story of God's redemption by the power of his mighty hand and empowering Spirit, giving revelations, performing signs and wonders, and testifying to Yahweh's faithfulness in all things.

The book of Joshua shows us that we can go into the promised land of what God wants us to be. We can become the delight of God. The book of Joshua is the Ephesians of the Old Testament. Joshua was blessed with every earthly blessing in the land of Canaan. We are blessed with every heavenly blessing in Christ (see Eph. 1:3). Joshua lays out a road map to victory for us so that we can advance into our destiny; and our true destiny is for the better Joshua, Jesus, to lead us into his kingdom (see Eph. 1:13–14).

PURPOSE

The book of Joshua contains an important and fascinating part of Israel's history. It describes the transition of God's chosen people from wilderness wanderers to courageous conquerors. Joshua is written as more than history. It is a "sermon" meant to activate believers today. We have an inheritance that we must fight for in faith. We have every blessing heaven contains (see Eph. 1:3), but we must claim and implement those blessings.

The church today needs the courage to conquer. Many modern believers act more like prisoners of war instead of passionate conquerors. Followers of Jesus must see themselves as soldiers in a disciplined army prepared to fight spiritual battles. The book of Joshua is a book of conquest, emboldening the church to move from passivity to passion. Like Joshua, our battles are spiritual battles, for we fight not against flesh and blood but against forces of darkness (see footnote on Josh. 24:11).

AUTHOR AND AUDIENCE

Joshua was one of the twelve spies who first went into the land of Canaan. Along with Caleb, Joshua was the only one to give a good report. Indeed, Israel recognized Joshua as their prophet and something similar to a "king,"[a] although they had not yet come into possession of their kingdom. According to the Jewish historian Josephus, Joshua succeeded Moses when he was eighty-five. He was a military commander who conquered seven nations (kingdoms) in seven years. He died at the age of one hundred and ten and was buried in Timnath Serah.

Joshua's original name was Hoshea, but Moses changed it to *Yehoshua* (see Num. 13:8, 16), which can be translated as "Yahweh is salvation" or "Yahweh save." In fact, the name Yehoshua is nearly the Hebrew equivalent of the name Jesus (Yeshua). The Greek word for Jesus is *Iesous* and means the same as the name Joshua. One could almost say there is a book in the Bible named *Jesus*. That's one book I would want to read, wouldn't you?

Although certain portions were added after Joshua's death, translators believe the author was Joshua himself for several reasons: Certain episodes of the book

---

a See Rashi, *Yoma* 73b; Rambam, *Hil. Melachim* 1:3, 3:8; *Hil. Sanhedrin* 18:6.

bear the mark of an eyewitness, such as where the author states "we" passed through the waters on dry ground in chapter three; Joshua's description of Canaanite wickedness parallels the well-known Ras Shamra tablets, written in Joshua's time; Joshua's list of boundaries for the twelve tribes (see Josh. 13–19) accurately reflect the known situation of Canaan prior to the Jewish monarchy; descriptions of certain cities, such as Jerusalem still being a Jebusite city (see 15:63) and Gezer still being a Canaanite city (see 16:10), imply the author was living in the time of Joshua; and the author seems to write about things that happened in his lifetime, not about anything happening previously.

For the people of Israel, the book of Joshua was an important "hinge book" between the Torah and Prophecy. This conquering military hero who ushered in the salvation of Yahweh wrote this book to a people wrestling with establishing the nation in the land Yahweh provided, understanding God's divine revelation-word of promise, and waiting for the fullness of his provision and promises to be realized. Similarly, we, too, wait for Yahweh's promises to be fully realized, awaiting the day of his promised-land rest!

MAJOR THEMES

The Land of Promise and Promised Gift. The book of Joshua is the book of the land. It is this long-ago-promised gift of a specific land by Yahweh that is the central animating theme. The verses offered just after Israel takes possession of the land could be a fair summary of the entire book: "So Yahweh gave Israel all the land he had promised their ancestors. They took possession of the land and settled there. Yahweh kept his promise and gave them peace in the land. . . . Not one of their enemies could stand against them. Yahweh didn't break a single promise that he made to the people of Israel" (21:43–45).

This central theological theme in Joshua is intimately connected with Israel's national and ethnic identities and to Yahweh's fulfillment of his promises to the patriarchs Abraham, Isaac, and Jacob to gift their generations such a land of promise. We find six aspects of this gift throughout the book of Joshua: (1) God promised the land-gift to the forefathers; (2) God gave the gift to Israel; (3) Joshua divided it as an inheritance for the people; (4) this gift was closely connected to the land on the east side of the Jordan River; (5) it would not be difficult to take from those still living there because God had caused its inhabitants to tremble with fear; and (6) the land-gift was filled with other gods who tempted Israel.

The promised land wasn't just *land*; it was a *gift*. A gift a good Father (Yahweh) gave to his beloved children (Israel). God promised this gift from the day he called out the man (Abraham) who would birth the nation, and he ultimately fulfilled that promise in this wonderful book. But God also extends this gift to committed hearts and obedient hands today. The book illustrates the tragedy of neglecting this gift, offering a foreshadowing of Israel's wandering ways that would ultimately lead to exile from the land and separation from the gift of Yahweh.

Covenant and the Obedience of God's People. The promised land given to the children of Israel as a promised gift is at the heart of a covenant Yahweh made with them generations ago. Genesis 17:7–9 outlines the terms of this covenant:

"I will be your children's God, just as I am your God.
I will give to you and your seed
the land to which you have migrated.
The entire land of Canaan will be yours and your descendants'
as an everlasting possession.
 And I will be their God forever!"

 God explained to Abraham, "Your part of the covenant is to obey its terms, you and your descendants throughout the ages."

Throughout the book of Joshua, the ark of the covenant went before the people as a constant reminder of this relationship, symbolizing Yahweh's mercy, power, and holiness. At every juncture of Israel's journey in this book—from the floodwaters of the Jordan to the gates of Jericho and to the covenant's renewal at Mount Ebal—they were to march in a new manner, with their eyes on the ark and their hearts set on Yahweh.

Obedience was at the core of this covenantal relationship, realized and renewed in Joshua. The people who still lived in the land, with their pagan gods and pagan ways, constantly challenged the obedience of God's people. Israel was to worship and obey Yahweh alone, practices which Joshua outlined in several ways: they were to meditate on the Torah day and night, learn the commands of Yahweh, practice circumcision, keep the Passover, worship at the place of Yahweh's choosing, and obey the written laws of Yahweh.

Perhaps the climax of the covenant in the book comes at the end, just before Joshua's death was reported. He led the people in renewing their relationship with Yahweh at Shechem and put into the starkest terms possible Israel's need to fully embrace their covenantal relationship with Yahweh and obey him completely: "Make your decision today which gods you will worship—the gods which your ancestors worshiped in Mesopotamia or the gods which the Amorites worship in the land where you are now living—but I and my family, we will give our lives to worship and serve Yahweh" (Josh. 24:15).

The ark not only beautifully illustrates God's covenant with Israel, it is also a wonderful picture of Jesus Christ, who "is the catalyst of a better covenant which contains far more wonderful promises" (Heb. 8:6). The power of Christ within us enables us to pass over into our full inheritance. Jesus, our forerunner, leads us in, and we are to join with the same obedient voices as those of Israel, declaring "We, too, will worship and serve Yahweh, for he alone is our God" (Josh. 24:18).

The Typology of Jesus. To read the book of Joshua and not see Jesus would be unfortunate. Joshua is a clear type of Jesus, for he took the Israelites into a realm that the law (Moses) was unable to experience. The church father Eusebius offers this connection between the name Joshua and the name Jesus:

Moses was inspired by the divine Spirit to foresee clearly the name of Jesus; and he deemed this name of special honor. Till it was made known to Moses, it had never been on man's lips before. He bestowed the name of Jesus on him first of all, and only on him, who he knew would succeed, in type and symbol, after his death. His successor had not previously been called Jesus, but his parents had called him Hoshea.[a]

For the believer, the typology of Joshua is apparent. First, the name Joshua is wonderfully similar to Jesus (Yeshua). Secondly, the promised land for the follower of Christ becomes a picture of the untold blessings that are ours in Christ (see Eph. 1:3). Canaan was a fertile land. It symbolizes the abundant life of the victorious believer. Canaan had to be conquered, and so our promises and blessings must be claimed by faith. The law of Moses did not attain Canaan but only the grace of God did. Heathen hordes inhabited Canaan, and God's people had to purge the land of the powers of darkness and idolatry, just as we must purge our hearts (see Eph. 6:12; Heb. 9:23).

The miracle-crossing of the Jordan River typifies crossing over into a life of abundance and union with Jesus Christ. Our Savior was the One who descended into judgment for our sins. The Jordan was miraculously rolled back all the way to a town called Adam; Jesus rolled back the waters of judgment all the way back to the sin of Adam. The rending of the Jordan corresponds to the rending of the veil in the Holy of Holies when Jesus was crucified (see 2 Cor. 3:1–18; Heb. 10:20). We are now those who cross over into union and intimacy with God.

Additionally, the pushing back of the waters (as the dividing of the Red Sea previously) displayed the power of Israel's God over all other gods, including those of the seas and rivers (that were believed to be untamable in the ancient world). Yahweh showed his power to destroy every other power and authority in carrying out his victory of life for a people he had made his own. This is what caused fear to enter the hearts of the inhabitants of the land who had previously heard of the strong and mighty outstretched arm of Yahweh that split the Red Sea in two and now divided the river. No god can stand before this God! This is even more significant when gods are associated with particular territories or spheres of influence. This God travels and has power over all territories and powers.

Aside from the clear name association, we can see Jesus in the book of Joshua in a number of ways:

The Heavenly Joshua (Heb. 4:8)
The Pioneer of Our Salvation (Heb. 2:10)
The Crimson Rope (Josh. 2:18)
The Ark of the Covenant of the Lord of All the Earth (Josh. 3:11)
The Memorial of Twelve Stones (Josh. 4:19–24)
The Passover Lamb (Josh. 5:10–12; 1 Cor. 5:7–8)
The Altar (Josh. 8:30–35; Heb. 13:10)
The Commander of Yahweh's Armies (Josh. 5:13–15; Eph. 6:12–18)
The Heavenly Refuge (Josh. 20:1–9; Heb. 6:19–20)

Conquest and God's Character. The book of Joshua is a road map, a manual for conquest. It contains the secrets of conquest with its amazing, jaw-dropping

---

[a] See *Hist. Eccles.* I 3.

victories and sadly disappointing defeats. And yet, many point to the book of Joshua as an example of God behaving badly because of this theme of conquest, which seems to touch a raw nerve. Some view these battles as morally dubious, filled with nationalistic violence and terror. However, note several things about the context of the time in which this history of Israel's conquests unfolds.

First, war was a normal fact of life; it still is. The Bible reminds us there is a time for war (see Eccl. 3:8) and a justifiable war (see Gen. 14), which the book of Joshua illustrates. However, the modern military cannot claim the right to destructive warfare based on Israelite wars, for they served a divine purpose in unfolding Yahweh's plans. Also the sort of holy war we find in Joshua was not invented by Israel nor limited to the nation. Further, the Canaanites were by no means innocent, for their sexual perversion, child sacrifice, and pagan idolatry could not go unpunished by a righteous God.

Finally, the theme of conquest reveals the character of God. In the book of Joshua, we see God's mercy unfold, such as in his sparing of Rahab and her family. Also, consider the fact that Yahweh mercifully waited hundreds of years before commencing the conquest, giving the inhabitants of the land ample time to repent (see 2 Pet. 3:9). God waited until their cup of iniquity was filled. No doubt this aspect of Joshua can be troubling. However, in this way the conquest shows us God's anger, justice, and wrath—important elements of his character.

God's character is further unfolded through the many conflicts that arise. We discover, along with Israel, that God not only initiates covenant relationships, but he also punishes disobedient people. He also gives his people victory over their enemies on their way toward possessing the land and nationhood. This God is a God who fights for his people, standing with them in the midst of their oppression and suffering, raising them up to the plateau of victory, and assuring them they have no reason to "yield to fear nor be discouraged, for I am Yahweh your God, and I will be with you wherever you go!" (Josh. 1:9).

JOSHUA

A New Beginning

Joshua's Great Commission

1 And[a] after Moses, Yahweh's servant, died,[b] Yahweh spoke to Joshua[c] son of Nun,[d] Moses' *faithful* assistant, and said,[e] 2"My servant Moses is dead. Now get up! Prepare to cross the Jordan[f] River, you and all the people. *Lead them*[g] into the land that I am giving to the Israelites. 3Every part of the land where you march[h] I will

---

a 1:1 The book of Joshua begins with the word "And." What writer uses the connective "And" to start a new production? This indicates the close connection between the books of Deuteronomy and Joshua. In the Hebrew text every book from Joshua through 2 Kings (with the exception of Ruth) begins with "And," demonstrating that the history of Israel is one connected narrative and inspired by one divine author, the Holy Spirit.

b 1:1 Jewish tradition states that Moses died on the seventh of Adar, the twelfth month of the Jewish calendar. The book of Joshua takes up the story right after the thirty-day mourning period for Moses (see Deut. 34:5–8). Leaders may die, but God's prophetic promises live on.

c 1:1 Joshua is the name Moses gave him, changing it from Hoshea to Joshua (*Yehoshua*), which means "Yahweh is salvation," "may Yahweh save," "Yahweh makes triumphant," or "Yahweh is the Deliverer."

d 1:1 *Nun* means "eternal," "perpetual," "to re-sprout," or "eternal increase." Joshua was the son of Nun. One greater than Joshua is Jesus, Son of the Eternal God. Joshua is introduced into the story as the "son of Nun." In western culture we are identified by our profession, by what we do or have accomplished. But in Hebrew culture, we are introduced in the language of sonship—as a son or daughter. In English, we, too, use patronyms to identify persons, which is nearly the same as "son of."

e 1:1 Seventeen times in Joshua we read the words "Yahweh spoke to Joshua" or "Yahweh said." Perhaps it was through an audible voice, in a dream, in a vision, in a divine encounter, through a prophecy, through the Urim and Thummim (see Num. 27:21), or by some other way. God has multiple ways of speaking to his servants.

f 1:2 Jordan comes from two Hebrew root words meaning "to descend" and "to judge."

g 1:2 Joshua was the successor to Moses. The leadership of Israel was given not to one of Moses' children but to the one whom God chose, prepared, and anointed. Leadership is not hereditary but established by the call of God on one's life. God chose Joshua in part because of his lifetime of service to Moses and his longing to be in the presence of God. See Ex. 33:11. Moses (representing the law) was not able to take God's people into their inheritance, but Joshua (representing Jesus) could.

h 1:3 Or "Every place you put the sole of your foot upon," a figure of speech for the power to conquer. To place the sole of your foot upon the land or upon your enemies was a metaphor for military victory. See Gen. 49:8; Josh. 10:24.

give you, as I promised Moses.[a] [4]Your borders will extend from the *southern* desert to the *northern* mountains of Lebanon, and from the great river Euphrates *in the east*, to the Mediterranean[b] in the west—including all the land of the Hittites.[c] [5]Joshua, no one will be able to defeat you for the rest of your life! I will be with you as I was with Moses,[d] and I will never fail[e] nor abandon you. [6]You must be strong and brave. You will lead the people to acquire and apportion the land that I promised their ancestors I would give them. [7]You must remain very strong and courageous![f] Be faithful to obey all the teaching[g] that my servant Moses commanded you to follow. Do not deviate from him[h] to the right or to the left, so that you will have overwhelming success[i] in everything you undertake. [8]Recite this scroll of the law constantly.[j] Contemplate it[k] day and night and be careful to follow every word it contains; then you will enjoy incredible prosperity and success.[l] [9]I repeat,[m] be strong and brave! Do not yield to fear nor be discouraged, for I am Yahweh your God, and I will be with you wherever you go!"[n]

Preparation to Cross Over

[10]Joshua ordered the leaders of the people: [11]"Go through the camp and

a 1:3 See Deut. 11:24.

b 1:4 Or "the Great Sea."

c 1:4 God mentioned the Hittites because they were the strongest and most warlike of the tribes, but in this passage, they are representative of all the seven tribes of the land. There were other inhabitants of the land as well—seven particular tribes are listed in several texts, including Deut. 7. The Hittites controlled a vast empire (with a capital far off to the north in modern Turkey) whose population stretched to the borderlands of Egypt (this very region that was now no longer under Egyptian domination).

d 1:5 What an amazing promise God gave to Joshua! In the same way Yahweh was with Moses (think burning bush, hearing God's voice, speaking "mouth to mouth" with God [Ex. 33:11], performing miracles, divine encounters, defeating enemies), so he would be with Joshua. Throughout this book, God repeatedly assured Joshua of his presence (see Josh. 2:24; 3:7, 10; 4:14; 6:27; 10:14, 42; 13:6; 14:12; 21:44; 23:3, 10).

e 1:5 Or "I will not weaken you" or "allow you to be weak." At least one Jewish scholar renders it, "I will not part from you." (See Reuven Drucker, *Yehoshua*, Art Scroll Tanach Series, 1988.)

f 1:7 To be courageous means to translate your convictions into bold actions.

g 1:7 Or "law [Torah]."

h 1:7 This phrase could mean "Don't deviate from [the instruction of] Moses" or "Don't turn from Yahweh."

i 1:7 Or "be prosperous," "push forward," or "break out."

j 1:8 Or "Don't let this book of the law depart from your mouth."

k 1:8 Or "meditate," "ponder," "imagine," "mutter," or "talk to oneself." See Ps. 1:2; Prov. 3:1–2.

l 1:8 Or "understanding." See Prov. 3:4.

m 1:9 Or "Have I not commanded you?"

n 1:9 God gave Joshua seven promises: (1) He would possess a vast territory (see vv. 3–4). (2) No one would be able to defeat him (see v. 5). (3) God would be with him as he was with Moses (see v. 5). (4) God would never fail him (see v. 5). (5) God would never abandon him (see v. 5). (6) He would enjoy prosperity and success (see v. 8). (7) God would be with him wherever he went (see v. 9). Remember, what God promised Joshua, he also promises you, for all that was promised to this Joshua is fulfilled in the better Joshua (Jesus) in whom we are included for receiving all of God's promises as yes and amen.

instruct the people, 'Pack your bags;[a] for within three days you will cross the Jordan to conquer and occupy the land that Yahweh your God is giving you to possess.' "[b]

[12]Then Joshua addressed the Reubenites, the Gadites, and the half-tribe of Manasseh:[c] [13-14]"Remember the words that Yahweh's servant Moses commanded you: 'Yahweh your God is giving you this land on the east side of the Jordan as your homeland.'[d] Therefore, your wives, your little ones, and your livestock[e] may remain here, but all your *valiant* warriors must cross over with us armed.[f] They will take the lead and help their brothers [15]until they take possession of the land that Yahweh your God is giving them as their homeland.[g] Afterward, you will be free to return to your own land and possess the land that Moses, Yahweh's servant, gave you here on the east side of the Jordan."[h]

[16]They answered Joshua: "We will do everything you have told us and will go wherever you send us. [17]We always obeyed Moses, and we will always obey you. May Yahweh your God stand beside you as he stood with Moses. [18]And anyone who questions your authority or disobeys whatever you command[i] shall be put to death. So, Joshua, be strong and brave!"[j]

Joshua Sends Spies into Jericho

Then Joshua son of Nun secretly sent out two spies[k] from their camp

---

a 1:11 Or "Prepare supplies" or "Gather what you need."

b 1:11 Many scholars conclude that Joshua did not give this command until after the spies he sent out in ch. 2 had returned.

c 1:12 See Num. 32:28–32; Deut. 3:18–20.

d 1:13–14 Or "[as] a place of rest."

e 1:13–14 The order here is significant: "your wives, your little ones, and your livestock." When the two and a half tribes asked Moses to remain on the other side of the Jordan, they displayed a warped sense of their values by speaking of their possessions before their wives and children. See Num. 32:16.

f 1:13–14 Forty thousand warriors from these two and a half tribes crossed over to fight for their brothers (see Josh. 4:13). From Num. 26:7, 18, 34, we learn that about ninety thousand people of these tribes remained on the east side of the Jordan, including the women, children (those under the age of twenty), and the old men. Their new settlement was vulnerable, and they needed a fighting force to remain in case of attack.

g 1:15 The unity of God's people is in focus in vv. 12–15. Similarly, we must be willing to fight for our brother's victory as much as we fight for our own (see 1 Sam. 23:16; Phil. 2:3–4; Heb. 10:25). This is one of the very points where the people would fail when we begin to read Judges. Everyone began to do what they wanted rather than to work together for the benefit of the whole community.

h 1:15 Joshua the prophet foresaw the complete victory of possessing the land of their enemies. In vv. 12–15 we learn that the land-takers were required to be united. Neither one individual nor one tribe could take the land; it required all God's people going in together and fighting as one. Battles are won as God's people unite. But unity alone isn't enough; we must be prepared for a battle over our complete inheritance. There must be no rest until everyone has received his or her inheritance. See Eph. 4:11–16.

i 1:18 Literally "your mouth."

j 1:18 Or "be determined and confident!"

k 2:1 Joshua was one of the twelve spies sent out publicly by Moses (see Deut. 1:22–23). Some scholars believe that one of the spies could have been Salmon, who married Rahab, and whose son was Boaz. See Matt. 1:5.

at Acacia.[a] He told them, "Go and explore the land of Canaan, especially Jericho."[b] They went and *arrived at Jericho and* entered the house of Rahab the prostitute and lodged there.[c] 2The king of Jericho was told: "Some Israelites have come into the city tonight to spy out the entire land. *They're in Rahab's house.*" 3So the king sent messengers to Rahab, who said to her: "Turn over the men who entered your house. They're here to spy out our land." 4But Rahab had already hidden the two men.

"Yes," she said. "The men came to me, but I had no idea where they were from. 5They left at sundown, just before the city gates were closed at night. Who knows where they went. Quick! Go after them, and maybe you can catch them!"[d] 6(Rahab had hidden the men on her rooftop under stalks of flax[e] she had spread out *to dry* on the roof.) 7So the men of Jericho went out to search for the spies, and the city gates were shut behind them. They searched for them as far as where the path crosses the Jordan.

Rahab's Pact with the Spies
8Before the spies had gone to sleep, Rahab went up to the rooftop 9and said to them, "I know that Yahweh has given you this land. Everyone is absolutely terrified, and we are all paralyzed with fear[f] because of you. 10We've heard of *the miracles that accompany you* and how Yahweh dried up the waters of the Red Sea[g] for you when you left Egypt. We've heard how you utterly

---

a 2:1 Archaeologists identify the location of Acacia with Tell el-Kefrein in modern Jordan. The Hebrew word for "Acacia" is *shittim*, which means "piercing" or "thorny." The acacia is a flowering hardwood tree. It was used to make the tabernacle furniture, including the ark of the covenant.

b 2:1 The Hebrew word for "Jericho" is *Yericho*, which means "moon." Jericho was known as "The City of the Moon" because of its occult worship of the moon god/goddess. The city, with its high double walls, was a capital of Canaanite worship. They considered their king to be a divine being. So when Yahweh gave the king over to be killed by Joshua and his men (see 6:2), they were, in effect, killing a "son of god." The earliest object of worship in the Canaanite religion was that of the male moon god Yerach. (See W. F. Albright, *Archaeology and the Religion of Israel*, especially pp. 83 and 92; John Gray, *The Canaanites*, p. 125.)

c 2:1 Although Josephus mentions that Rahab was an innkeeper (*Ant*. 5.1.2), the book of James clearly states she was a prostitute (see James 2:25). It may be that she was both. *Rahab* means "overcome" or "overcomer." The Hebrew word *rahab* is also found in Song. 6:5. The Shulamite has "rahab" (overcome) the heart of the Beloved. The church fathers noted that Rahab possessed the spirit of prophecy, which the Jewish historian Josephus also mentions (see Josephus *Ant. Jud.* 5.1.13). She had a revelation that God was giving the land to Israel (see Josh. 2:9, 12). Rabbinical tradition states that Rahab was rewarded by having prophets and kings as her descendants.

d 2:5 Rahab protected the spies at the risk of her own life. She was a woman of faith. See Heb. 11:31; James 2:25.

e 2:6 Flax is a plant from whose stem a fiber was made that was woven into linen cloth. The valiant and virtuous woman (representing the radiant bride of Christ) also worked with flax. See footnote on Prov. 31:13.

f 2:9 Or "everyone's heart melts with fear."

g 2:10 Or "the Sea of Reeds."

annihilated*a* the two Amorite kings, Sihon*b* and Og,*c* *and their kingdoms* who were on the other side of the Jordan.*d* ¹¹As soon as we heard it, our hearts melted with fear, and we were left with no courage among us*e* because of you. Yahweh, your God, is the true God *who rules* in heaven above and on earth below.*f* ¹²Please, solemnly swear to me by the name of Yahweh that you will show kindness to my family because I have shown kindness to you. Give me a sure sign ¹³that you will spare the lives of my father and mother, my brothers and sisters, and all their families. Don't let us be killed!"

¹⁴The men answered, "If you don't disclose our mission to anyone, we'll pledge our lives for yours. Then, when Yahweh gives us this land, we'll honor our promise and treat you kindly."

¹⁵Rahab's house was built into the city wall,*g* so she let them down from the window by a rope. ¹⁶She told them, "Head for the hill country and hide. The men chasing you won't find you there. Hide for three days until they have returned, then you'll be safe to go your way."

¹⁷But the men warned her, "*You must do what we say, or* we will not be bound to the oath you made us swear. ¹⁸When our invasion begins, bring all your family together in your house—your father and mother, your brothers and sisters, and all their families. And tie this crimson rope*h* in the same window through which you let us down. ¹⁹Remember, if anyone ventures outside your house, his death will be his own fault,*i* not ours! But if anyone inside your house is harmed,

---

a 2:10 This is the Hebrew word *cherem*, meaning "totally devoted, consumed, dedicated and given over to Yahweh." This term plays a significant role in the stories that follow concerning Jericho, Ai, and Achan.

b 2:10 *Sihon* means "to strike down." Sihon was an Amorite king who ruled over the city-state of Heshbon. *Heshbon* means "intelligence"; this town represents the mind of man. In Num. 21:27–30, the ballad singers wrote songs about Heshbon and its king, which indicates how far the fame of Sihon has spread. The tribe of Gad eventually settled in the territory where Sihon once reigned. Jewish tradition states that Sihon and Og were both giants. The Jewish apocryphal book *The Book of Giants*, part of the Dead Sea Scrolls discovered at Qumran, states that Sihon and Og (Ogias) were brothers.

c 2:10 *Og* means "long-necked," "pride," or "intimidation." Og was the king of Bashan. Moses had fought and conquered his kingdom, which included over sixty fortified cities (see Deut. 3:1–7, 11). He was also a Rephaite giant or "terrible one." His iron bed was "nine cubits long and four cubits wide" (thirteen and a half feet long and six feet wide). A man needing this size of bed was at least ten or eleven feet tall. See Deut. 2:20–21. One of the cities the Israelites took from Og was Golan, which later became a Levitical city and a city of asylum (see Josh. 21:27).

d 2:10 See Num. 21:21–35.

e 2:11 Or "everyone's spirit no longer rose up."

f 2:11 Rahab was a pagan Canaanite woman, yet she declared her faith in Yahweh. She is commended as a woman of faith. See Heb. 11:31; James 2:25.

g 2:15 That is, a section of the city wall formed the outside wall of Rahab's house. Since this clause is not found in the Septuagint, some scholars believe it was a later scribal addition to the text.

h 2:18 This crimson rope can be seen in the light of the New Testament as an emblem of the blood of Jesus. Faith in Christ's blood brings us salvation. Rahab experienced a personal "Passover" because of the blood (crimson) applied to her house. Both Passover blood and the crimson rope were described in Hebrew as *oth*, "a sign." See Ex. 12:13; Josh. 2:12.

i 2:19 Literally "his blood will be on his own head."

then we will be held responsible. ²⁰And if you disclose our mission, we will be released from the oath you made us swear."

²¹Rahab replied in agreement, "Let it be as you say." And she sent them away, and after they departed, she tied the crimson rope in her window.

²²The spies went straight to the hill country and hid there for three days, until the pursuers turned back. The king's men had scoured the countryside without finding them.

²³Then the two men*ᵃ* came down from the hills and crossed back over *the Jordan to their camp.* They reported to Joshua son of Nun all that had happened to them: ²⁴"Yahweh has certainly handed over the entire land into

our hands! All the people of the land melt in fear before us!"

The Miracle-Crossing of the Jordan

3 Joshua was up bright and early the next morning.*ᵇ* They broke camp, and Joshua led the Israelites from Acacia to *the eastern bank of* the Jordan.*ᶜ* There they set up camp and waited until they crossed over. ²After three days,*ᵈ* the leaders of the people went throughout the camp ³giving orders to the people, "Watch for the priests of the tribe of Levi to lift the ark of the covenant of Yahweh*ᵉ* your God. When it starts moving, follow it ⁴so you'll know which way to go, since you've never marched this way before.*ᶠ* Follow about a half mile*ᵍ* behind the ark; don't go near it."

---

a 2:23 The two spies represent "two witnesses" to establish and confirm their report. See Num. 13–14; Rev. 11:3–12.

b 3:1 What an exciting day this was for Joshua and the people. They left their days of wandering in the wilderness behind. A new beginning was now before them. All but two men were under forty years old and had been born in the desert; now they would cross over into a fertile land. Anticipation was in the air! After three days of waiting before a flooding river, they were about to see a miracle! (For more examples of rising early, see Josh. 6:12; 7:16; 8:10; Mark 1:35; Luke 4:42.)

c 3:1 This was a journey of about eight or nine miles, a day's walk with a crowd of a million people.

d 3:2 The reference to three days points us to the resurrection of Jesus Christ. The biblical significance of the number three refers to Jesus' resurrection after three days.

e 3:3 The ark is the center of this story. It is mentioned or alluded to twenty-one (or 3 × 7) times in chapters 3 and 4. Twenty-one, in the language of biblical numbers, signifies a complete manifestation of God. The ark is a wonderful picture of our Lord Jesus Christ. The power of Christ within us enables us to pass over into our full inheritance. Jesus, our forerunner, leads us in. The ark was a constant reminder that God is powerful, holy, and to be obeyed. The ark also symbolizes God's mercy, for it had a mercy seat as a lid, or cover. Jesus is our Mercy Seat, or atoning sacrifice (see 1 John 2:2). Notice that it wasn't only the ark (Jesus) that went into the dry riverbed but also all of Israel. In the same manner, every believer today is co-crucified with Christ (see Gal. 2:20), and our "Adam-nature" was dismantled by the work of the cross (see Rom. 6:6).

f 3:4 The Hebrew word *derek* can mean "way" or "manner." They were to march in a new manner—with their eyes on the ark (see Col. 1:10). A new order for a new day. Before they crossed the Jordan, the ark had always been covered. Beginning when they crossed the Jordan and entered the promised land, the ark was in plain sight. In the Old Testament, Jesus was concealed; in the New Testament, Jesus is revealed. Without all the covering, the weight on the priests' shoulders would have been less. See Matt. 11:28–30.

g 3:4 Or "two thousand cubits."

⁵Joshua instructed the people, "Get yourselves ready! Set yourselves apart[a] for Yahweh! Tomorrow, Yahweh will perform for us *great* miracles!"[b]

⁶Joshua told the priests, "Raise up the ark of the covenant and step out ahead of the people." So they lifted the ark *onto their shoulders* and marched in front of the people.

⁷Yahweh said to Joshua, "This very day I will begin to exalt you in the sight of all Israel[c] so that they will realize that I am with you[d] in the same way I was with Moses. ⁸You are to command the priests who carry the ark of the covenant with these words: 'Carry the ark to the edge of the Jordan and wade into the water.' "[e]

⁹Joshua told the Israelites, "Come closer and listen to the words of Yahweh your God. ¹⁰This is how you will know for sure that the Living God is among you. *As you advance into the land,* he will drive out before you the Canaanites, Hittites, Hivites, Perizzites, Girgashites, Amorites, and Jebusites.[f] ¹¹Look! The ark of the covenant of the Lord of all the earth will go before you

---

a 3:5 Or "Sanctify yourselves," implying an inward attitude of purity and an outward washing and ritual purification. See 2 Cor. 7:1; 2 Tim. 2:21; Heb. 10:22; 1 John 3:3. Both distance and attitude were important to God as the people followed the ark. We need both whole-hearted devotion and heart purity in our worship of God today. See 2 Cor. 11:3.

b 3:5 Some scholars are puzzled over the use of the plural word for miracles when it was only one miracle (parting the river). The plural implied the beginning of a new season of miracles and wonders as they crossed over.

c 3:7 The place of the miracle-crossing was the very place where John baptized Jesus (our Joshua).

d 3:7 God was with Joshua and God is with you. This would imply God's comforting presence, his power, and his delight to be at our side.

e 3:8 Or "stand still in the Jordan."

f 3:10 See Deut. 7:1–5. The Canaanites and Amorites (see Gen. 15:16; Amos 2:9) were the largest and most powerful tribes inhabiting the land. The Canaanites dwelt in the lowlands, and the Amorites were in the hill country (see Num. 13:29). The Hittites lived in the northernmost parts of the land (see Josh. 1:4). The Hivites were associated with Shechem and Gibeon (see Gen. 34:2; Josh. 9:7; 11:19). The Jebusites had their stronghold at Jerusalem (see 18:25–28). The Perizzites are related to the Rephaites ("giants," 17:15). The Girgashites were a branch of the Hivites and lived in the western region of the land. These seven tribes could also represent seven strongholds that must be conquered in the life of a believer: (1) The Hebrew word for "Canaanites" means "those who traffic in materialism," "merchants," or "pirates"; they represent the love of money. (2) The Hebrew word for "Hittites" means "those broken in pieces," "terror," or "dread"; they represent anger and violence. (3) The Hebrew word for "Hivites" means "life born of effort" or "beastly life"; they represent human effort and reliance upon self. (4) The Hebrew word for "Perizzites" means "rustic," "country dwellers," or "backwoods"; they represent lack of vision and initiative. (5) The Hebrew word for "Girgashites" means "dense, condensed marshy ground"; they represent ignorance, unwillingness to learn. (6) The Hebrew word for "Amorites" means "those who live on high" or "summit dwellers"; they represent pride and arrogance. (7) The Hebrew word for "Jebusites" means "trampled down under foot"; they represent fear and anxiety that cripple spiritual growth. Jesus, our heavenly Joshua, is more than enough to empower us to overcome these inner strongholds.

and prepare a way for you through the Jordan.*ᵃ* ¹²Now select twelve men from among the people, one man from each tribe.*ᵇ*

¹³ᵃ"The moment the feet of the priests carrying the ark of Yahweh, the Lord of all the earth, touch the water of the Jordan, *a great miracle will happen!* The water flowing downstream toward you will stop and pile up as if behind a dam."

¹⁴⁻¹⁵Now it was time for the early harvest,*ᶜ* and the river was overflowing at flood stage. When the people broke camp to cross the Jordan, the priests went in front of them carrying the ark of the covenant *on their shoulders*. The very moment the priests with the ark dipped their feet in the river's edge, ¹⁶the water coming downstream toward them stopped flowing and piled up in a solid wall as far upstream as Adam, a place near Zarethan.*ᵈ* Yahweh completely cut off the flow of the river so that it drained downstream toward the Desert Sea (the Dead Sea).*ᵉ* So the people crossed over opposite Jericho. ¹⁷Now the priests stood firmly on dry ground in the riverbed with the ark *on their shoulders.*ᶠ* The entire nation

---

a 3:11 Joshua was expressing to Israel that if God can roll back the waters of a raging river, he can repel the attacking armies of Canaan. This miracle reminded these children of the Israelites who saw the waters of the Red Sea rolled back that they could experience the same wonder-working God moving on their behalf. Further, it signaled to the inhabitants of the land that the God of Israel was supreme over the gods of the waters (gods which were untamable and uncontrollable to the Canaanites). As Yahweh had overthrown the gods of Egypt, so he would overcome the gods of Canaan.

b 3:12 On the discourse level, this verse is somewhat out of place. The twelve men are not Levitical priests but representatives of the tribes. Further details of their duties are given in the next chapter (see 4:2–3).

c 3:14–15 The tributaries of the Jordan, swollen with the spring snowmelt from Mount Hermon, flooded the river valley. The width of the flooding river could have been up to a mile at the time of the miracle-crossing. (See 1 Chron. 12:15.) By comparing Josh. 3:14–15; 4:19 with Ex. 9:31, we learn that Israel's miracle-crossing took place in the spring when both barley and flax were harvested, four days before Passover.

d 3:16 Adam is seventeen miles north of the place of the miracle-crossing, and Zarethan is another twenty miles north. The waters were held back and formed a lake that would have extended for almost forty miles. Notice the name "Adam." The Jordan represents the death of Jesus on the cross and the price he paid to save us. The word for "Jordan" is a compound word joining the words for "to descend" and "judging" (judgment; see Gen. 30:6 and footnote). Jesus, pictured as the ark, descended into judgment for our sins and rolled the river of guilt, shame, and judgment all the way back to Adam! The root word for *Zarethan* is a verb that means "piercing" or "bleeding of the veins." Judgment was abated to Adam by the one who was "pierced" for our rebellious deeds. It was both the ark and the people who crossed over. Our old Adam-life was buried figuratively at the crossing, and we were "resurrected" with him to possess our inheritance as a people set free (see Rom. 6:3–4).

e 3:16 Or "the Sea of Arabah (Salt Sea)." A very wide path opened for the people to cross over on dry ground. The "waters of death and judgment" stopped flowing when Jesus our Savior was crucified. Now, when we believe, the fountain of living waters opens within us.

f 3:17 We are also "priests" of God (1 Pet. 2:9; Rev. 5:9–10) who "stand firm" in the finished work ("dry ground") of the cross and resurrection of Christ and who carry the ark of his glory in our hearts (see Col. 1:26–27).

passed by the ark as they completed their *miracle*-crossing on dry ground.*[a]*

Two Stone Memorials Established

4 When the entire nation had finished their miracle-crossing of the Jordan, Yahweh said to Joshua, [2]"Choose twelve men,*[b]* one from each of the *twelve* tribes of Israel. [3]Instruct each of them to take a stone from the riverbed, twelve stones from the very place where the priests stand *with the ark*. Have them carry the stones over to the place where you camp tonight."

[4]So Joshua summoned the twelve men he had selected from the Israelites, one per tribe. [5]Joshua instructed them, "Walk out to the middle of the riverbed to the ark of Yahweh your God. Each of you choose a stone and lift it up onto your shoulder—one stone for each tribe. [6]The stones will always be a sign to you. Someday, when your children ask you, 'Why are these stones so important?' [7]tell them, 'The Jordan stopped flowing in front of the ark of the covenant of Yahweh—the floodwaters were completely cut off.' These stones will serve as a memorial for Israel forever."

[8]The Israelites did as Joshua commanded them. They took twelve stones according to the number of the tribes of Israel, from the middle of the riverbed, and carried them to the camp and put them there.

[9]Joshua set up the memorial stones *that they had taken from* the exact spot*[c]* where the priests stood bearing the ark in the riverbed. They remain there to this day.*[d]*

[10]While the priests remained standing in the middle of the Jordan with the ark *on their shoulders*, the people hurried across. All the instructions Yahweh had given to Joshua were carried out*[e]*—just as Moses had told Joshua.*[f]* [11]And when Israel had finished crossing, the ark of Yahweh and the priests crossed as the people looked on.

[12]The Reubenites, the Gadites, and half the tribe of Manasseh went

---

a 3:17 The miracle-crossing of the Jordan bore many similarities to the parting of the Red Sea. (1) Both involved water. (2) Both were witnessed by the entire nation of Israel. (3) Both involved an act of a servant of God—Moses stretched out his rod over the water, and Joshua commanded the priests and the people. (4) Both removed a barrier to the forward advance of God's people. (5) Both miracles vindicated God's leader (see Ex. 14:31; Josh. 4:14). (6) Both required the obedience of God's people (see Ex. 14:15; Josh. 3:3). (7) Both miracles enabled Israel to cross over on dry ground (see Ex. 14:22). (8) Both miracles were performed while God's people stood still (see Ex. 14:14; footnote on Josh. 3:8). (9) Both the waters of the Red Sea and of the Jordan were restored to their places. (10) Both miracles became a hinge of history, marking a new beginning. (11) Both miracles revealed God's tremendous power to defeat his enemies. (12) Both miracles resulted in songs of praise (see Ex. 15; Ps. 114; Hab. 3).

b 4:2 Jesus, our heavenly Joshua, likewise chose twelve men to be his disciples.

c 4:9 Or "Joshua set up the stones in the exact spot," which would imply there may have been a second set of memorial stones (one set on land and another on the riverbed).

d 4:9 The Talmud states that these stones were still at that very spot even a generation after the destruction of the Second Temple, and that three rabbis stood on top of them (Talmud, *Sotah* 34a).

e 4:10 For the priests to stand still for many hours with the heavy ark on their shoulders was a test of their strength, patience, and courage. We also are priests in the kingdom of God, and we are called upon to possess those same qualities.

f 4:10 See Deut. 31:7–8.

across, armed and ready for battle, in front of the Israelites, as Moses had commanded them.[a] [13]In all, about forty thousand men were equipped for battle. And they all marched before Yahweh to wage war on the plains of Jericho.

[14]On that day, Yahweh exalted Joshua before all the people. As they had stood in awe of Moses, so they stood in awe of Joshua for the rest of his life.

The Jordan Returns to Flood Stage

[15]Yahweh said to Joshua,[b] [16]"Command the priests carrying the ark of the covenant[c] to come up from the Jordan." [17]So Joshua did as he was commanded, [18]and the priests carrying the ark of the covenant of Yahweh came up from the riverbed. And the moment their feet touched the western bank of the Jordan, the floodwaters surged back in place where they were before and returned to flood stage.

[19]The people experienced the miracle-crossing of the Jordan on the tenth day of the first month *of the Jewish calendar.*[d] They established their base camp at Gilgal,[e] east of Jericho,[f] [20]where Joshua set up a *memorial with* the twelve stones taken from the Jordan. [21]He told the Israelites, "In time to come, when children ask their fathers, 'Why are these stones so important?' [22]tell them, 'Here is the place where the Israelites crossed the Jordan on dry ground!' [23]For your God, Yahweh, dried up the waters of the Jordan before your eyes until you crossed over,[g] just as Yahweh your God did for us *years ago*; he dried up the Red Sea while we crossed over! [24]He has done these *miracles* so that all the earth will be in awe[h] of the mighty power[i] of Yahweh and that you might always obey[j] Yahweh your God!"

---

a 4:12 See Num. 32:20–22.
b 4:15 Joshua heard the voice of God in real time.
c 4:16 Or "the ark of testimony [instruction]."
d 4:19 The "first month" is the month of Abib, which began with the first new moon occurring after March 11 on the Gregorian calendar, so the crossing occurred between March 21 and April 18. It was on this same day forty years earlier that Israel set apart the Passover Lamb in Egypt (see Ex. 12:2–3, 18). (See Keil, *Joshua*, 51.)
e 4:19 *Gilgal* means "circle" or "rolling away."
f 4:19 Or "on the east border of Jericho," which was about halfway between the Jordan and Jericho.
g 4:23 Elijah had a repeat of this miracle-crossing (see 2 Kings 2:7–8). Those who walk in the "spirit of Elijah" today can likewise expect miracles in their ministry. Elisha, who had a double portion of the spirit of Elijah, also performed the miracle-crossing (see 2 Kings 2:9–14; cf. John 14:12).
h 4:24 Or "know firsthand" from the Hebrew word *yada*.
i 4:24 Or "hand."
j 4:24 Or "fear," which has a varied universe of meanings in Hebrew. The two miracles—the parting of the Red Sea and the miracle-crossing of the Jordan—carry a message for the entire world to learn. As believers in our heavenly Joshua, our Lord Jesus, we can learn from the symbolism of these miracles. The Red Sea parting shows us deep lessons of our salvation from sin, and so does the Jordan crossing. We were co-buried with Christ in baptism into his death (Jordan), and now we are co-raised with him on the "dry ground" of resurrection territory (see Rom. 6:4–5; Col. 2:12).

God's People at Gilgal

5 All the Amorite kings west of the Jordan and all the Canaanite kings along the coast of the Mediterranean Sea became terrified of the Israelites. For when they heard how Yahweh miraculously dried up the Jordan so that the Israelites could cross over, all their courage melted away.

²At that time, Yahweh commanded Joshua,ᵃ "Make knives of flint and circumcise*ᵇ* the men of Israel again."*ᶜ* ³So Joshua made stone knives and circumcised all the men at *a place they named* Circumcision Hill.*ᵈ*

⁴⁻⁶Joshua had to circumcise all the men and boys—all the fighting men. Although they had been circumcised before leaving Egypt, the male children born during the forty years they spent in the wilderness had not been circumcised. Also, by the end of that forty years, all the fighting men who had come out of Egypt had died because they had not listened to the voice of Yahweh. So Yahweh had made an oath that they would not see the land he had promised to give their ancestors, a fertile land. ⁷So he raised up their sons in their place, and Joshua circumcised them because they had not been circumcised on the way.

⁸After the circumcision was completed, the whole nation waited in the camp until their wounds had healed. ⁹Then Yahweh said to Joshua, "Today, I have rolled away your disgrace from *being slaves in* Egypt." For that reason, the place is named Gilgal*ᵉ* to this day.

¹⁰While encamped at Gilgal, not far from Jericho,*ᶠ* the Israelites celebrated the Feast of Passover*ᵍ* in the evening of the fourteenth day of the month *of Abib.ʰ* ¹¹The very next day, they ate for the first time food grown in Canaan—roasted grain and flatbread

---

a 5:2 Yahweh and Joshua were friends. How wonderful to know that God will converse with his servants.

b 5:2 Circumcision, the cutting off of the foreskin from the penis, was the sign of the covenant that God made with Abraham (see Gen. 17:9–14). The reason for doing this is given in Josh. 5:4–7. The male children born while Israel was wandering in the wilderness for forty years had not been circumcised. This would leave Israel vulnerable for a number of days as the men healed.

c 5:2 Or "the second time." All male Israelites had been circumcised before their exodus from Egypt (see Ex. 12:44–51), so this would be the nation's second time.

d 5:3 Or "Gibeath Haaraloth." *Gibeath Haaraloth* means "Hill of Foreskins." There could have been more than a half million men who were circumcised at that time. The Hebrew word for "circumcision" is *muwl*, which means "to cut short," "to blunt," "to destroy," or "to cut in pieces." The principle of circumcision is that the flesh (human nature apart from divine influence) must be cut off and removed if God's people are to enter into the fullness of their spiritual inheritance (see Col. 2:10–11; 3:9). Circumcision was performed on the eighth day after birth (see Luke 2:21). Eight is the number of a new beginning. The circumcision of the heart (see Deut. 10:16; 30:6; Jer. 4:4; Rom. 2:29) frees us to hear from God, to live in the Spirit of God (see Phil. 3:3), and to enter into the fullness of God (see Rom. 6:1–14).

e 5:9 *Gilgal* means "circle" or "roll away." It became their headquarters during the early days of their conquest of Canaan.

f 5:10 Or "in the plains of Jericho."

g 5:10 The Feast of Passover commemorated their deliverance from slavery in Egypt. See Ex. 12:1–14.

h 5:10 Abib was the first month of the Jewish ecclesiastical calendar and was later changed to Nisan after the Babylonian captivity. It is roughly April in the Gregorian calendar.

made without yeast. [12]On that day, when they ate the produce of the land, the manna[a] stopped falling *from heaven*. The Israelites never ate manna again, but that year they enjoyed the fruit of the land of Canaan.

The Commander of the Armies of Heaven

[13]When Joshua was near Jericho, he looked up and saw standing in front of him a man holding a drawn sword.[b] Joshua approached him and said, "Are you on our side or on our enemies'?"

[14]"Neither," he replied. "I have not come *to take sides but* to take charge.[c] I am the Commander of Yahweh's armies."[d] *At once*, Joshua threw himself facedown to the ground and worshiped,[e] and he said to him, "I will do whatever you command, my Lord."

[15]The Commander of Yahweh's armies said to Joshua, "Remove your sandals, for you are standing on holy ground!" And Joshua obeyed.[f]

The Capture of Jericho

6 Now the gates of Jericho were bolted and barred because of the Israelites; no one could get in or out.

[2]Yahweh commanded Joshua,[g] "See, I have given Jericho, its king

---

a 5:12 *Manna* means "what is it?" See Ex. 16:14–15, 31. For forty years, God supernaturally fed his people in the wilderness (see Ex. 16:35). Manna is also called "angels' food" (Ps. 78:25).

b 5:13 There is nothing in the text to indicate that this was a vision. Joshua physically saw this tangible man before him.

c 5:14 This encounter was not a matter of Joshua gaining the allegiance of the Lord but of the Lord gaining the allegiance of Joshua.

d 5:14 No doubt, the imposing walls of Jericho that stood before Israel intimidated Joshua. Suddenly the Commander came to take over the leadership of his armies. Also, these armies were not only earthly but also the greater armies of the angelic host that stood ready to follow their heavenly Commander into battle. See 2 Kings 6:15–17. He was about to give Joshua a supernatural and illogical strategy for taking the city of Jericho.

e 5:14 Joshua worshiped this "Commander," showing that he was neither an angel nor a human messenger but Jesus. This was a Christophany (a pre-incarnate appearing of Christ). Furthermore, the Commander called the ground Joshua was upon "holy" because of the presence of the Holy One. Compare Gen. 16:7; 18:22; 32:24–32; Ex. 3:5; Judg. 2:1; 6:12–18; 13:3–22.

f 5:15 See Ex. 3:5. This chapter teaches us many principles to prepare us to enter our own spiritual "promised land" to claim our endless spiritual blessings (see Eph. 1:3). First, we cross over into a new day, burying our old identity in Jordan's flood. Second, we submit our hearts to Jesus (Joshua), cutting off flesh, experiencing the circumcision of the heart. Third, we enjoy a Passover Feast, receiving full deliverance from sin and victory over our enemies (see 1 Cor. 5:6–8). Fourth, we get a new diet for conquerors (see Heb. 5:11–6:3). Manna (the life of Christ while he was on earth) has ceased, and the new roasted grain has become our feast. Jesus passed through the fires of God's judgment for our sins and has now become the grain of wheat who fell into the ground (see John 12:24–26). Now he is raised with many grains of wheat (our co-resurrection with Christ, see Eph. 2:6). We eat the unleavened bread of single-hearted devotion and purity in the love feast we enjoy in Christ (see 2 Cor. 11:3). Fifth, we encounter the Commander of Yahweh's armies, knowing that he will lead us forward in "endless triumph" (2 Cor. 2:14). These principles prepare us to enter into our spiritual promised land and into a new dimension of spiritual warfare (see Josh. 6).

g 6:2 If we see v. 1 as parenthetical, then Joshua was still in the presence of the Commander of Yahweh's armies, identified here as Yahweh.

and mighty warriors into your hands.ᵃ ³March around the city with all your men of war once a day for six days. ⁴Have seven priests carry shofars in front of the ark. On the seventh day, march around the city seven times, with the priests blowing the shofars. ⁵When you hear the blare of the shofars, have all the people shout with a mighty shout of joy!ᵇ Then the wallsᶜ of the city will collapse *before your eyes*, and your whole army must charge straight in!"ᵈ

⁶So Joshua son of Nun summoned the priests and instructed them: "Take up the ark of the covenant, and have seven priests carry seven shofars in front of the ark of Yahweh."

⁷And to the people he said, "Forward! March around the city and set an advance guard of armed men to march ahead of the ark of Yahweh."

⁸At Joshua's order, the seven priests carrying seven shofars advanced before Yahweh. The ark of the covenant of Yahweh followed them as they made long blasts on their shofars. ⁹The advance guard marched in front of the priests who were blowing the shofars, the rear guard marched behind the ark, and the shofars blared the whole time! ¹⁰Now Joshua had commanded the rest of the people, "Do not shout! Remain silent! Don't make a sound until the moment I command you to shout. Then lift up a shout *with all your might!*" ¹¹So the ark of Yahweh circled the city once, then they all came back to the camp *in Gilgal* and spent the night.

¹²Joshua rose bright and early the next morning, and the priests took up the ark of Yahweh. ¹³The armed men and the seven priests carrying the seven shofars marched in front of the ark of Yahweh blowing their shofars continually, and the rear guard followed the ark of Yahweh, while the trumpets kept sounding. ¹⁴On the second day, they circled the city once and again returned to the camp. They repeated this *pattern* for six days.

¹⁵On the seventh day, everyone rose at daybreak, and they marched around the city in the same manner seven times. ¹⁶After their seventh time around, when the priests were about to blow the shofars, Joshua commanded the people: "Shout a shout *of joy*! Yahweh has given you the

---

ᵃ 6:2 Faith will see "what is still unseen" (Heb. 11:1). God gave Joshua a promise upon which to rest his faith.

ᵇ 6:5 The Hebrew word for "shout" is *teruw'ah* and can be either a war cry or a shout of joy.

ᶜ 6:5 The walled city of Jericho could represent the stronghold of the natural mind and every high thought that exalts itself against the knowledge of the true God (see 2 Cor. 10:3–5). Walls represent our inner "walls" and arguments we erect against learning something new. The mind of man is opposed to the ways of God (see Isa. 55:8; Rom. 8:7). The door to truth is not the intellect but rather the spirit yielded to God. Daniel saw the writing on the wall, and knew the walls of Babylon would fall (see Dan. 5:4–9, 25–31). Ezekiel dug through the "wall" to uncover the abominations that were hidden (Ezek. 8:7–18). The prophet Joel saw an army that would run upon and climb up the "walls" (Joel 2:1–9). David was a champion who leapt over the "wall" (2 Sam. 22:30; see Ps. 18:29). And similarly, Joshua was a prophetic leader who shouted so that the "walls" could topple (Josh. 6:1–20).

ᵈ 6:5 The perimeter of Jericho was about four miles. God designed this unorthodox military strategy to demonstrate his power (see Ps. 80:1–2), to discourage all forms of self-reliance, and to bring all the glory to himself (see Ps. 115:1). The thick, impenetrable walls (see Num. 13:28; Deut. 1:28–30) were nothing against the power of God!

city! [17]Jericho and everything in it are to be a devoted offering to Yahweh.[a] But spare Rahab the prostitute and everyone in her house because she hid our spies. [18]You must not take for yourselves[b] anything that is dedicated to Yahweh or you will bring trouble and destruction to the entire Israelite camp![c] [19]Everything made of silver, gold, bronze, and iron is sacred and devoted to Yahweh; place all of it in Yahweh's treasury!"

[20]The people were ready to shout with a great shout when they heard the shofars. As soon as they heard the blast of the shofars, they raised a massive shout of jubilee *like a thunderclap*, and all at once the *thick* walls of Jericho collapsed! Everyone rushed straight ahead[d] and captured the city. [21]They utterly destroyed all that was in Jericho, men and women, young and old, livestock and donkeys—everything was destroyed with the sword.[e]

Rahab and Her Family Are Spared

[22]Joshua told the two spies who had entered Jericho, "Go to the prostitute's house and rescue her and everyone in her house, just as you promised her." [23]So the two spies brought out Rahab, her father, mother, brothers and sisters, and all who belonged to her, and gave them refuge outside the camp of Israel.

[24]Then they burned Jericho to the ground and all that was within it. Only the silver and gold, brass, and iron were placed into the treasury of Yahweh's house. [25]Yet Joshua spared Rahab the prostitute, her father's family, and all that belonged to her. She lives among the Israelites to this day[f] because she hid the two men Joshua sent to spy out Jericho.

[26]Afterward, Joshua pronounced this solemn oath:

"May Yahweh curse anyone
who attempts to rebuild this city, Jericho!
He will pay for laying its foundation
with the life of his oldest son,
and for setting up its gates with his youngest son!"[g]

[27]Yahweh's presence was with Joshua, and he became famous throughout the land.

Achan's Sin

7 But the Israelites violated the commandment regarding the wealth of Jericho that was to be set apart *for*

---

a 6:17 The Hebrew term for "devoted offering" is *cherem* and implies things or persons who were entirely and irrevocably consecrated to God, often by total destruction. See Lev. 27:28–29.

b 6:18 Or "keep away from."

c 6:18 See Deut. 7:25–26.

d 6:20 Or "everyone ascended." By comparing v. 20 with 1 Thess. 4:16–17, we see that both events have the Lord himself (see Josh. 6:8), a shout, a trumpet blast, and the people ascending. There are a number of "sevens" in this chapter: seven priests, seven shofars, seven days circling the city, seven times the city was to be encompassed on the seventh day. Seven represents completion, fullness, and perfection.

e 6:21 Or "by the mouth of the sword." See Heb. 4:12.

f 6:25 This shows that the book of Joshua was written not long after the events of the book.

g 6:26 This curse was fulfilled 550 years later in the time of Ahab by Hiel the Bethelite (see 1 Kings 16:34). In contrast, our heavenly Father laid the foundation of the church (see 1 Cor. 3:10–11) with the death of his Firstborn (see Rom. 8:29). The younger son is the overcomer, the many sons brought to glory, we who will also lay down our lives to rebuild the gates of Zion.

the Lord. Achan[a] son of Carmi,[b] grandson of Zimri,[c] of the clan of Zerah,[d] from the tribe of Judah, stole some of the devoted things for himself. This ignited Yahweh's anger against Israel.

[2]Joshua sent spies from Jericho to Ai (a *small city* near Beth Aven,[e] southeast of Bethel), with orders to spy out the land. So the spies left for Ai.[f] [3]When they returned to Joshua, they reported to him, "There is no need to trouble the whole army to conquer Ai. The people are so few that two or three thousand men could attack it *and take the city*."[g] [4]So Joshua sent three thousand troops to attack the city, but they were routed by the men of Ai. [5]The men of Ai chased them from the city gates, down the hill as far as the quarries,[h] cutting them down as they fled. They killed thirty-six of Joshua's men,

and when Israel heard of their defeat, their hearts melted away with fear![i]

[6]Joshua and the elders of Israel tore their clothes and threw dust over their heads to show their sorrow.[j] They threw themselves facedown to the ground in front of the ark of Yahweh until the evening *sacrifice*.[k] [7]Joshua cried out, "O Lord Yahweh, why did you lead these people across the Jordan? To be defeated? To be killed by the Amorites? If only we had been content to stay on the other side of the Jordan! [8]O Lord, what can I say now that Israel has retreated from its enemies? [9]When the Canaanites and everyone else in the land hear about *our defeat*, they will gang up on us and wipe us off the face of the earth. And what then will you do about your great name?"[l]

---

a 7:1 *Achan* means "one who brings trouble." Just as there was a snake in the garden (see Gen. 3:1), Judas among the followers of Christ (see Matt. 10:4), and Ananias and Sapphira in the church (see Acts 5:1–11), so there was "one who brings trouble" in the midst of Israel. See 1 Cor. 5:6.

b 7:1 *Carmi* means "my vineyard."

c 7:1 Or "Zabdi" or "Zabri" (see 1 Chron. 2:6 LXX).

d 7:1 Through Zerah, Achan was the descendant of Judah's sexual sin. See Gen. 38:6–30.

e 7:2 *Beth Aven* means "house of wickedness."

f 7:2 Ai was about fifteen miles north of Jericho. Tradition identifies the site known as et-Tell as biblical Ai. *Ai* means "heap of ruins."

g 7:3 Nothing in our spiritual life is so small that we can war against it in our own strength without God.

h 7:5 Or "Shebarim." *Shebarim* means "quarries" or "ravines."

i 7:5 Or "melted away and turned to water." It is interesting to note that after a great spiritual victory, we are all susceptible to a painful defeat. Only as we walk in divine strength and become aware of our weakness can we experience victory (see Isa. 2:22). This event warns us all of the sins of pride and presumption. All our fountains are in Christ (see Ps. 87:7).

j 7:6 Tearing one's clothes and throwing dust on one's head were ancient acts of mourning. See Gen. 37:34; 2 Sam. 1:2; 13:31; Job 1:20; 2:12.

k 7:6 This was the time of the evening sacrifice of a lamb.

l 7:9 That is, "What will you do to protect your great reputation?" Joshua pleaded with God to consider that his reputation was at stake over the success and protection of his people.

¹⁰Yahweh spoke to Joshua: "Stand up! Why are you groveling before me? ¹¹Israel has sinned!ᵃ They have broken the covenant which I had commanded them to keep. They have taken forbidden plunder. They have stolen from me, taken what is mine, hidden it among their belongings, and lied about it. ¹²Cursed things are among you! That is why Israel is powerless, has retreated from their enemies, and is in danger of annihilation. If you do not get rid of these cursed things from among you, I will not go with you any longer. ¹³Get up and purify the people in preparation for tomorrow.ᵇ Tell them, 'This is what Yahweh, the God of Israel says: "O Israel, you have in your midst what must be devoted entirely to me! You cannot stand against your enemies until you remove the devoted things from your midst!" ¹⁴Tomorrow morning, you shall present yourselves by tribes. Yahweh will indicateᶜ which tribe must come forward by clans. Yahweh will indicate which clan must come forward by families. And Yahweh will indicate which family must come forward one by one. ¹⁵Then finally, Yahweh will expose the man caught with the devoted things, which must be destroyed by fire. Everything that man ownsᵈ you must likewise destroy by fire, for he has violated the covenant of Yahweh and committed an outrageous act in Israel!' "

¹⁶Joshua was up at the crack of dawn and had Israel come forward by tribes, and Yahweh indicatedᵉ the tribe of Judah. ¹⁷Joshua then had the clans of Judah come forward, and Yahweh picked out the clan of Zerah. Joshua then had the clan of Zerah come forward and Yahweh indicated the family of Zimri. ¹⁸Joshua then had Zimri's family come forward one by one, and Yahweh picked out Achan, the son of Carmi, son of Zimri, son of Zerah, of the tribe of Judah.

¹⁹Then Joshua said to Achan, "My son, give glory to Yahweh, the God of Israel,ᶠ and confess.ᵍ Tell me the truth and do not hide anything from him. What have you done?"

²⁰"It's true," Achan said. "I've sinned against Yahweh, the God of Israel. This

---

a 7:11 The defeat at Ai was not just because they did not pray and trust God; it was because there was sin in the camp of Israel and they had lost God's favor. Although it was one individual, Achan, who sinned, God viewed them as a unit. We are one body in Christ, and the victory of one is the victory of all, and the sin of one is the sin of all. See 1 Cor. 5:1–7. For the righteousness of one (Rahab), the whole of her family was saved. For the sin of Achan, the whole of his family was condemned. Thus it is imperative that we belong firmly to the family of God in Christ Jesus, our eldest brother and representative head.

b 7:13 See Joel 2:15–16; Amos 4:12.

c 7:14 Or literally "catch by lot."

d 7:15 Or "All who belong to him."

e 7:16 Although Joshua does not record the manner in which Yahweh picked out Judah, we know that it was through a supernatural act of communication, possibly the Urim and Thummim. (*Urim* means "lights" and *Thummim* means "perfections.") See Ex. 28:30; Num. 27:21; Ezra 2:63. During the entire process, Achan had ample time to step forward and repent.

f 7:19 "Give glory to God!" was a Hebraism by which Joshua demanded the truth from Achan. (See footnote on John 9:24.)

g 7:19 Or "give him praise." To admit our sin before God in heartfelt confession is equated with giving praise to God.

is what I did: ²¹I saw among the plunder an exquisite robe from Babylon,ᵃ two hundred pieces of silver, and a fifty-shekel bar of gold.ᵇ I wanted them badly, so I took themᶜ and buried them in my tent with the silver underneath."

²²Joshua sent messengers who ran to the tent, and there it was! They found it buried in the middle of the tent with the silver underneath. ²³They took the stolen objects from the tent,ᵈ brought them to Joshua and all the Israelites, and displayed them in the presence of Yahweh.ᵉ ²⁴Then Joshua, and all Israel with him, took Achan son of Zerah along with the silver, the robe, the bar of gold, and all that belonged to him—his sons, daughters, donkeys, oxen, sheep, tent—everything. Joshua led them all to the Valley of Troubleᶠ ²⁵and said, "Why have you brought all this trouble on us? Yahweh will bring trouble on you today!"

Then all the people stoned Achan and his family to death. They burned up the bodies and all Achan's possessions. ²⁶They raised over him a huge mound of stones that remains to this day. That is why the place was called the Valley of Trouble ever since.

Afterward, Yahweh's anger subsided against Israel.ᵍ

Ai Conquered

8 Yahweh said to Joshua, "Do not yield to fear nor shrink back *because of Israel's failure.* Now, get up, take all your soldiers with you, and march against Ai. See, I have handed over to youʰ the city, the king, his people, and his land. ²Do to Ai what you did to Jericho and its king, except

---

a 7:21 Or "Shinar." See Gen. 10:10; 11:2; 14:1. Babylonia was recognized for its splendid, costly robes of many colors. It is possible that this robe had idolatrous figures embroidered on it. It may have been the royal robe of the king of Jericho. See Jonah 3:6.

b 7:21 This was equivalent to about five pounds of silver and one pound (or twenty ounces) of gold.

c 7:21 Achan followed the same order in his sin as Adam and Eve: he saw, he wanted them, and he took them. See Gen. 3:6; Col. 3:5; James 1:14–15. This is in the heart of sinful creation in rebellion against the goodness of God's generosity and holiness. Similarly, Achan sought to hide himself (he did not come forward but required Yahweh to expose him). Similarly, the family of Achan was condemned for his sin in the same fashion that the descendants of Adam are condemned for his sin.

d 7:23 Buried in our dust, in our "tent-life" (see 2 Cor. 5:1–5), we often try to hide our sins. It is always better to live without shame and without hidden things. Joshua's (Jesus') messengers will uncover the hidden things and bring them to the light (see Num. 32:23) so that victory may be restored. Our sins affect not only ourselves but those around us as well.

e 7:23 Most likely, the stolen objects were laid in the tabernacle before the ark of glory.

f 7:24 Or "the Valley of Achor." *Achor* (related to Achan) means "trouble" or "disaster." But judgment is not the end of the story. For the believer today, God's loving heart will open a door of hope for us even in the Valley of Trouble (see Hos. 2:15; Isa. 65:10). Jesus turns the Valley of Trouble into a door of hope. He took our judgment that we might rise up in resurrection's hope. See Isa. 53:5–6; Phil. 3:10–11.

g 7:26 Leadership lessons we can learn from this chapter include: (1) There are times the advice of others can lead us astray (see v. 3). (2) It is dangerous for leaders to be presumptuous, to be self-confident, and to ignore sin (see v. 5). (3) We can never take anything that has been devoted to God (see v. 11). (4) Our message to the people must bring them into purity (see v. 13). And (5) keeping ourselves pure will restore favor and blessing to God's people (see v. 26).

h 8:1 Or "I have delivered into your hands."

this time, you may take the plunder, including livestock. Set an ambush behind the city."

³Joshua and his entire army set out to attack Ai. He chose thirty thousand valiant warriors and sent them ahead by night ⁴with these instructions: "Now pay attention. Set an ambush behind Ai, but don't hide very far away. Stay alert and ready for battle! ⁵I'll lead the rest of the army and make a direct assault on the city, and when they come out to fight us, we'll flee from them as we did the first time. ⁶When this happens, they'll say to themselves, 'Look! They're running away from us, just like last time!' And they'll keep chasing us until we've lured them away from the city. While we're running away from them, ⁷jump up from your hiding place, race into Ai, and seize it. Yahweh, your God, will deliver the city into your hands! ⁸When you've captured the city, set it on fire. Now that you have your orders, go and do as Yahweh has commanded!"

⁹Joshua then sent them off, and they proceeded to take up a concealed position west of Ai, between Ai and Bethel, while Joshua spent the night with the rest of the troops.

¹⁰So early the next morning, Joshua mustered his troops. He and the leaders of Israel went in front of the army and led them toward Ai. ¹¹The entire fighting force with Joshua advanced until they were near the city and encamped north of Ai,ᵃ with a valley between them and the city. ¹²He placed *a smaller force* of about five thousand men west of the city to set an ambush between Bethel and Ai.ᵇ ¹³The main fighting force north of the city prepared for battle, while the rear guardᶜ held a concealed position west of the city. Joshua spent the night in the valley.ᵈ

¹⁴At dawn, when the king of Ai saw the Israelites, he and his army rushed out to fight. They ran to attack Israel at a predetermined place en route to the Arabah, not knowing that an ambush had been set against them behind the city. ¹⁵Joshua and all the main fighting force fled toward the wilderness as though they were being overcome. ¹⁶*Joshua's tactic* drew all of Ai's reinforcements out of the city, and they set off in hot pursuit of Joshua *and his men.* ¹⁷Not a man remained in Ai or in Bethelᵉ who did not go out in pursuit of Israel, leaving their city undefended.

¹⁸Then Yahweh spoke to Joshua and said, "Now, take the spear in your hand and point it toward Ai, for I will hand the city over to you!" So Joshua pointed his spear toward the city, ¹⁹and when Joshua gave this signal, all the men waiting in ambush behind the city jumped up from their position and poured into Ai. They quickly captured it and set it on fire.

²⁰⁻²¹When the men of Ai looked back, they saw the smoke of their city rising to the sky. Joshua and his men also saw the smoke and knew that the other Israelite soldiers had captured the city and had set it on fire. The army of Ai

---

a 8:11 Joshua encamped in plain sight of the enemy.

b 8:12 Some Jewish scholars (Rashi, David Kimchi) suggest that Joshua set a double ambush, one closer to the city than the other. One consisted of five thousand and the larger ambush, thirty thousand.

c 8:13 Or "his heel."

d 8:13 The Septuagint omits v. 13 entirely.

e 8:17 The reference to Bethel is omitted in the Septuagint.

had no place to escape, so Joshua and his men turned on them and began killing them. ²²The men who had taken the city came out and joined the battle, so the Israelites had them surrounded. Israel cut them down, leaving neither survivors nor fugitives. ²³But they captured the king of Ai alive and brought him to Joshua.

²⁴Joshua's men killed all the inhabitants of Ai in the fields and in the wilderness where they had chased them. They all fell by the sword. Then the Israelites turned to attack Ai and killed those who were still there.ᵃ ²⁵⁻²⁶Joshua kept his spear pointed at Ai until the destruction was complete. Ai's entire population, twelve thousand men and women, fell that day. ²⁷However, the Israelites took the livestock and the goods captured in the city as Yahweh had instructed Joshua.

²⁸Then Joshua burned Ai to the ground and reduced it to a mound of ruins for all time. It remains desolate to this day. ²⁹And he hanged the king of Ai on a tree until sunset. Then at sunset, Joshua had the corpse taken down and left it lying in front of where the city gates *once stood*. They raised a large pile of stones over his corpse, *where it remains* to this day.

Renewal of the Covenant at Mount Ebal

³⁰Afterward, Joshua built near Mount Ebal a stone altarᵇ to Yahweh, the God of Israel. ³¹He made it according to the teaching in the law of Moses, Yahweh's servant. Moses had commanded them to build an altar using stones that had not been cut with iron tools.ᶜ On it they offered to Yahweh burnt sacrifices and fellowship offerings.ᵈ ³²And with the Israelites looking on, Joshua inscribed on stones the law which Moses had written.

³³All Israel, including their elders, officials, and judges, stood on either side of the ark. Both native-born citizens and immigrants alike faced the ark of the covenant of Yahweh and the Levitical priests who carried it. In front of half of them stood Mount Gerizim,ᵉ

---

a 8:24 God did a miracle for Israel with Jericho's walls crumbling, but with the battle of Ai, it was God's brilliant strategy carried out by Joshua's men that won the victory. Every battle in our lives requires that we seek God's face and obey his instructions so that we will taste the joys of victory. Obedience to God's plan is the key. Though God assured Israel of victory, they still had to discharge their responsibility.

b 8:30 This altar was built at Shechem, about twenty miles from Ai, between Mount Ebal and Mount Gerizim. *Ebal* means "stripped of all covering," "bare," "naked," or "barren." The law etched upon stones exposes sin, leaves us guilty, and produces death (see 2 Cor. 3:7).

c 8:31 See Deut. 27:1–26. Building the altar without the tools of people teaches us that God alone made the ultimate altar, the cross of Jesus. Salvation is not through the hands of humankind but by the mercy of God (see Titus 3:5). The altar was to be on Mount Ebal, the place where the curses were read. God has provided an altar of salvation even when sin's curse defeats us. Mercy's altar stands on Ebal even when we feel stripped, bare, naked, and barren.

d 8:31 Or "peace offerings," "offerings of well-being," or "communion sacrifices." The fellowship offerings were given in gratitude to God. Only the fat was burned (see Lev. 7:29–34), and the rest was consumed by the people (see Lev. 10:14).

e 8:33 *Gerizim* means "cut up" or "shorn place." Jesus took our curse and was "shorn" and "cut up" for our sins (see Isa. 53:7–8). Israel renewed their covenant with Yahweh in the valley between Mount Ebal (*ebal* means "stripped of all covering," a picture of the law) and Mount Gerizim (*gerizim* means "cut up," a picture of the cross of Jesus Christ). The new covenant, the Spirit of Life, is now written upon our hearts. See Jer. 31:33; 2 Cor. 3:3; Heb. 8:10; 10:16.

and in front of the other half stood Mount Ebal, as Yahweh's servant Moses commanded at first to bless the people of Israel.*ᵃ ³⁴Afterward, Joshua read aloud all the words of the law, the blessings and the curses,ᵇ exactly as it was written in the scroll of the law. ³⁵Joshua read aloud every word that Moses had commanded, and all the assembly of Israel heard it, including the women, the children, and the foreigners who accompanied them.ᶜ

The Gibeonites Deceive Joshua

9 Now when all the kings west of the Jordan heard about these things—those in the hill country,ᵈ in the western foothills, and along the entire coast of the Great Sea as far as Lebanon (the kings of the Hittites, Amorites, Canaanites, Perizzites, Hivites, and Jebusites)— ²they came together to make war against Joshua and Israel. ³When the inhabitants of Gibeonᵉ learned how Joshua had destroyed Jericho and Ai, ⁴they resorted to a ruse: They sent a delegation disguisedᶠ *as messengers from a distant land*. They loaded their donkeys with worn-out sacks and old, patched wineskins. ⁵They wore old, patched sandals on their feet and old, tattered clothes, and took along dry, moldy bread. ⁶When they arrived at Israel's camp at Gilgal, they said to Joshua and the Israelites: "We've come from a far country to propose that you make a treaty with us."

⁷The men of Israel asked the Hivites, "Perhaps you live nearby. Why should we make a treaty with you?"ᵍ

⁸"We are willing to be your servants," they answered Joshua.

Joshua questioned them further, "Who are you and where are you from?"

⁹The Gibeonites replied: "Your servants come from a very distant land because we've heard of the fame of your God, Yahweh. We've heard of his wonders and all that he did in Egypt. ¹⁰We've also heard of all he did to help you defeat the two Amorite kings on the other side of the Jordan—King Sihon of Heshbon and King Og of Bashan, who lived in Ashtaroth.ʰ ¹¹Therefore, our leaders and all the inhabitants of our land sent us to find you with these instructions: 'Get food ready for your long trip, and go to the Israelites and say to them, "Make a treaty with us. We're willing to be your servants." ' ¹²Look at our bread! It was still warm when we left home with it. See how dry and moldy it's become! ¹³These wineskins were new when we

---

a 8:33 See Deut. 11:29.

b 8:34 See Lev. 26; Deut. 27–28.

c 8:35 See Neh. 8:1–12.

d 9:1 This was a hilly area on the west of the Jordan called the Shephelah. The kings of the highlands could represent those today who occupy the high ground of pride and fleshly confidence. They look down from their elevated position on anyone unlike them.

e 9:3 The kings mentioned in this passage could represent those today who oppose God's ways: *Gibeon* means "hill city," representing human pride, *Hivite* means "human effort," and *Ai* means "heap of ruins." Gibeon was the capital of the Hivites, a large city about seven miles from Ai and nearly twenty miles from Israel's camp at Gilgal. It has been identified with modern al-Jib, a Palestinian village about six miles northwest of Jerusalem.

f 9:4 Or possibly "They collected provisions." The meaning of the Hebrew is uncertain.

g 9:7 See Ex. 23:32; Deut. 7:2.

h 9:10 They did not mention the more recent miraculous conquests of Jericho and Ai.

filled them. See how they've dried up and burst! And look, our clothes and sandals are worn out from our long journey."*a*

¹⁴The leaders of Israel ratified a peace treaty with the Gibeonites by sharing a meal together,*b* but they failed to consult with Yahweh.*c* ¹⁵Joshua agreed to let them live. He made a peace treaty with them, and the leaders of the assembly sealed it with an oath.

¹⁶But three days after the treaty had been made, the Israelites learned*d* *that they had been deceived*. In fact, the Gibeonites were from the local area and lived nearby. ¹⁷So the Israelites set out at once, and on the third day, they came to their cities: Gibeon, Chephirah,*e* Beeroth,*f* and Kiriath Jearim.*g* ¹⁸But the Israelites did not attack them because the leaders of the assembly had sworn an oath to them in the name of Yahweh, the God of Israel.

This caused Israel to grumble against their leaders, ¹⁹but the leaders told the assembly of Israel, "We cannot touch them, for we swore an oath to them in the name of Yahweh, the God of Israel. ²⁰⁻²¹We must let them live for fear that God's anger will come upon us because of the oath we swore to them." So they became woodcutters and water carriers for the community of Israel, as their leaders had decreed.

²²Joshua summoned the Gibeonites and asked them, "Why did you deceive us? You told us that you lived very far from us, but we now know for a fact that you live right here near us. ²³Therefore, *we will spare your lives*, but you will live under a curse, and you will be condemned to perpetual servitude. You will serve the house of

---

a 9:13 The Gibeonites with old wineskins (religious systems), old clothing (old nature), old worn-out shoes (old methods), and moldy bread, represent counterfeit traditions and deceptions of religion. Their bread was moldy, not fit for consumption. The boast of their "long journey" parallels the ecclesiastical history of many church traditions today that have confidence in their long history more than the authority of Scripture. We can make no alliance with the old as we move forward to possess our inheritance. A new victory requires that we eat the fresh bread of heaven with a renewed mind that hears what God is saying today to his people.

b 9:14 Literally "The men took some of their provisions." This was not simply eating the moldy bread but also a sharing of a fellowship meal to ratify the peace treaty.

c 9:14 Or "they did not ask the mouth of Yahweh." Some Jewish scholars believe that meant they did not ask the Lord to show them what to do through the Urim and Thummim. If we lack wisdom and ask God, he will give us his heart (see James 1:5).

d 9:16 Or "heard." It is possible that Israel supernaturally heard that the Gibeonites were lying, perhaps through a dream or from a prophet among them who heard from God.

e 9:17 *Chephirah* means "lioness." It has been identified with the modern Khirbet el-Kefireh, about ten miles west of Jerusalem.

f 9:17 *Beeroth* means "wells."

g 9:17 *Kiriath Jearim* means "city of dense thickets" (representing the mind of man). Kiriath Jearim is also called Kiriath Baal (see Josh. 15:60). The four cities in this verse were clustered close together: Beeroth was about five miles northeast of Gibeon; Chephirah was about five miles southwest of Gibeon, and Kiriath Jearim was a bit farther away in the same direction.

my God by cutting wood and carrying water for us."[a]

[24]They answered Joshua, "We lied, sir, because we greatly feared for our lives. We know for certain all about Moses and how he served Yahweh, your God. We know for certain that Yahweh will honor his promise to Moses and give you all these lands as your own. And we know for certain that he commanded you to wipe out all the inhabitants living here and thus take possession of this land. [25]Now we are at your mercy, so do with us what you consider right and proper."

[26]So Joshua *had mercy* and saved them[b] from being killed by the Israelites. [27]That day, he made them woodcutters and water carriers to serve the community of Israel for the altar of Yahweh at his divinely chosen place.[c] And that is what they do to this day.

When the Sun Stood Still

10 [1-2]Adoni-zedek,[d] the king of Jerusalem,[e] was struck with fear when he[f] heard how Joshua had totally destroyed the kings and cities of Ai and Jericho and that the people of Gibeon had made a peace treaty with Israel and were living alongside them. The city of Gibeon was larger than Ai, as large as any of the cities that were ruled by a king, and all its men were known as great warriors. [3]So King Adoni-zedek of Jerusalem sent messages to King Hoham[g] of Hebron,

---

a 9:23 See Deut. 29:10–11. Cutting wood and carrying water were the tasks of women in the culture of that day. The implication is that the Gibeonites would have had to disband their army and depend on Israel for their defense. Furthermore, cutting wood and carrying water would be very important tasks for tabernacle worship when Israel set up their base in Shiloh (see Josh. 18:1). Though they were considered servants and uncircumcised gentiles, they would be close in proximity to the worship of Yahweh in the tabernacle and serve the needs of the sacrificial system. Historically, the Gibeonites retained their treaty rights with Israel for more than four hundred years, until the close of David's reign. One violation of their treaty occurred under Saul's reign, and it brought Israel three years of famine as God's judgment. See 2 Sam. 21:1–9. Principles of any covenant are very important to God.

b 9:26 Israel's sons once made a treaty with the people of Shechem but broke it and killed the people (see Gen. 34:13–31). Here Joshua made a peace treaty and kept his oath. Like Joshua, leaders must always keep their promises and show mercy to others. At times, our past sins do affect our lives. The consequences of our sins may later surface so that we can learn from the past and break off its influence by the power of the Holy Spirit.

c 9:27 See Deut. 12:11, 14, 26; 15:20; 17:8; 31:11.

d 10:1–2 The high-sounding names of the five kings mentioned in this chapter all speak of human pride, self-righteousness, and the natural life with its five senses. *Adoni-zedek* means "lord of righteousness." There is only one Lord of Righteousness, and it wasn't he.

e 10:1–2 This is the first mention of Jerusalem in the Bible. *Jerusalem* means "foundation of peace" or "city of peace." The city was originally known as the stronghold of Jebus or Jerus. Later, in about 1010 BC, David captured the stronghold of the Jebusites and established Jerusalem as the capital of his united kingdom. See 1 Chron. 11:4–7.

f 10:1–2 Or "they." This was not only the people of Jerusalem but the four other kings as well (see v. 3). The kings of that land were struck with fear because of God's miracles that accompanied Israel. See Ex. 23:27; Deut. 11:25.

g 10:3 *Hoham* means "driven [forced]" or "he crushed." He ruled as king of Hebron, twenty miles south of Jerusalem. *Hebron* means "alliance."

King Piram of Jarmuth,[a] King Japhia of Lachish,[b] and King Debir of Eglon:[c] [4]"The people of Gibeon have made peace with Joshua and the Israelites. Come and help me attack them."

[5]The five Amorite kings joined forces—the kings of Jerusalem, Hebron, Jarmuth, Lachish, and Eglon.[d] Their combined armies surrounded Gibeon and attacked it.

[6]The Gibeonites sent out a call for help to Joshua[e] at the camp in Gilgal: "Don't abandon us, for we are your servants! Come quickly and save us! Help us, for the Amorite kings of the hill country have surrounded us!"[f] [7]So Joshua and all his fighting men, all the mighty warriors of Israel, left Gilgal *to aid the Gibeonites.*

[8]Yahweh spoke to Joshua:[g] "Do not fear the Amorite kings and their armies, for I have decreed your victory over them; not one will withstand you!"

[9]Joshua and his fighting force marched all night long from Gilgal *to Gibeon*[h] and took them all by surprise! [10]Joshua inflicted a crushing defeat on them at Gibeon, for Yahweh threw the Amorites into a panic at the sudden sight of Israel's army! Yahweh *empowered Joshua*[i] *and his army* to chase them in the direction of the Beth Horon ascent,[j] *and they slaughtered the*

---

a 10:3 *Piram* means "wild donkey" or "fierce." Piram ruled as king of Jarmuth (modern Khirbet el-Yarmuk), which is eighteen miles southwest of Jerusalem. *Jarmuth* means "high place." These high places could also include "every arrogant attitude that is raised up in defiance of the true knowledge of God" (2 Cor. 10:5).

b 10:3 *Japhia* means "one who enlightens" or "elevated." Japhia ruled as king of Lachish, fifteen miles west of Hebron. *Lachish* means "invincible." Archeologists believe that Tell el-Hesy is ancient Lachish.

c 10:3 *Debir* means "speaker" or "oracle." Debir was the king of Eglon, ten miles west of Hebron. *Eglon* means "young bull."

d 10:5 The combined forces of these five city-states would have been quite intimidating, to say the least. However, it was in fact God's plan to bring them together and to defeat them in one epic battle. This chapter describes the miraculous way in which their coalition was defeated and how the God of Israel gave victory to Joshua.

e 10:6 Even though the men of Gibeon were "great warriors," they didn't trust in their own strength but called for help to Joshua (Jesus). See Isa. 31:1; 2 Cor. 12:10.

f 10:6 The five kings occupied the high ground, standing above everyone else. Their elevated position is a picture of pride in a perceived higher status. Many believers today look down on others who are not like themselves. See Isa. 40:4; Phil. 2:5–10; 3 John 9–10.

g 10:8 Once again, Yahweh spoke to his servant, Joshua. We need leaders today who hear the voice of our Champion-God and help others to hear God's voice for themselves. See 1 Sam. 3:1–21; John 10:27.

h 10:9 This march, over rough, uphill country, took about nine hours to complete.

i 10:10 The Hebrew text indicates that Yahweh is still the subject in vv. 10–11. Yahweh empowered the army, after an all-night march, to fight victoriously over the coalition of the Amorites. Yahweh also empowered them to run for many miles when Israel's fighting force turned south from Beth Horon all the way to Azekah and Makkedah. This was a supernatural event not accomplished by the might of Israel's army alone. They were given supernatural strength by faith (see Heb. 11:33–35).

j 10:10 Beth Horon was two towns. Upper Beth Horon was about five miles northwest of Gibeon. There was a mountain pass that descended to lower Beth Horon.

kings' armies all the way to Azekah[a] and the city of Makkedah.[b] [11]As the Amorites raced down the hill to Beth Horon, Yahweh hurled large hailstones on them from the sky![c] The hail continued to fall all the way to Azekah; in fact, more men died from *Yahweh's* hailstones than by the swords of the Israelites.

[12]Yahweh gave the men of Israel victory over the Amorites that day, the day when Joshua stood before the people and prayed to Yahweh:

"Sun, stand still[d] over Gibeon!

Moon, stay where you are over the valley of Aijalon!"[e]

[13]And so the sun stood still in the middle of the sky and was in no hurry to set until one day *became two.* And the moon halted while the nation triumphed[f] over its enemies—as it is *also* recorded in the Scroll of the Upright One.[g] [14]It was the day Yahweh himself fought for Israel! There has never been a day like it before or since—a day when Yahweh obeyed the voice of a man!

[15]*After their victory,*[h] Joshua and his fighting men returned to their camp at Gilgal.

Joshua Captures the Five Amorite Kings

[16]Meanwhile, the five Amorite kings fled and hid in a cave at Makkedah. [17]When Joshua was told that the five kings

---

a 10:10 The exact site of Azekah is unknown, but it is believed to be in or near the Valley of Elah. David famously fought Goliath in the Valley of Elah, about fifteen miles southwest of Bethlehem, probably modern Wadi es-Sant.

b 10:10 The exact location of Makkedah is unknown, but it is believed to be el-Mughar, twenty-five miles from Gibeon. *Makkedah* means "shepherd's field."

c 10:11 God supernaturally directed the hailstones to hit the Amorites, but not the Israelites (see Ps. 91:7). There have been reports in human history of record hailstones weighing over 120 pounds. The largest hailstone in recent history fell in South Dakota, US, and was nearly the size of a volleyball. Hail is a biblical symbol of God's truth and justice that destroy the refuge (web) of lies. See Ex. 9:18–35; Isa. 28:17; Rev. 11:19.

d 10:12 Or "Sun, wait silently."

e 10:12 *Aijalon* means "field of deer" or "a strong place." The fiery passion of the Lord (see Isa. 9:7; 37:32) consumed Joshua as he spoke to the sun and moon so he could finish the fight. What faith we see in his decree! Imagine if that zeal came upon you.

f 10:13 Or "exacted vengeance." This chapter contains perhaps the most amazing miracle recorded in Israel's history. By the decree of a mortal, the entire cosmos paused as Yahweh himself fought for his people! God will go to any length to see you win your battles as you live in faith and obedience to him. God is the engineer of the universe and holds its controls in his hands. He can accelerate or slow down the created order he set in place. See Job 9:7; Isa. 38:7–8; Hab. 3:11.

g 10:13 Or "Jashar." See 2 Sam. 1:18. Jashar is from the Hebrew word *yashar*, which means "upright," "correct," or "pleasing." The scroll's name can also be translated "the Song of Heroes" or "the True Record." The *Scroll of the Upright One* was a book likely containing war songs, prayers, and exploits of Israel. The Jewish sage Rashi believed "Jashar" was a symbolic name for the Torah. Others believe it is the same as the book of the wars of the Lord (see Num. 21:14). There has been no manuscript found containing the *Scroll of the Upright One*. There are other books by that name, but they are not the same as the one mentioned here.

h 10:15 Scholars debate whether or not this is a scribal error, mistakenly copied from v. 42 and placed here. Regardless, the narrative doesn't end yet, for the battle continued as they captured the kings of the opposing forces and executed them.

had been found hiding in a cave at Makkedah, [18]Joshua ordered his men, "Seal up the mouth of the cave with large stones and post guards in front of it. [19]But don't stop! Pursue your enemies! Cut off their retreat and don't let them reach their cities, for Yahweh your God has given them into your hand!"

[20]So Joshua and the Israelites nearly killed them all—almost to a man—although a few escaped into the fortified cities. [21]The whole army returned safely to Joshua at the camp in Makkedah. No one dared speak against the Israelites.[a]

[22]Then Joshua ordered, "Open up the cave and bring the five kings out to me." [23]So Joshua's men removed the five kings from the cave, the king of Jerusalem, the king of Hebron, the king of Jarmuth, the king of Lachish, and the king of Eglon, and brought them before Joshua.

[24]Joshua summoned all of Israel and ordered his army officers, "Place your feet on the necks of these kings." So they placed their feet upon their necks! [25]Then Joshua said to his officers, "Never be afraid of your enemies or let them discourage you. Be strong and filled with courage! Yahweh is going to do to all your enemies what he's done to these kings!"

[26]Then Joshua had the kings executed and hanged on five trees, and he left them there until evening. [27]At sunset, Joshua ordered them taken down from the trees and thrown into the cave where they had been hiding. He had large stones rolled over the mouth of the cave, and they remain there to this day.[b]

The Capture of the Cities of the South

[28]That day, Joshua captured Makkedah, annihilated the inhabitants, and put its king to the sword, leaving no survivors. And he did to its king what had been done to the king of Jericho.

[29]From Makkedah, Joshua and his army marched *southwest* to the city of Libnah[c] and attacked it. [30]*By the power of* Yahweh, the city and its king were handed over to the Israelites. They annihilated all the inhabitants with the sword, leaving no survivors. And they did to its king what they had done to the king of Jericho.

[31]From Libnah, Joshua and his army marched south to *the city of*

---

a 10:21 Or "no one so much as snarled [or 'sharpened their tongue'] at the Israelites."

b 10:27 Joshua had imprisoned the five Amorite kings and set men as guardians over the cave until he had defeated their armies. Then his men opened the cave and brought out the kings, and he invited the men of war to put their feet on the necks of these enemies as a symbol of total victory. Joshua executed the five kings, hanging them on five trees. Without revelation, our five natural senses rule and limit us. A mind set on the five senses (metaphorically represented by the five kings) is like a cave and tomb of darkness. In the same way Joshua shut the mouth of the cave with stones, Jesus (our Joshua) set guardians over the church (see 1 Cor. 12:28; Eph. 4:11). Jesus pounds our enemies to a pulp under our feet (see Rom. 16:20; Heb. 10:12–13), a total victory. In the same way Joshua executed the five kings, Jesus has silenced all the voices accusing and condemning us (see Rom. 8:1–6) and has set us free from the curse of legalistic self-effort (see Gal. 3:13). He crucified our old identities, and they are dead and buried. We no longer live submitted to sin's power because Jesus gives us new life and new identities, empowered by his faith (see Rom. 6:6; Gal. 2:20).

c 10:29 *Libnah* means "pavement" or "whiteness." Libnah lies about seven miles southwest of Makkedah.

Lachish and attacked it. ³²*By the power of* Yahweh, the city was handed over to Joshua on the second day of the battle. They annihilated all the inhabitants of the city, just as they had done to Libnah. ³³Meanwhile, Horam,ᵃ king of Gezer,ᵇ had marched out to help Lachish, but Joshua defeated him and his army, leaving no survivors.

³⁴Then Joshua and all the Israelite army marched on from Lachish to attack *the city of* Eglon.ᶜ ³⁵*By the power of* Yahweh, they captured the city in one day and destroyed its inhabitants, just as they had done to Lachish.

³⁶Then Joshua and all the Israelite army marched from Eglon and attacked Hebron.ᵈ ³⁷*By the power of* Yahweh, they captured the city, the king, and nearby villages, and totally wiped out all the inhabitants, leaving no survivors, just as they had done to Eglon.

³⁸Lastly, Joshua and all the Israelite army turned around and attacked Debir. ³⁹*By the power of* Yahweh, they captured the city, the king, and nearby villages, and totally wiped out all the inhabitants, leaving no survivors. They did to Debir and its king as they had done to Libnah and its king and to Hebron.

⁴⁰*Yahweh empowered* Joshua to conquer the whole region,ᵉ including the hill country, the southern desert,ᶠ the western foothills, and the mountain slopes. He conquered all the kings of the land and left no survivors. Everything that breathed was slaughtered—as Yahweh, the God of Israel, had commanded.ᵍ ⁴¹Joshua's conquest stretched from Kadesh Barnea to Gaza, and from Goshen to Gibeon. ⁴²Joshua conquered all their kings and their lands in a single campaign, for Yahweh, the God of Israel, fought for his people. ⁴³Finally, Joshua and all the Israelite army returned to their base camp in Gilgal.

Joshua's Northern Conquest

11 When the news of Israel's *southern* victories reached King Jabinʰ of Hazor,ⁱ he *organized a massive coalition to fight against Israel.* He sent messages to:

---

a 10:33 *Horam* means "exalted."

b 10:33 *Gezer* means "steep"; it is about twenty-two miles north of Lachish.

c 10:34 *Eglon* means "bull-like"; it is about ten miles west of Lachish.

d 10:36 *Hebron* means "alliance"; it is in the highlands about twenty-two miles from Eglon.

e 10:40 These seven victories (including the defeat of Horam's army) established the Israelites in the land and made the name of Yahweh famous.

f 10:40 Or "Negeb."

g 10:40 The utter destruction of the cities and people of the land God gave to Israel reflects our need to identify and destroy absolutely everything in our lives that hinders God's grace from subduing and conquering our hearts. No doubt it was not a pleasant task for Israel, nor is it a pleasant task for a believer today. Nevertheless, we must set apart the "promised land" of our hearts for God alone, with neither compromise nor hidden sin. It is our responsibility to seek out and destroy anything in our lives that might corrupt a single-hearted devotion and pure love for a holy God (see Matt. 5:29–30; 2 Cor. 11:3). With God's divine grace, nothing is impossible (see Matt. 19:26; Luke 1:37). We will share the likeness of Jesus and become the radiant, look-alike partners to the Son of God (see Rev. 19:7–8).

h 11:1 *Jabin* means "discerner" or "wise one."

i 11:1 *Hazor* means "fortified" or "castle." It was a major city-state that lay about nine miles north of Lake Galilee.

King Jobab of Merom,[a]
the king of Shimron,[b]
the king of Achshaph,[c]
[2]the kings of the northern hill country,[d]
the kings of the Jordan Valley south of Lake Galilee,[e]
the kings of the foothills,
the western kings in the heights of Dor,[f]
[3]the eastern and western Canaanite kings,
the Amorite kings,
the Hittite kings,
the Perizzite kings,
the Jebusite kings in the highlands,
and the Hivite kings who lived near Mount Hermon in the land of Mizpah.[g]
[4]They came out in full force with a multitude of horses and chariots. Their vast armies were as numerous as the grains of sand on the seashore.[h] [5]All these kings and their enormous armies joined forces[i] and encamped at Lake Merom[j] to fight against Israel.

[6]Yahweh spoke to Joshua, saying, "Don't be afraid of them; by this time tomorrow, I, Yahweh, will have them all lying slain before Israel. After the battle, cripple their horses and burn their chariots."[k]

[7]Joshua launched his surprise attack, and all his army pounced on them at their camp at Lake Merom. [8]Yahweh fought[l] alongside Joshua's fighting men to defeat them. Part of the Israelite army attacked and pursued the retreating forces as far north as the cities of Misrephoth Maim[m] and Sidon.[n] Another part of the Israelite army pursued the enemy as far east as the valley of Mizpah and crushed

---

a 11:1 Or "Madon." *Madon* means "strife." Some scholars, because of historical and archaeological evidence, prefer to read "Merom" (v. 5) here and in 12:9–24. Merom was three miles west of Lake Galilee.

b 11:1 *Shimron* means "extreme vigilance." It was a city-state of the Lower Galilee region and the Jezreel Valley. It is identified today as Tell Samunia or Tell Shimron.

c 11:1 *Achshaph* means "incantation" or "sorcery." The exact location of Achshaph is unknown, but it is believed to be about thirty miles from Hazor.

d 11:2 The northern hill country would be the modern district of Galilee.

e 11:2 Or "Arabah south of Chinneroth [Galilee]." In biblical times, Arabah referred both to the Jordan Valley between Lake Galilee and the Dead Sea, and also to an area south of Judah.

f 11:2 Or "the foothills of the Carmel range." This was the region west of Lake Galilee toward the Mediterranean coastal plains south of Mount Carmel. *Dor* means "lofty place"; it was the chief city.

g 11:3 *Mizpah* means "watchtower."

h 11:4 According to Josephus, the armies of these ten kingdoms were more than three hundred thousand foot soldiers, ten thousand horses, and twenty thousand chariots (see *Ant.* 5.1.18). Joshua confronted these armies and defeated them all with only an infantry and Yahweh!

i 11:5 Or "met by appointment."

j 11:5 Or "the waters of Merom," most likely modern Lake Huleh. Josephus called it "the lake of Semechonitis" (see *Ant.* 5.5.1).

k 11:6 Yahweh did not want Israel to trust in the might of horses or chariots but in him alone. See Ps. 20:7; 33:17.

l 11:8 Or "Yahweh delivered them into their hands."

m 11:8 *Misrephoth Maim* means "lime kilns by the waters." It was a city on the border of Israel and Lebanon.

n 11:8 Or "Great Sidon," an important Phoenician city north of Israel on the Mediterranean coast.

them all, leaving no survivors. [9]Afterward, Joshua crippled their horses and burned their chariots as Yahweh had commanded.

[10]Because Hazor at that time was the most powerful of all these kingdoms, Joshua circled back after the battle and conquered it.[a] [11]They killed the king, burned Hazor[b] to the ground, and annihilated all its inhabitants. They spared not one breathing thing, leaving no survivors.

[12]Joshua conquered all those royal cities and their kings. He destroyed them all, as Yahweh's servant Moses had commanded. [13]However, of all the cities built on mounds,[c] Joshua burned down only Hazor. [14]The Israelites kept all the spoils of these towns, including the livestock, but the inhabitants they killed with the sword. There were no survivors. [15]Just as Yahweh commanded his servant Moses, so Moses commanded Joshua, and Joshua obeyed everything[d] that Yahweh commanded Moses.

The Territory Taken by Joshua

[16]So Joshua conquered the entire region: the Judean hills, the southern desert, all the land of Goshen, the foothills, the lowlands of the Jordan Valley, the northern hill country of Israel including its lowlands— [17]everything from Mount Halak,[e] which rises toward Seir, all the way to Baal-Gad[f] in the Lebanon Valley below Mount Hermon.[g] Joshua captured all their kings and executed them.

[18]Joshua waged war with all those kings over a long period.[h] [19]Apart from the Hivites living in Gibeon, not one city made peace with Israel. By the power of Yahweh, Joshua conquered them all. [20]Yahweh himself hardened their hearts and made them obstinate so they would attack Israel. Yahweh had determined to wipe them out and condemn them to destruction without mercy, just as he had commanded Moses.

[21]Joshua also drove out the Anakim,[i] a race of giants, from the hill country (including the cities of Hebron, Debir, and Anab)—from the entire hill country of Judah and Israel. Joshua destroyed the Anakim and their towns [22]so that there were no surviving Anakim in Israelite territory. Some survived but only in the Philistine cities of Gaza,

---

a 11:10 Or "struck them down with the mouth of the sword."

b 11:11 The destruction of Hazor has been dated by recent excavations to around 1225 BC. Solomon later rebuilt the city (see 1 Kings 9:15).

c 11:13 That is, cities that were rebuilt on the ruins of earlier settlements.

d 11:15 The words "obeyed everything" should be the goal and ambition of our lives. Our calling is not simply to be successful but also to be obedient. See Luke 1:38; John 2:5.

e 11:17 Mount Halak means "bare mountain"; it is likely Jebel Halaq.

f 11:17 Baal-Gad means "the god of fortune."

g 11:17 The southern limit of Joshua's conquest was Mount Halak, near Edom, south of the Dead Sea; the northern limit was the town of Baal-Gad, not far from Mount Hermon.

h 11:18 The "long period" was about seven years. There are spiritual battles we fight that we do not win easily or quickly. Thankfully, God will ultimately make us victorious in all things. See 1 Sam. 17:47; 1 Cor. 15:57; Gal. 6:9; Eph. 6:10–13.

i 11:21 The Anakim were descendants of Anak. They are mentioned in Num. 13 as intimidating giants that kept the Israelites fearful in unbelief, which led to their wandering in the wilderness. Here we read that Joshua eliminated these giants and enabled the tribes of Israel to possess their inheritance, just as Jesus does today to the giants keeping us from full faith. Giants are nothing compared to God's omnipotence.

Gath, and Ashdod.*a* *23*Joshua conquered the whole land, just as Yahweh had promised Moses. Joshua assigned portions of the land to each of the tribes of Israel, and the Israelites lived in peace throughout the land.*b*

The Kings Defeated by Moses

12 On the east side of the Jordan, *Moses and* the Israelites had conquered two kings, *Sihon and Og.* The Israelites occupied their territory, which extended from the Arnon Valley *in the south* to Mount Hermon *in the north*, including the entire eastern desert.*c*

*2*Sihon, king of the Amorites, reigned in Heshbon*d* and ruled over *the southern* half of Gilead, from Aroer on the edge of the Arnon River Valley *in the south* to the River Jabbok *in the north*, which is the border of the Ammonites. *3The western area of* his kingdom included the eastern desert from Lake Galilee to the Dead Sea (the Salt Sea). His territory included the area east of the Dead Sea as far as the town of Beth Jeshimoth*e* and as far south as Mount Pisgah.

*4*Og, the king of Bashan,*f* was one of the last of the race of giants.*g* He reigned in the cities of Ashtaroth and Edrei.*h* He ruled over all of Bashan, the northern half of Gilead, to the boundary of Sihon, king of Heshbon. *5*His territory included Mount Hermon *in the north* and Salecah *in the east*, and *south* to the boundary of the Geshurites and the Maacathites. *6*Moses and the Israelites conquered the two kings, Sihon and Og. Moses, the servant of Yahweh, divided their land *east of the Jordan* among the tribes of Reuben, Gad, and half the tribe of Manasseh.

The Kings Defeated by Joshua

*7*On the west side of the Jordan, Joshua and the Israelites defeated *thirty-one* kings, from Baal-Gad in the Lebanon Valley in the north to Mount Halak in the south near Edom.*i* Then Joshua divided this land among the tribes of Israel and gave them their portions as permanent possessions—*8*the hill country, the western foothills, and the Jordan Valley, the mountain slopes, the wilderness *of Judea,j* and the southern desert region—*the land*

---

a 11:22 *Gaza* means "fortified" or "strength," *Gath* means "wine press," and *Ashdod* means "stronghold." These three cities were Philistine cities. The giant Goliath was from Gath (see 1 Sam. 17:23).

b 11:23 Or "the land had rest from war."

c 12:1 Or "all the eastern Arabah [dry and desolate area]."

d 12:2 Heshbon, the capital city of the Amorites, was about fifteen miles northeast of the northern end of the Dead Sea. *Heshbon* means "reasoning" or "stronghold" and hints at the mind of man.

e 12:3 Or "House of Deserts."

f 12:4 *Bashan* means "snake." It is the region east and northeast of Lake Galilee.

g 12:4 Or "Rephaites [giants]." For the defeat of King Og, see Num. 21:33–35.

h 12:4 Ashtaroth (also the name of a Canaanite goddess) and Edrei are two cities to the east and southeast of Lake Galilee. *Edrei* means "by force" or "power."

i 12:7 Or "which rises toward Seir," a mountainous region of Edom.

j 12:8 Or "the eastern slopes."

of the Hittites, Amorites, Canaanites, Perizzites, Hivites, and Jebusites.

⁹⁻²⁴*Here is the list of the thirty-one[a] kings destroyed by Joshua:*

1. The king of Jericho
2. The king of Ai near Bethel
3. The king of Jerusalem
4. The king of Hebron
5. The king of Jarmuth
6. The king of Lachish
7. The king of Eglon
8. The king of Gezer
9. The king of Debir
10. The king of Geder
11. The king of Hormah
12. The king of Arad
13. The king of Libnah
14. The king of Adullam
15. The king of Makkedah
16. The king of Bethel
17. The king of Tappuah
18. The king of Hepher
19. The king of Aphek
20. The king of Lasharon
21. The king of Madon
22. The king of Hazor
23. The king of Shimron Meron
24. The king of Achshaph
25. The king of Taanach
26. The king of Megiddo
27. The king of Kedesh
28. The king of Jokneam in Carmel
29. The king of Dor on the coast
30. The king of Goyim[b] in Galilee
31. The king of Tirzah[c]

---

a 12:9–24 The number *thirty-one* is also found in 2 Kings 22:1 in reference to the righteous reformer King Josiah (similar in Hb. to Joshua) who reigned thirty-one years.

b 12:9–24 The Hebrew word *goyim* means "peoples."

c 12:9–24 Our heavenly Joshua (Jesus) has defeated every principality, power, and stronghold that resists our advance in Christ. The name of God, El (Mighty God), according to its gematria (the numerical value in Jewish culture), equals thirty-one. The meaning of the names of the principalities of these thirty-one kings could represent the thirty-one strongholds that dull our understanding of the finished work of Christ for us: (1) Jericho represents walls, impossibilities, limitations. (2) *Ai* means "heap of ruins" (representing the world system). (3) *Jerusalem* means "lord of righteousness" (counterfeit spirituality, under the rule of Adoni-zedek). (4) *Hebron* means "fellowship"; *Hoham* means "he crushed" (broken fellowship with God). (5) *Jarmuth* means "lifted up"; *Piram* means "wild donkey" (pride and arrogance). (6) *Lachish* means "impregnable"; *Japhia* means "splendid, bright" (human ingenuity). (7) *Eglon* means "bull-like" (human arguments and oratory). (8) *Gezer* means "steep, precipitous" (sharp tongue, stinging words). (9) *Debir* means "speaker, oracle" (political spirit). (10) *Geder* means "wall" (defensiveness). (11) *Hormah* means "destroyed, laid waste" (defeat, depression). (12) *Arad* means "wild fugitive" (rebellions, lawlessness). (13) *Libnah* means "white" (self-righteousness, hypocrisy). (14) *Adullam* means "justice of the people" (approval of others, insecurity). (15) *Makkedah* means "place of shepherds" (false shepherds, selfish leadership). (16) *Bethel* means "house of God" (religious spirit). (17) *Tappuah* means "apple, distillation" (drunkenness). (18) *Hepher* means "pit, well" (shame, condemnation). (19) *Aphek* means "strength, fortress" (self-sufficiency). (20) *Lasharon* means "like the plain" (complacency, passivity). (21) *Madon* means "strife, contention" (divisive, argumentative). (22) *Hazor* means "enclosed, fortified"; *Jabin* means "intelligent" (human wisdom, mind of man). (23) *Shimron Meron* means "guardian of arrogance" (traditions, prideful opinions). (24) *Achshaph* means "enchantment" (occult, witchcraft). (25) *Taanach* means "hard to pass, sandy" (soulish, double mindedness). (26) *Megiddo* means "place of troops, crowded place" (distraction, anxiety). (27) *Kedesh* means "sacred, purity" (man-made holiness standards). (28) *Jokneam* means "possessed by the people" (celebrity worship). (29) *Dor* means "dwelling, habitation" (worldly comfort). (30) *Gilgal* means "circle" (dull of heart, refusing to change, going nowhere). (31) *Tirzah* means "delight, pleasing" (loving worldly pleasures more than loving God). Jesus sets us free from each of these thirty-one strongholds!

Yahweh Speaks to Joshua

13 Many years passed, and Joshua was a very old man.[a] One day, Yahweh spoke to him: "Although you have reached a ripe old age, a great deal of land remains for you to conquer. [2]The territory *waiting for you to possess* includes all the land of the Geshurites[b] and the Philistines. (The kings of the Philistines lived at Gaza, Ashdod, Ashkelon, Gath, and Ekron.)[c] [3]And also all the territory of the Avvites[d] to the south. (The land from the stream of Shihor,[e] at the Egyptian border, as far north as the border of Ekron was considered Canaanite.) [4]There is still all the Canaanite territory from the Sidonian city of Mearah[f] (which belonged to the Sidonians) as far as the Amorite border city of Aphek.[g] [5]*You have still not conquered* the land of the Gebalites,[h] all the land eastward to Lebanon, from the city of Baal-Gad, which is south of Mount Hermon, to Hamath Pass.[i] [6]*You still must conquer* the land of the Sidonians who live in the hill country between the Lebanon Mountains and Misrephoth Maim.[j] As the people of Israel advance, I myself will drive out these peoples from before you! Divide the land among the tribes of Israel exactly as I have commanded you. [7]Divide among the other nine tribes and the other half-tribe of Manasseh the territory *west of the Jordan* to possess as their inheritance."[k]

The Division of the Land East of the Jordan

[8]The tribes of Reuben, Gad, and the half-tribe of Manasseh had already received their portion of the land on the east side of the Jordan, which Yahweh's servant Moses had assigned to them.[l] [9]These tribes occupied the land

---

a 13:1 Joshua had spied out the land forty-five years earlier (see Num. 13–14). He was over eighty years old at the time of this encounter with Yahweh. Despite all of Joshua's victories, there remained more territory to conquer. Believers today, although complete in Christ, have yet more spiritual blessings to possess.

b 13:2 *Geshurites* means "those who see themselves as proud." These people lived in the extreme southwest of Canaan reaching as far south as the Egyptian border and are not to be confused with the Geshurites mentioned in 12:5.

c 13:2 Philistia consisted of a federation of the five city-states mentioned in this verse. *Ekron* means "plucked up by the roots." It was on the northeast border of Philistia, possibly the modern village of Akar.

d 13:3 Or "Hivites."

e 13:3 Some identify Shihor as an eastern tributary of the Nile, known as Wadi el-Arish. See 1 Chron. 13:5; Jer. 2:18. *Shihor* means "dark."

f 13:4 *Mearah* means "cave."

g 13:4 *Aphek* means "strong enclosure"; it was a city northeast of Beirut, Lebanon (modern Aphaca).

h 13:5 *Gebal* means "boundary" or "limit" and was also known as "Babylus," a city north of Beirut, Lebanon. Gebal was the center of worship of the god Dumuzid, later known as Tammuz.

i 13:5 Or, if a proper noun, "Lebo Hamath."

j 13:6 See Josh. 11:8 and footnote.

k 13:7 The word "inheritance" is the Hebrew word *nachalah*, taken from the root word *nachal*, which has a homonym meaning "a flowing stream." We can interpret inheritance to mean wealth flowing from one generation to the next.

l 13:8 See Num. 32:1–42.

as far southeast as the city of Aroer on the edge of the Arnon Valley, including the city in the middle of the valley and the plain from Dibon in the south, north to Medeba.[a] [10]Their territory went as far east as the border of Ammon, including all the cities over which King Sihon, the Amorite king, ruled over from Heshbon. [11]It also included Gilead, the land of the Geshurites and Maacathites, all of Mount Hermon, and all of Bashan to *its eastern boundary of* Salecah. [12]It encompassed the entire kingdom of Og (the last of the Rephaites) in Bashan, who ruled from Ashtaroth and at Edrei. Moses had defeated them and possessed their lands, [13]except for the Geshurites and Maacathites, who still live among the Israelites to this day. [14]However, Moses did not assign any land as an inheritance to the tribe of Levi, for their inheritance was to share in the sacrificial offerings[b] made to Yahweh, the God of Israel, as he promised them.

The Territory Assigned to Reuben

[15]The land Moses assigned to the families of the tribe of Reuben [16]extended from Aroer, on the edge of the Arnon Valley, including the city in the middle of the valley, the whole plain of Medeba, [17]Heshbon and all its surrounding towns on the plain, including Dibon, Bamoth Baal,[c] Beth Baal Meon,[d] [18]Jahaz,[e] Kedemoth, Mephaath, [19]Kiriathaim, Sibmah,[f] Zereth Shahar on the hill in the valley, [20]Beth Peor, the slopes of Pisgah, and Beth Jeshimoth, [21]including all the cities of the plain, and the whole kingdom of Sihon the Amorite, who had ruled at Heshbon. Moses defeated him and the Midianite tribal chiefs, Evi, Rekem, Zur, Hur, and Reba, who dwelt in the land as princes of Sihon. [22]Among those the Israelites killed in battle was the fortune-teller Balaam son of Beor.[g] [23]The *western* boundary of the Reubenites was the Jordan River. These cities and their surrounding villages comprised the inheritance of the families of the tribe of Reuben.

The Territory Assigned to Gad

[24]The land Moses assigned to the families of the tribe of Gad [25]included Jazer, all the cities of Gilead, and half the Ammonite country as far as Aroer, near Rabbah.[h] [26]It extended *north* from the city of Heshbon to Ramath Mizpah and Betonim, continuing on to the city of Mahanaim, and to the borders of Lo-Debar.[i] [27]In addition, the tribe of Gad received the land along the eastern side of the Jordan River as far north as the southern end of Lake Galilee. This included the cities of Beth Haram, Beth Nimrah, Sukkoth, and Zaphon, all of which were in the Jordan Valley.

---

a 13:9 The Moabites eventually recaptured Dibon and Medeba, the two principal towns of Moab.

b 13:14 Or "fire offerings." The people of Israel brought offerings to the Levites to support them in their priestly functions. See Num. 18:20–26.

c 13:17 Or "the high places of Baal."

d 13:17 Or "the house of the lord of Meon," a likely reference to the local deity worshiped at Meon.

e 13:18 This was the location where Sihon fought with Israel (see Num. 21:23) and later became a Levitical city (see 1 Chron. 6:63–64).

f 13:19 Sibmah is possibly modern Sumeih.

g 13:22 See Num. 22–24; 31:8.

h 13:25 *Rabbah* means "the great," and is the shortened form of Rabbah Ammon (modern Amman, Jordan).

i 13:26 Or "Debir." See 2 Sam. 9:4–5; 17:27.

[28]These cities and their surrounding villages comprised the inheritance of the families of the tribe of Gad.

The Territory Assigned to East Manasseh

[29]The land Moses assigned to the families of the half-tribe of Manasseh [30]extended *north* from the city of Mahanaim, including all of Bashan and the sixty villages of Jair.[a] King Og of Bashan had once ruled over all this territory. [31]*Moses had given* half of Gilead to this half-tribe of Manasseh, which descended from Manasseh's son Machir, including the cities of Ashtaroth and Edrei, where king Og had once ruled.

[32]Moses had distributed all the territory of Moab in the Jordan Valley east of Jericho as the inheritances *of these two and a half tribes of Israel.* [33]But Moses gave no inheritance of land to the tribe of Levi, but said to them, "Yahweh, the God of Israel, is to be your inheritance."

The Division of the Land West of the Jordan

14 Eleazar the priest,[b] Joshua son of Nun, and the Israelite tribal leaders divided the land west of the Jordan among the people of Israel as their inheritance. [2]By drawing lots, Eleazar assigned territory to the nine and a half tribes, as Yahweh had commanded Moses.[c] [3-4]The descendants of Joseph were divided into two tribes, Manasseh and Ephraim. Moses had already granted land east of the Jordan, but the tribe of Levi did not receive land as their inheritance. However, they were assigned cities in which to live and pasturelands for their property and livestock.[d] [5]So the Israelites divided the land as Yahweh had commanded Moses.

Caleb

[6]*One day*, while Israel was encamped at Gilgal, the people of Judah approached Joshua, including Caleb[e] son of Jephunneh[f] from the Kenizzite[g]

---

a 13:30 *Jair* means "forest"; he was the son (or possibly "descendant") of Manasseh. The villages of Jair were villages he conquered (see Num. 32:41).

b 14:1 Eleazar was the son and successor of Aaron (see Deut. 10:6). Yahweh had instructed Moses to include the tribal leaders in the allotment of land to the Israelites. See Num. 34:16–29. Eleazar was mentioned before Joshua because the high priest presided over the drawing of lots, for he bore the Urim and Thummim on his breastplate. A traditional account of this event is stated in the Talmud: "Eleazar was wearing the Urim and Thummim, while Joshua and all Israel stood before him. An urn containing the names of the tribes and an urn containing descriptions of the boundaries were placed before him. Animated by the Holy Spirit, he gave directions, exclaiming, 'Zebulun is coming up and boundaries of Acco came up with it.' Thereupon, he shook well the urn of the tribes and Zebulun came up in his hand. Likewise, he shook well the urn of the boundaries and boundary of the line of Acco came up in his hand; . . . and so with the other tribes." (See Bava Batra 122a.)

c 14:2 See Num. 26:52–56.

d 14:3–4 See Num. 35:1–15.

e 14:6 The name *Caleb* can be translated "dog." However, because the name is actually a compound word in Hebrew, alternate meanings are "faithful," "devoted," "wholehearted," "bold," and "brave."

f 14:6 *Jephunneh* means "he will behold."

g 14:6 *Kenizzite* (see Gen. 15:19) means "possessor," "spear-thrower," or "hunter." The descendants of Kenaz (Kenizzites), a non-Israelite people group, were later incorporated into the Judahite genealogy (see Judg. 1:13).

clan. Caleb said to Joshua, "Remember what Yahweh said to Moses about you and me while we were still at Kadesh Barnea. [7]I was forty years old when Moses, Yahweh's servant, sent me from Kadesh Barnea to spy out the land *of Canaan*,[a] and I brought back an honest and accurate report.[b] [8]I have been faithful and obedient to Yahweh, my God.[c] But my fellow spies who went with me only *discouraged the people* and made their hearts shrink back with fear. [9]On that day, Moses made an oath and promised me, 'Every part of the land your feet tread upon shall be an inheritance for you and your descendants forever because you were loyal to Yahweh, my God.'[d]

[10]"*So here I am*. It's been forty-five years since Yahweh made this promise to Moses, when Israel journeyed through the wilderness. Yahweh has preserved me, an eighty-five-year-old man, to this day. [11]I'm still as strong today as on that day when Moses sent me out! I'm just as fit to go out to battle now as I was then. [12]Now give me the hill country that Yahweh promised me on that day. You yourself were there and heard the report that the Anakim lived there in strong and fortified cities. I know that with the power of Yahweh helping me, I will drive them out, just as Yahweh said!"[e]

[13]Joshua spoke *God's* blessing over Caleb son of Jephunneh and gave him Hebron as his inheritance. [14]So Hebron has belonged to Caleb son of Jephunneh the Kenizzite ever since because he passionately followed Yahweh, the God of Israel. [15](Hebron used to be called the City of Arba, after Arba, the most famous of all the Anakim.) Then the land was free of war.

Judah's Inheritance

15 Here is the land allotted to the families of the tribe of Judah: Their territory extended southward to the Wilderness of Zin, which belonged to Edom. [2]Their boundary started from the bay at the southern end of the Dead Sea, [3]crossed south of Scorpion Pass, continued to Zin, and went on south of Kadesh Barnea. Then it went past Hezron up to Addar and curved around to Karka, [4]continued to Azmon and followed the stream on the border of Egypt in a northwesterly direction to the Mediterranean Sea. That is the southern border *of all the tribes of Israel*.

[5]The Dead Sea formed the eastern border *of Judah*, and its territory lay to the west *toward the Mediterranean Sea*. Their northern border began there [6]and went up to Beth Hoglah and continued north of the ridge overlooking the Jordan Valley.[f] From there it went up to the Stone of Bohan, *named after Bohan*, Reuben's son. [7]The boundary then went up to Debir from the Valley of Achor[g] and turned north to Gilgal, which faces Adummim Pass south of

---

a 14:7 See Num. 13.

b 14:7 Or "as it was in my heart" or "according to my convictions."

c 14:8 Or "I filled [myself] up with Yahweh, my God."

d 14:9 See Num. 14:24, 30. Inheritance is based on obedience to the Lord.

e 14:12 Caleb's courage at eighty-five was incredible! He was neither weary nor intimidated by any giant. He knew God had promised him that land, and no giant was going to get in his way. Caleb was a giant-killer. Some scholars believe that he lived another twenty-five years enjoying his inheritance.

f 15:6 Or "north of Beth Arabah."

g 15:7 Or "Valley of Trouble." *Achor* (Achan) means "trouble." See 7:25–26.

the gorge. It continued along to the waters of En Shemesh and ended at En Rogel. ⁸Then the boundary ran through the Hinnom Valley along the southern slope of Jebus (now known as Jerusalem). From there it went to the top of the hill west of the Hinnom Valley at the northern end of the Valley of Rephaites.ᵃ ⁹It continued from the top of the mountain to the spring of the waters of Nephtoah, and from there to the town of Mount Ephron and on to Baalah, which today is called Kiriath Jearim. ¹⁰It then turned west from Baalah to Mount Seir and ran along the northern shoulder of Mount Jearim (that is, Kesalon), descended to *the city of* Beth Shemesh, and crossed to *the city of* Timnah. ¹¹The border then went north to the ridge of *the city of* Ekron, turned toward *the city of* Shikkeron, crossed to Mount Baalah, and came out at *the city of* Jamnia.ᵇ The border ended at the *southern end of the Dead Sea.*

¹²The western boundary was the Mediterranean coastline. This was the territory that belonged to the families of the tribe of Judah.

Caleb Conquers Hebron and Debir

¹³Yahweh had commanded Joshua, "Give a share of the territory from the tribe of Judah to Caleb son of Jephunneh." So Joshua gave him the city of Hebron which was founded by Arba, the ancestor of Anak. ¹⁴Caleb drove out three Anakim from Hebron: Sheshai, Ahiman, and Talmai—descendants of Anak.ᶜ ¹⁵From Hebron, he marched out and fought against the people of Debir, which used to be called Kiriath Sepher.

¹⁶Caleb once promised, "Whoever succeeds in capturing Kiriath Sepherᵈ may marry my daughter Achsah." ¹⁷Caleb's nephew Othniel, the son of his brother Kenaz,ᵉ took the city, so Caleb gave him the hand of his daughter Achsah in marriage.

¹⁸One day, Achsah came and charmed her father so that she could ask him for a gift. When she got down from her donkey, Caleb said to her, "What would you like *for a wedding present?*"

¹⁹"Father," she replied, "give me a special gift. You have already given me land, but it's in arid country. Please, also give me some springs of water." So Caleb gave her the upper and lower springs *near the city of Hebron.*

The Cities of Judah

²⁰These are the cities given as an inheritance to the families of the tribe of

---

a 15:8 Or "the Valley of the Giants."

b 15:11 Or "Jabneel."

c 15:14 The descendants of Anak were the giants in the land. *Sheshai* means "whitewashed"; he represents hypocrisy. Jesus called the religious scholars of his day and the Pharisees hypocrites and "tombs painted over with white paint" (Matt. 23:27). *Ahiman* means "brother of my right hand" or "my brother is a gift"; he represents an exaggerated spirituality. *Talmai* means "brave"; he represents arrogance and false confidence. If we find these giants in the "land" of our hearts, then we must cast them out.

d 15:16 *Kiriath Sepher* means "the city of the book." *Debir* (v. 15) means "oracle" or "the word of God." The one who conquers "Book City" and changes it to the "word of God" will get the daughter of Caleb. *Achsah* means "anklet" (beautiful feet of the evangelist, see Isa. 52:7).

e 15:17 Kenaz was possibly Caleb's half brother. *Othniel* means "lion of God"; this nephew of Caleb became the first "deliverer" or "judge." See Judg. 3:9–11.

Judah.ª ²¹The cities *of the first district* in the extreme south near the border of Edom included

Kabzeel, Eder, Jagur,
²²Kinah, Dimonah, Adadah,
²³Kedesh, Hazor, Ithnan,
²⁴Ziph, Telem, Bealoth,
²⁵Hazor Hadattah, Kerioth Hezron (that is, Hazor),
²⁶Amam, Shema, Moladah,
²⁷Hazar Gaddah, Heshmon, Beth Pelet,
²⁸Hazar Shual, Beersheba, Biziothiah,
²⁹Baalah, Iyyim, Ezem,
³⁰Eltolad, Kesil, Hormah,
³¹Ziklag, Madmannah, Sansannah,
³²Lebaoth, Shilhim, Ain, and Rimmon—a total of twenty-nine towns and their villages.

³³The cities *of the second district* in the western foothills included

Eshtaol, Zorah, Ashnah,
³⁴Zanoah, En Gannim, Tappuah, Enam,
³⁵Jarmuth, Adullam, Socoh, Azekah,
³⁶Shaaraim, Adithaim, and Gederah (or Gederothaim)ᵇ—fourteen towns and their villages.

³⁷*The cities of the third district included*
Zenan, Hadashah, Migdal Gad,
³⁸Dilean, Mizpah, Joktheel,
³⁹Lachish, Bozkath, Eglon,
⁴⁰Cabbon, Lahmas, Kitlish,
⁴¹Gederoth, Beth Dagon, Naamah, and Makkedah—sixteen towns and their villages.

⁴²*The cities of the fourth district included*
Libnah, Ether, Ashan,
⁴³Iphtah, Ashnah, Nezib,
⁴⁴Keilah, Aczib, and Mareshah—nine towns and their villages.

⁴⁵*The cities of the fifth district included*
Ekron, with its surrounding settlements and villages;
⁴⁶from Ekron westward, all the towns in the vicinity of Ashdod, together with their villages;
⁴⁷Ashdod, and its surrounding settlements and villages;
and Gaza, its settlements and villages, as far south as the Wadi of Egypt and as far west as the coastline of the Mediterranean Sea.

⁴⁸The cities *of the sixth district in* the *Judean* hills included
Shamir, Jattir, Socoh,
⁴⁹Dannah, Kiriath Sannah (that is, Debir),
⁵⁰Anab, Eshtemoh, Anim,ᶜ
⁵¹Goshen, Holon, and Giloh—eleven towns and their villages.

⁵²*The cities of the seventh district included*
Arab, Dumah, Eshan,
⁵³Janim, Beth Tappuah, Aphekah,
⁵⁴Humtah, Kiriath Arba (that is, Hebron), and Zior—nine towns and their villages.

⁵⁵*The cities of the eighth district included*
Maon, Carmel, Ziph, Juttah,

---

a 15:20 From here through ch. 19, Joshua gives us detailed geographical descriptions of the inheritances of the tribes of Israel. Many of the places mentioned are never referenced again in Scripture, thus making them difficult to identify. Judah is mentioned first, for it was the leader-tribe of Israel. See Num. 2:9; 1 Chron. 5:1–2.

b 15:36 Or "and its sheepfolds," which would make a total of fourteen cities.

c 15:50 The Septuagint adds another district at the end of verse 50, as follows: "Tekoa, Ephrath (that is, Bethlehem), Peor, Etam, Culon, Tatam, Shoresh, Cerem, Gallim, Bether, and Manach: eleven cities, along with the towns around them." Many scholars believe that the Septuagint preserves the original text here. Some modern translations include the addition.

⁵⁶Jezreel, Jokdeam, Zanoah,
⁵⁷Kain, Gibeah, and Timnah—ten towns and their villages.

⁵⁸*The cities of the ninth district included* Halhul, Beth Zur, Gedor,
⁵⁹Maarath, Beth Anoth, and Eltekon—six towns and their villages.

⁶⁰*The cities of the tenth district included* Kiriath Baal (that is, Kiriath Jearim) and Rabbah—two towns and their villages.

⁶¹The desert *cities of the eleventh district* included

Beth Arabah, Middin, Secacah,
⁶²Nibshan, the City of Salt,ᵃ and En Gedi—six towns and their villages.ᵇ
⁶³The people of Judah could not dislodge the Jebusites from Jerusalem, and they live among the people of Judah to this day.

The Land Given to Joseph's Descendants

16 The territory assigned to Joseph's descendants began east of the springs of Jericho near the Jordan, then turned north through the desert and into the hill country as far as Bethel. ²From Bethel (that is, Luz),ᶜ it crossed over to Arkiteᵈ territory at Ataroth.ᵉ ³It then descended westward to the territory of the Japhletites as far as the border of Lower Beth Horon and Gezer, ending at the Mediterranean Sea. ⁴Ephraim and Manasseh, the descendants of Joseph, inherited this entire territory.

The Land Given to Ephraim's Descendants

⁵The southern boundary of the territory of the tribe of Ephraim went from Ataroth Addar in the east to Upper Beth Horon ⁶then westward to the Sea. The northern boundary went from Michmethath to the east of Taanath-Shiloh and going further to the east of Janoah.ᶠ ⁷From Janoah the border descended to Ataroth and Naarah. It touched Jericho and came out at the Jordan River. ⁸⁻⁹From Tappuah, it proceeded westward to the Kanah Ravine and ended at the Sea. The inheritance of the families of the tribe of Ephraim also included the towns and villages set apart for them within the territory of West Manasseh.ᵍ ¹⁰However, the Ephraimites did not drive out the Canaanites from the city of Gezer, but they conscripted the Canaanites to serve them to this day.

The Half-Tribe of West Manasseh

17 Joshua assigned land to the descendants of Manasseh, Joseph's firstborn son. Joshua allotted Gilead and Bashan to Machir the firstborn of Manasseh, the father of Gilead, because he was a *brave* warrior.

---

a 15:62 The Hebrew is *'Ir-hammelach*, possibly in later times the site of the Qumran community of Essenes.

b 15:62 There are 110 cities mentioned in this chapter, one city for every year of Joshua's life. See 24:29.

c 16:2 As translated from the Septuagint. The Hebrew reads "From Bethel to Luz."

d 16:2 The Arkites were descendants of Arki, a son of Canaan and grandson of Ham (see Gen. 10:15–17).

e 16:2 Or "Ataroth Addar."

f 16:6 Scholars identify Janoah with modern Yanun, eight miles southeast of Nablus.

g 16:8–9 See 17:8–10.

²And Joshua assigned land *west of the Jordan River* to the rest of the tribe of Manasseh. The male descendants of Manasseh were Abiezer, Helek, Asriel, Shechem, Hepher, and Shemida. All of these men were heads of families, *and each of their families received territory west of the Jordan River.*

³Manasseh's grandson Gilead had a son named Hepher who had a son named Zelophehad,ᵃ who had no sons.ᵇ But he did have five daughters: Mahlah,ᶜ Noah,ᵈ Hoglah,ᵉ Milcah,ᶠ and Tirzah.ᵍ ⁴They came before the priest Eleazar and Joshua son of Nun and the leaders, and said, "Yahweh commanded Moses to give us an inheritance among our relatives." So according to Yahweh's commandment, he gave an inheritance to them as he did to their uncles. ⁵⁻⁶Since Joshua assigned land to both Manasseh's male and female descendants, the tribe of Manasseh received ten shares of land on the west side of the Jordan River and two on the east (the territories of Gilead and Bashan).

⁷The northwest territory of Manasseh reached from Asher to Michmethath, which is east of Shechem; the boundary went southward to the inhabitants of the spring of Tappuahʰ ⁸and divided the land of Tappuah belonging to *the tribe of* Manasseh from the town of Tappuah belonging to the Ephraimites. ⁹⁻¹⁰From there, the southern border followed the Kanah Stream westward

to the Mediterranean Sea. The main territory of Manasseh lay north of the stream of Kanah, but south of it were some cities that belonged to the tribe of Ephraim even though they were located inside the territory of Manasseh. In the northwest, Manasseh bordered on the tribe of Asher, and in the northeast, it bordered on the tribe of Issachar. ¹¹Within these two territories, there were several cities together with their surrounding towns that belonged to Manasseh: Beth Shean, Ibleam, Dor, Endor, Taanach, and Megiddo. These constituted three regions.ⁱ ¹²Yet the men of Manasseh failed to take possession of those towns, and the Canaanites continued to live in that land. ¹³Later, when the Israelites grew strong, they put the Canaanites to forced labor but did not utterly drive them out.

The Tribes of Ephraim and West Manasseh Request More Land

¹⁴One day, the descendants of Joseph came to Joshua and said, "Yahweh has blessed us with many people, but you have given us only one part of the land. We ought to have more land!"

¹⁵Joshua said to them, "If the hill country of Ephraim is too small for the large number of people in your tribes, then go into the forests which belong to the Perizzites and the Rephaites, and clear ground for yourselves there."

---

a   17:3 *Zelophehad* means "first one [to break through]" or "firstborn."

b   17:3 See Num. 27:1–7.

c   17:3 *Mahlah* means "smooth," "polished," "caressing," or "pleasing."

d   17:3 *Noah* is found here as a woman's name and means "rest," "call," "quiet," or "peace."

e   17:3 *Hoglah* means "hopping bird" or "quail."

f   17:3 *Milcah* means "queen," "rule," or "counsel."

g   17:3 *Tirzah* means "pleasure," "delight," "loving," or "graciousness."

h   17:7 *Tappuah* means "apple."

i   17:11 The Hebrew meaning is uncertain.

[16]The descendants of Joseph answered, "Indeed, there's not enough room for us in the hill country of Ephraim. Yet all the Canaanites who live in the plain have chariots with iron-rimmed wheels, both those in Beth Shean and its villages, and those in the Valley of Jezreel."

[17]Then Joshua said to the tribe of Ephraim and the half-tribe of Manasseh,[a] "There are indeed many people in your tribes, and for that reason, you are very powerful. I will give you more than one share of land. [18]Therefore, I will give you the hill country as well. It is a forest, but *Yahweh will empower* you to take possession of it and clear it from one end to the other. You will conquer all the Canaanites even though they not only have iron chariots but also are a strong people."

The Tabernacle at Shiloh

18 After the Israelites had conquered the land, all of them gathered at Shiloh,[b] and *the priests* set up the tabernacle. [2-3]Joshua addressed the seven tribes that remained[c] who had not yet received their inheritance: "How much more time will you waste until you go out and possess the land that Yahweh, the God of your ancestors, has given you? [4-7]The tribes of Gad, Reuben, and the half-tribe of Manasseh have already received their allotted land east of the Jordan which Moses, Yahweh's servant, assigned them. The tribe of Judah already has its territory in the south, and the descendants of Joseph have their territory in the north. So *let each of the seven remaining tribes* select three men and send them to me. I will send them out to survey and make a map of the entire land. Divide the territory into seven districts and bring the description of each district to me. Then I will draw lots before Yahweh our God to determine which section he has chosen for each tribe to receive. But the Levites will not have an allotted portion among you, for their inheritance is to serve as Yahweh's priests."

[8-9]*The tribes each selected three men*, and as they set out on their journey, Joshua told them, "Go through all the land and write down its description. When you bring the description back here to me, I will ask Yahweh in Shiloh to divide the land among your tribes." So the men went through all the land and divided it into seven sections. They wrote a description of each section and also made a list of the towns within each section and returned to Joshua at Shiloh. [10]Then Joshua cast

---

a 17:17 Or "Then Joshua said to the house of Joseph."

b 18:1 After seven years of conquest, the Israelites moved the tabernacle that Moses had constructed in the wilderness from Gilgal to Shiloh, where it remained for 369 years. Shiloh became the center of worship throughout the time of the Judges (also the time of the book of Ruth). *Shiloh* means "whole," "sound," "quiet," "secure," "health," or "abundance." It was the place where Hannah prayed to have a son and then dedicated her miracle son, Samuel, to God (see 1 Sam. 1:3–24). He became the first of the prophets of Israel. The origins of the prophets can be traced back to the ancient pre-Jerusalem capital of Israel, Shiloh. See Judg. 18:31; 21:12–21; 1 Sam. 3:21; 4:3–12; 1 Kings 2:27; 14:2–4; Ps. 78:60. Jesus is our Shiloh (see Gen. 49:8–12).

c 18:2–3 Judah plus Gad, Reuben, and the (eastern) half-tribe of Manasseh were the four tribes so far possessing their inheritance. Benjamin (see vv. 11–28), Simeon (see 19:1–9), Zebulun (see 19:10–16), Issachar (see 19:17–23), Naphtali (see 19:32–39), and Dan (see 19:40–48) were the "remaining seven" tribes. Levi, of course, did not inherit land (see vv. 4–7). In addition, Joshua inherited a city, Timnath Serah (see 19:49–51).

lots in Yahweh's presence at Shiloh and assigned a section of the land to each of the remaining tribes of Israel.

The Tribal Land of Benjamin

[11]The first lot came out for the families of Benjamin. So the first tribe that received territory was the tribe of Benjamin. Joshua assigned them land which lay between the tribe of Judah *on the south* and the descendants of Joseph *on the north*. [12]Their northern border began in the east at the Jordan River and went up the slope north of Jericho and westward through the hill country as far as the desert *near the city* of Beth Aven. [13]The border then went to the slope on the south side of Luz (that is, Bethel) then down to Ataroth Addar on the mountain south of Lower Beth Horon. [14]The border then turned south from the western side of this mountain and went to the city of Kiriath Baal, which is also called Kiriath Jearim, a town of Judah. [15]From the outskirts of Kiriath Jearim, the boundary extended to Mount Ephron[a] and went from there to the fountain of the Waters of Nephtoah. [16]It continued down to the foot of the mountain on the north side of the Valley of Rephaites, where the Hinnom Valley begins. From there it went south through the Hinnom Valley to the south slope of Jerusalem[b] and then downward to En Rogel.[c] [17]From there the boundary turned sharply northward to En Shemesh and on to Geliloth, facing the ascent of Adummim, and descended to the Boulder of Bohan, son[d] of Reuben. [18]Then it passed north of the ridge[e] overlooking the Jordan Valley. From there it descended into the valley, [19]passing north of the ridge of Beth Hoglah. The southern border ended where the Jordan River empties into the Dead Sea. [20]The eastern border was the Jordan River. The families of the tribe of Benjamin received as their possession the land within these borders.

[21-24]There were twelve cities, along with the towns around them, which belonged to the tribe of Benjamin:

Jericho, Beth Hoglah, Emek Keziz,
Beth Arabah, Zemaraim, Bethel,
Avvim, Parah, Ophrah,
Chephar Ammoni, Ophni, and Geba.

[25-28]There were another fourteen cities, along with the towns around them, which also belonged to the tribe of Benjamin. These cities were

Gibeon, Ramah, Beeroth,
Mizpah, Chephirah, Mozah,
Rekem, Irpeel, Taralah,
Zela, Haeleph, Jebus (or Jerusalem),[f] Gibeah, and Kiriath. Joshua assigned this land and all these cities to the tribes of Benjamin.

---

a 18:15 The Hebrew text is uncertain. The Masoretic text reads "westward," which is not correct. The Septuagint is transliterated as "toward Gasin." Some translations omit "westward" or "Mount Ephron" entirely. Other scholars suggest "toward Iyyim" or "toward the ruins of Mount Ephron" as the intended meaning of the text.

b 18:16 Or literally "the slope of the Jebusites."

c 18:16 En Rogel is identified with the modern 'Ain Ummel-Daraj, a name which means "the fountain of the virgin." David's spies hid at En Rogel during Absalom's uprising. See 2 Sam. 17:17.

d 18:17 Or possibly "grandson." Bohan apparently distinguished himself by fighting the Canaanites at this large rock.

e 18:18 Or possibly a place named "Cheteph."

f 18:25-28 It is interesting that Jerusalem was not given to the tribe of Judah but to the tribe of Benjamin.

The Tribal Land of Simeon

19 The families of the tribe of Simeon received the second assignment of land, which was located within the territory of Judah. ²⁻⁶Their inheritance included the towns of

Beersheba,ᵃ Moladah, Hazar-Shual, Balah, Ezem,

Eltolad, Bethul, Hormah, Ziklag, Beth Marcaboth, Hazar-Susah,

Beth Lebaoth, and Sharuhen—thirteen towns with their villages.

⁷In addition, they received four other cities, along with the villages around them: Ain, Rimmon, Ether, and Ashan. ⁸Simeon's territory included all the cities and villages as far south as the town of Baalath Beer, which is also known as Ramah in the Negeb. ⁹The families of Simeon received their inheritance from Judah's share of land because Judah's portion exceeded what they needed. So the inheritance of the families of Simeon was within the territory of Judah.ᵇ

The Tribal Land of Zebulun

¹⁰The families of the tribe of Zebulun received the third assignment of land. Their boundary reached as far southeast as *the city of* Sarid. ¹¹Going west, it ran to Maralah, touched Dabbesheth, and extended to the stream near Jokneam. ¹²In the other direction, the boundary line went east to the border of Chisloth-Tabor, and from there to Daberath and Japhia; ¹³then it continued east of Gath-Hepher,ᶜ Eth Kazin, Rimmon, and turned toward Neah. ¹⁴The northern boundary of Zebulun passed Hannathon and ended at the valley of Iphtah El. ¹⁵Their land encompassed twelve cities, including Kattath, Nahalal, Shimeon,ᵈ Iralah,ᵉ and Bethlehem.ᶠ ¹⁶Zebulun's families inherited all these towns and their villages.

The Tribal Land of Issachar

¹⁷The families of the tribe of Issachar received the fourth assignment of land. ¹⁸⁻²¹Their inheritance included

Jezreel, Kesulloth, Shunem, Hapharaim, Shion, Anaharath,

Rabbith, Kishion, Ebez, Remeth, En Gannim, En Haddah, and Beth Pazzez.

²²Their border touched Tabor, Shahazumah, and Beth Shemesh, and ended at the Jordan River—sixteen towns and their villages. ²³Issachar's families inherited all these cities and their towns.

The Tribal Land of Asher

²⁴The families of the tribe of Asher received the fifth assignment of land. ²⁵Their territory included the city of Helkath to Hali, Beten, Achshaph, ²⁶Allammelech, Amad, and Mishal. Their border touched Carmel to the west and Shihor Libnath. ²⁷The eastern

---

a 19:2–6 Or "Beer Sheba" or "Sheba." The Masoretic text inserts "Sheba" here, which may be a scribal error, for its addition makes the total number of towns fourteen rather than thirteen. Most modern translations include "Sheba."

b 19:9 Simeon's portion of land was scattered throughout the territory of Judah, fulfilling Jacob's prophecy (see Gen. 49:7). See also Judg. 1:3.

c 19:13 Gath-Hepher (three miles northeast of Nazareth) was the birthplace of the prophet Jonah. See 2 Kings 14:25.

d 19:15 Or "Shimron." See 11:1; 12:9–24.

e 19:15 Or "Idalah."

f 19:15 This is not the famous Bethlehem south of Jerusalem. This Bethlehem was a town about seven and a half miles (twelve kilometers) west of Nazareth. See Judg. 12:8–10.

border went north from the city of Beth Dagon. It touched the territory of the tribe of Zebulun and the Valley of Iphtah El to the north, Beth Emek and Neiel, and extended to Cabul on the north. ²⁸It went to Abdon,ᵃ Rehob, Hammon, and Kanah, as far as Greater Sidon. ²⁹The boundary then turned back toward Ramah and went to the fortified city of Tyre, turned toward Hosah and came out at the sea in the region of Aczib, ³⁰Ummah, Aphek, and Rehob—twenty-two towns and their villages. ³¹Asher's families inherited this entire region.

The Tribal Land of Naphtali

³²The families of the tribe of Naphtali received the sixth assignment of land. ³³The *northern* border of its territory went from the town of Heleph to the oak near the town of Zaanannim, then continued to Adami Nekeb, Jabneel, and on to Lakkum, and ended at the Jordan River. ³⁴It turned westward to Aznoth Tabor, extended from there to Hukok, touched Zebulun on the south, Asher on the west, and the Jordan on the east. ³⁵⁻³⁸The fortified towns of Naphtali included

Ziddim, Zer, Hammath, Rakkath, Kinnereth,

Adamah, Ramah, Hazor, Kedesh, Edrei, En Hazor,

Iron, Migdal El, Horem, Beth Anath, and Beth Shemesh—nineteen towns

and their villages. ³⁹Naphtali's families inherited this entire region.

The Tribal Land of Dan

⁴⁰The families of the tribe of Dan received the seventh assignment of land. ⁴¹⁻⁴⁶Its area included the towns of

Zorah, Eshtaol, Ir Shemesh, Shaalabbin, Aijalon, Ithlah,

Elon, Timnah, Ekron, Eltekeh, Gibbethon, Baalath,

Jehud, Bene Berak, Gath Rimmon, Me Jarkon, and Rakkon,

as well as the territory around Joppa. ⁴⁷The Danites had difficulty taking possession of their territory, so they went up and attacked Leshem, took it, killed its inhabitants, and occupied it. Then they renamed the city after their ancestor Dan. ⁴⁸Dan's families inherited this entire region.

The Land Given to Joshua

⁴⁹⁻⁵¹All the people of Israel gathered in front of the tabernacleᵇ at Shiloh so that Eleazar the priest, Joshua, and the leaders of the tribes could divide all the land *west of the Jordan River*. They used lots to find out how Yahweh wanted them to divide the land. When they finished dividing the land into its regions, the Israelites gave *their warrior-chief*, Joshua son of Nun, his inheritance. As Yahweh had instructed, they gave him the city he requested—Timnath Serahᶜ in the

---

a 19:28 Or "Ebron."

b 19:49–51 Or "tent of meeting [assembly]."

c 19:49–51 *Timnath Serah* means "an extra portion." It is taken from the verb *mana*, meaning "to count" or "to assign" and the noun *serah*, meaning "excess." The Israelites, following God's instructions, gave Joshua what he longed for: an extra portion. Those who minister to God's people and serve them are worthy of double honor. See 1 Tim. 5:17. Jesus is our heavenly Joshua who waits for the fullness of his inheritance until his people have received theirs. Receiving in us the fullness of his inheritance was the joy that was set before him (see Heb. 12:1–2). The church, his bride, is the "city" he desired. See Song. 6:4; Matt. 5:14; Rev. 21:2. He has built up this city and dwells there.

Ephraimite hill country. So he built up the city and lived there.

Six Cities of Asylum

20 ¹⁻³Yahweh instructed Joshua: "A person who accidentally and unintentionally kills someone will need a place of asylum—a city where he can run for safety. Otherwise, the dead man's relatives will kill him." So now Yahweh said to Joshua, "Tell the people of Israel to choose these cities of asylumᵃ as I instructed you through Moses. ⁴The one *who has committed manslaughter* shall escape for protection to one of these cities and stand at the entrance to the city gates and explain his case to the leaders of the city. The leaders must then receive him into their city and grant him asylum. ⁵When the one looking for revengeᵇ comes after him, the leaders of the city must protect him and not hand him over, for he killed the person accidentally and without premeditation. ⁶He must remain in the city until he has had a public trial; then he must remain protected in the city until the man who is high priest at that time has died. Afterward, he may return to his family and his own hometown."ᶜ

⁷So they dedicated three cities *on the west side of the Jordan River*: Kedesh in Galilee in the hill country of Naphtali, Shechem in the hill country of Ephraim, and Kiriath Arba (that is, Hebron) in the hill country of Judah. ⁸And beyond the Jordan east of Jericho, they dedicated Bezer in the desert plain belonging to the tribe of Reuben, Ramoth in Gilead, from the tribe of Gad, and Golan in Bashan, from the tribe of Manasseh.ᵈ ⁹These were the

---

a 20:1–3 Or "cities of refuge." The need for cities of asylum arose because it was the duty of the nearest relative of a man who had been killed to search out and kill the killer. When it was clearly not a murder (intentional killing) but manslaughter (accidental killing), then the killer could seek asylum in one of the six cities of asylum, three on the west side and three on the east side of the Jordan River. See Ex. 21:12–14; Num. 35:9–34.

b 20:5 Or "the blood-redeemer," that is, a relative of the one killed. See Gen. 9:6. The avenger of blood is a picture of the law (see Rom. 5:9–11; 6:7; 7:1–4; Heb. 7:23–25).

c 20:6 The protection of the manslayer would be based on the killer being proven innocent (accidental death). If found innocent, he would remain in the city until the death of the ruling high priest. See Num 35:25, 28. After the high priest's death, the manslayer would receive amnesty and permission to return home. However, if he were found guilty of premeditated murder, there was no protection for him—the leaders would turn him over to the avenging relative of the dead man. See Num 35:19.

d 20:8 Although Moses had already designated these three cities east of the Jordan (see Deut. 4:41–43), they were not officially appointed until Joshua had the people of Israel select three cities on the west side of the Jordan River.

designated cities of refuge.[a] Any Israelite or any foreigner[b] living among them who had accidentally killed someone could run to one of these cities for protection. He could live there safely until he had a fair trial, *and unless he had been proven guilty*, he could not be killed by the one seeking revenge.

The Cities of the Levites

2 1 [1-2]While the people of Israel camped at Shiloh in the land of Canaan, the ancestral heads of the Levites went to Eleazar the priest, to Joshua son of Nun, and to the heads of the families of all of the tribes of Israel and said, "Yahweh instructed through Moses for you to give us cities to live in and pasturelands around the cities for our livestock." [3]So the people of Israel obeyed Yahweh's command and gave the Levites some of their cities and pasturelands from their inheritance.

[4-5]Each clan of the Levites received its cities by drawing lots. First, the people of Israel gave to the descendants of Aaron the priest from the clan of Kohath[c] thirteen cities from the territories of Judah, Simeon, and Benjamin. They allotted to the rest of the clan of Kohath's descendants ten towns from the clans of the tribes of Ephraim, Dan, and half of Manasseh.

[6]By lot, the descendants of Gershon received thirteen cities from the tribe of Issachar, from the tribe of Asher, from the tribe of Naphtali, and from the half-tribe of Manasseh in Bashan.

[7]Clan by clan, the descendants of Merari received twelve cities from the tribe of Reuben, the tribe of Gad, and the tribe of Zebulun. [8]Yahweh had commanded through Moses to draw lots to see what cities the Levites would receive. So they drew lots, and the people of Israel gave them these cities together with the pasturelands around them.

[9-10]The members of the clan of Kohath, the descendants of Aaron, received *nine* cities from the tribes of Judah and Simeon. [11-16]They received the city of Hebron, which was also a city of asylum. It lay in the hill country of Judah and was named Kiriath Arba, after Arba the father of Anak. The

---

a 20:9 The six cities of asylum all point to Christ and his tender mercy (see Neh. 9:27; Pss. 103:13; 119:156; Mic. 7:18). The positioning of these six cities was meant to provide access to everyone from wherever they lived. They built roads to these cities to help the one fleeing from vengeance. See Deut. 19. The cities of refuge were situated on hills and high places so that the manslayer could easily see them and find them. Similarly, Jesus has been exalted to the highest place as our Champion and Savior, and yet he is accessible to all by faith. *Bezer* means "cut off," "fortification," or "strong city," and speaks of Christ as our secure refuge. *Ramoth* means "exaltation" or "heavenly," and speaks of Christ as our high and exalted refuge. *Golan* means "their rejoicing" (see Rom. 5:11), and speaks of Christ as our perfect refuge. *Kedesh* means "holy place," "sacred," "sanctified," or "holiness" (see Isa 9:7), and speaks of Christ as our holy refuge. *Shechem* means "between the shoulders," "burden bearer," or "strength," and speaks of Christ as our strong refuge (see Ps. 91:2; Nah. 1:7). *Hebron* means "united," "fellowship," "joined," or "communion" and speaks of Christ as our loving refuge who has joined himself to us. We are safe forever, for our High Priest will never die. See Heb. 6:17–20.

b 20:9 These refuge cities were to be available for all, even the gentiles (see Num. 35:15; Rom. 10:12).

c 21:4–5 The first lot fell to the descendants of Aaron. They were classified as priests (see v. 19), while the other descendants of Levi were not.

fields and towns around it had already been given to Caleb, but the city and its pasturelands were now given to the descendants of Aaron. They also received the cities and pasturelands of Libnah, Jattir, Eshtemoa, Holon, Debir, Ain, Juttah, and Beth Shemesh; nine cities from these two tribes.

¹⁷⁻¹⁸They received four cities from the territory of Benjamin: Gibeon, Geba, Anathoth, and Almon, along with the pastureland of each. ¹⁹The priests, the descendants of Aaron, received thirteen cities in all, with their pasturelands.

²⁰⁻²²The rest of the Kohathite clans of Levi received four cities with their pasturelands in the territory of Ephraim. One of these cities was Shechem, located in the hill country and one of the cities of asylum. The other three cities were Gezer, Kibzaim, and Beth Horon.

²³⁻²⁴The Levites also received four cities from the territory of Dan: Eltekeh, Gibbethon, Aijalon, and Gath Rimmon, along with the pastureland of each.

²⁵They also received two cities from the half-tribe of Manasseh: Taanach and Gath Rimmon, along with the pastureland of each. ²⁶The rest of the Kohathite clans received ten towns and their pasturelands.

²⁷The Levite clans of the Gershonites received two towns from the half-tribe of Manasseh: Golan in Bashan (a city of asylum for one who committed manslaughter) and Beeshterah, together with their pasturelands.

²⁸⁻²⁹*They received* four towns from the tribe of Issachar: Kishion, Daberath, Jarmuth, and En Gannim, together with their pasturelands.

³⁰⁻³¹*They received* four towns from the tribe of Asher: Mishal, Abdon, Helkath, and Rehob, together with their pasturelands.

³²*They received* three towns from the tribe of Naphtali: Kedesh in Galilee (a city of asylum for one who committed manslaughter), Hammoth Dor, and Kartan, together with their pasturelands. ³³All the Gershonite clans received thirteen towns, together with their pasturelands.

³⁴⁻³⁵The remaining Levites of the Merarite clans received four cities from the tribe of Zebulun: Jokneam, Kartah, Dimnah, and Nahalal, along with the pastureland of each.

³⁶⁻³⁷*They received* four cities from the tribe of Reuben: Bezer, Jahaz, Kedemoth, and Mephaath, along with the pastureland of each.

³⁸⁻³⁹*They received* four cities from the tribe of Gad: Ramoth in Gilead (a city of asylum for one who committed manslaughter), Mahanaim, Heshbon, and Jazer, along with the pastureland of each. ⁴⁰Merarite clans of the remaining Levites received twelve cities in all.

⁴¹⁻⁴²The Levites received from the other tribes of Israel a total of forty-eight cities, each with the pasturelands around them.

Israel Takes Possession of the Land

⁴³So Yahweh gave Israel all the land he had promised their ancestors. They took possession of the land and settled there. ⁴⁴Yahweh kept his promise and gave them peace in the land*ᵃ* just as he had promised to their forefathers. Not one of their enemies could stand against them. ⁴⁵Yahweh didn't break a single promise that he made to the people of Israel. He faithfully kept every promise he made to them.

---

a 21:44 Or "Yahweh gave them rest on every side." See Deut. 12:10.

The Eastern Tribes Return to Their Land

22 Then Joshua summoned all the men of the tribes of Reuben, Gad, and East Manasseh ²and said to them, "You have done all that Moses the servant of Yahweh commanded, and you have obeyed me in everything I commanded. ³Through it all, you've never deserted your fellow Israelites *and were always there to help them.* You've completed every task given to you by Yahweh your God. ⁴Yes, he has promised peace to your fellow Israelites, and he has kept that promise. So now, return to the homeland east of the Jordan which Moses, Yahweh's servant, assigned to you. ⁵Make sure you obey every command and instruction Moses, Yahweh's servant, gave you. Love Yahweh! He is your God, so walk in his ways and obey his commands! Cling to him and serve him diligently with all your heart and with all your soul!"

⁶Then Joshua spoke a blessing over them and sent them on their way, and they settled there.ᵃ ⁷To one half of the tribe of Manasseh, Moses had assigned land in Bashan. To the other half, Joshua assigned land on the west side of the Jordan with their fellow Israelites. Joshua blessed them and sent them off to their homes ⁸with these words: "You are free to go. You leave for your homes rich—with great herds of cattle, silver and gold, bronze and iron, and a great quantity of clothing! Share with your friends and families everything you took from your enemies."

⁹So the tribes of Reuben, Gad, and East Manasseh left their fellow Israelites at Shiloh in Canaan and returned to Gilead, their homeland. For Moses had told them before he died, "Yahweh wants you to take this land for your own."

The Tribes East of the Jordan Build an Altar

¹⁰On their way home, the tribes of Reuben, Gad, and East Manasseh came to the town of Geliloth near the Jordan River. So they built their own large, impressive altar there.ᵇ ¹¹When the rest of the Israelites heard that the people of the tribe of Reuben, Gad, and East Manasseh had built an altar at Geliloth at the entrance to the land of Canaan, ¹²they gathered at Shiloh to go to war against them.

¹³⁻¹⁴The Israelites of the ten western tribes sent a delegation to the tribes of Reuben, Gad, and East Manasseh in the land of Gilead. They sent Phineasᶜ son of Eleazar the priest, together with ten respected clan leaders, princes from each of their ten tribes. ¹⁵So they came to the people in the land of Gilead, to the tribes of Reuben, Gad, and East Manasseh. Phineas and the men with him said, ¹⁶"We speak to you on behalf of all Yahweh's people. Why did you rebel against Yahweh and build this altar for yourselves? Why did you quit following the God of Israel and do such an evil thing?

---

a 22:6 Or "they went to their tents."

b 22:10 The Hebrew text is somewhat ambiguous. Although some scholars (including the historian Josephus) believe the altar was on the east side of the river, it is more likely they built it on the west bank before they crossed over.

c 22:13–14 Phineas, the grandson of Aaron, was known for his zeal for Yahweh in resisting apostasy. See Num. 25:11–12; Mal. 2:4–6. The name *Phineas* means "mouth of brass [judgment]."

¹⁷Haven't we had enough trouble from the terrible sin*ᵃ* we committed at Peor? There a plague came upon us even though we belong to Yahweh. To this day, our conscience is stained and we still suffer*ᵇ* from our atrocious deeds. ¹⁸How dare you turn back from following Yahweh! If you rebel against him today, he will be angry with everyone in Israel tomorrow.*ᶜ* ¹⁹If you think your land is defiled, then come back to Yahweh's land, where his tabernacle stands *at Shiloh*. But don't rebel against Yahweh or us by building for yourself an altar. ²⁰Don't forget what happened to Achan! Yahweh told us, 'Destroy everything in the city of Jericho.' But Achan son of Zerah did not obey Yahweh's command regarding the devoted things, and so Yahweh punished us all. Achan died because of what he did, and so did many other Israelites because of Achan's sin."

Reconciliation of the Tribes

²¹The Reubenites, the Gadites, and the half-tribe of Manasseh answered the princes of the tribes of Israel: ²²"Yahweh is the God of all gods! Yahweh is the God of all gods! We appeal to God Almighty *as our witness*. He knows why we did this, and we want you to know too! If we rebelled or betrayed Yahweh, then you may take our lives today. ²³But we built this altar with no intention of burning any kind of sacrifices*ᵈ* on it. If we built this altar in rebellion against Yahweh or to break our covenant with him, then may Yahweh himself punish us. ²⁴⁻²⁵No! *We love Yahweh!* We were afraid that in the future your descendants will say*ᵉ* to our descendants, 'Who are you? What right do you have to worship Yahweh, the God of Israel? He has placed the Jordan River as a barrier between our people and your people. You Reubenites and Gadites have no part in *the worship of* Yahweh.' And your descendants may prevent ours from worshiping him. ²⁶We did build an altar, but not for burning sacrifices or making offerings. ²⁷We built this altar to show to our people and to your people and to the generations to come that we will worship Yahweh at his tabernacle. We will bring all our offerings into Yahweh's presence there so that your children may never say to our children in the future, 'You have no part in *the*

---

a 22:17 Or "Was that sin too little for us?" The implication is that building an altar to any god other than Yahweh would be worse than the sin the Israelites committed at Peor, which released an epidemic that killed twenty-four thousand. See Num. 25:1–9. *Peor* means "opening." Their sin at Peor became an opening for darkness and sickness among them. Peor was the mountain where Balak attempted to entice Balaam to pronounce a curse upon Israel. See Num. 23:28.

b 22:17 Or "we have yet to cleanse ourselves." This statement shows the depth to which their sin had rooted itself in the conscience of the nation.

c 22:18 They were asserting that the altar constituted a rebellion against God and against the unity of the nation which was to worship Yahweh at Shiloh. The centralization of the worship of God's people was at stake. Collective guilt can be a "plague" on the moral conscience of a nation.

d 22:23 Or "burnt sacrifices, grain offerings, or peace offerings." The evident intention of listing these three types of sacrifice is to be comprehensive.

e 22:24–25 When we are afraid of what people will say, we are walking in fear, not faith. This entire episode could have been prevented if the two and a half tribes had consulted with the others beforehand.

worship of Yahweh.' [28]We have decided among us that if that day should ever come, our descendants would reply: 'See the replica of the altar of Yahweh, which our fathers made here *at the border between us*—not for burnt offerings or sacrifices,[a] but as a witness *that we both serve the same God.*' [29]Far be it from us to rebel against Yahweh or to turn away from following him this day by building an altar on which to present offerings or make sacrifices to Yahweh our God. We would never build an altar to take the place of the altar which stands before his tabernacle, *the place of his presence.*"

[30]When Phineas the priest, and the princes of the tribes heard the explanation of the tribes of Reuben, Gad, and East Manasseh, they were satisfied. [31]Phineas son of Eleazar the priest said to them, "Now we know that Yahweh is among us! Since you have not rebelled against him, you have indeed saved the Israelites from Yahweh's punishment."

[32]Then Phineas and the ten princes of the western tribes returned to the land of Canaan and told the people of Israel everything that happened. [33]The outcome pleased the Israelites and they praised God. They spoke no more of going to war against the eastern tribes to destroy the land where they had lived. [34]The Reubenites and

the Gadites called the altar *Witness*, for they said, "The altar stands as a witness to us all that Yahweh is God."[b]

Joshua's Farewell at Shiloh

23 Many years had passed since Yahweh had given Israel rest[c] from all their enemies, and Joshua was very old.[d] [2]So Joshua called together all the Israelites, including all their leaders—elders, judges, and officials—and told them, "I'm now very old *and don't have much longer to live.* [3]Yahweh your God *has shown you his power* and fought against your enemies for you. You have seen all *the wonders* that he has done to all these nations because *he loves* you. [4]See, I have assigned to your tribes all the land from the Jordan River in the east to the Mediterranean Sea in the west. I have given you the land of all the nations that we've already conquered as an inheritance, and also the land of those nations that we've yet to conquer. [5]Yahweh your God will *absolutely* keep his promises to you. He will drive out all your enemies and make them retreat before you so that you will possess their land. [6]So be very strong and steadfast; be careful to obey fully what is written in the Scroll[e] of the teaching of Moses, without deviating from it.[f] [7]Do not intermingle with the nations that are left among you nor speak the

---

a 22:28 See Deut. 12:4; 13–14.

b 22:34 How soon we forget all that God has accomplished for us! In a little over four centuries, the meaning of the altar of witness had been forgotten. See 1 Chron. 5:25–26.

c 23:1 See Matt. 11:28; Heb. 4:1–11. Jesus brings us into the faith-rest life.

d 23:1 This was about twenty-five years later. Joshua was one hundred and ten when he made a final speech to the nation. As Jacob had blessed his sons (see Gen. 49) and Moses the people (see Deut. 33), so Joshua gave a final speech before he died.

e 23:6 Singular, not "Scrolls," which shows that Moses was the author of the Torah and that it is one book in five parts, a five-fold expression of God's instruction to Israel.

f 23:6 Or "turning aside from it neither to the right nor to the left." See Num. 20:17; Deut. 2:27; 2 Sam. 2:19–21. This signifies being steadfast in following God's Word.

names of their gods when you take an oath. And by all means don't worship or pray to them. ⁸As you have done until now, cling tightly to Yahweh, for he is your God. ⁹Yahweh has driven out great and powerful nations before you! No one was able to withstand you, ¹⁰for Yahweh your God fights for you as he promised he would! That is why just one of you causes a thousand of our enemies to run away.ᵃ ¹¹Above all else, keep watch over your hearts, so as to always love Yahweh your God.ᵇ

¹²"But if you ever turn away and make alliances with the nations that remain in your midst, and establish friendly relations with them and intermarry, ¹³then you may be sure that Yahweh your God will no longer drive them out before you. Instead they will become a snare and a trap for you! They will be like whips on your backsides and thorns in your eyes until you perish from the good land that Yahweh your God has given you.ᶜ

¹⁴"Now I am about to go the way of all humanity.ᵈ You know with all your heart and soul that not one promise of Yahweh your God has failed. Without a doubt, every promise he made to us he has kept; he has fulfilled them all.ᵉ ¹⁵Just as he has kept every *wonderful* promise he ever made to you, so Yahweh your God will carry out every threat and will obliterate you completely from this good land which he has given you. ¹⁶But if you break the covenant our God, Yahweh, made with you and worship other gods and bow down to them, his anger will blaze against you. He will punish you, and he will remove you from the face of this good land he has given you."

Renewal of the Covenant at Shechem

24 Joshua assembled all Israel's tribes at Shechem.ᶠ He summoned all the leaders—elders, judges, and officials of Israel—and they all stood in the presence of God.

---

a 23:10 See Lev. 26:8; Deut. 32:30.

b 23:11 To those under the law of Moses, God is to be loved (see Deut. 6:4–5), and so much more for those who have been set free to follow Jesus Christ, our Beloved. Serving God must be based on loving him with all our hearts.

c 23:13 See Deut. 4:25–26; 11:16–17.

d 23:14 Or "I am going the way of everything earthly." Joshua realized his mortality and knew he didn't have much longer to live. See 1 Kings 2:2–3.

e 23:14 See 2 Cor. 1:20.

f 24:1 Three locations in the promised land were of vital interest to Israel: Gilgal, Shiloh, and Shechem. Gilgal was their military headquarters during the invasion. For the believer today, Gilgal represents our beginning, our resurrection into new life, and our responsibilities and battles that come with it (see Josh. 10:43–11:23; Eph. 6:12). Gilgal was also a place of recovery and renewal, for the reproach of Egypt was rolled away at Gilgal. Shiloh was the pre-Jerusalem capitol and worship center for Israel, the spiritual pivot of national life. That is where God had manifested his grace, guidance, and power. It represents the holy realm of worship and devotion to God, where we receive divine revelation. Shechem was the political cradle of the nation due to its importance in the lives of the patriarchs. Shechem was not only the geographic center of Canaan but also the moral heart of the nation. At this city Abraham built the first altar to Yahweh within the land, and here God appeared to him and promised that Abraham's seed would inherit the promises (see Gen. 12:7). It is the place of building altars, renewing our covenant-love of God (see Gen. 35:1–4), and receiving our spiritual inheritance as sons and daughters of God.

²Then Joshua said to them all: "This is what Yahweh the God of Israel has to say to you: 'Long ago, your forefathers—Terah, father of Abraham and father of Nahor—lived beyond the Euphrates and worshiped other gods. ³I took your father Abraham from that land and led him through all the land of Canaan. I gave him a son, Isaac, and through Isaac I multiplied his descendants. ⁴I gave Isaac two sons, Jacob and Esau. To Esau and his descendants I gave the hill country of Edom*a* as their inheritance, while Jacob and his family went down to Egypt. ⁵*When the time of their captivity was complete*, I sent Moses and Aaron to Egypt *to deliver them*. I struck the land with great plagues, and afterward I led you*b* out from there. ⁶I freed your forefathers from Egypt and brought you to the Red Sea, but the Egyptians pursued them with chariots and horsemen. ⁷Then our people cried out to Yahweh for help, and he put a thick, dark cloud between you and the Egyptians. *When the Egyptians attempted to follow them*, I caused the sea to roll over them and drown them. You saw with your own eyes what I did to the Egyptians. Then you lived in the desert for many years. ⁸I brought you to the land of the Amorites, who lived east of the Jordan. When they fought against you, I gave them into your hands. As you advanced, I gave you victory over them, and you took possession of their land.

⁹"Later, when Balak son of Zippor, king of Moab, opposed Israel, he sent for *the prophet* Balaam son of Beor to come and curse you. ¹⁰But I refused to listen to Balaam. Instead he had to prophesy my blessings over you! I rescued you from his power.*c*

¹¹"Later, after you crossed the Jordan miraculously, you faced *another impossibility*—Jericho! The lords of Jericho,*d* as well as the Amorites, Perizzites, Canaanites, Hittites, Girgashites, Hivites, and Jebusites, fought with you, but I gave you victory over them all! ¹²I sent the hornet*e* ahead of you to run off the two Amorite kings.*f* Your weapons and strength had nothing to do with it! ¹³I gave you land on which you had not labored and cities that you had not built. You are now living in the land I gave you. You are eating grapes from vines that others planted and olives from trees planted by the people who lived there before you.'

Choose Whom You Will Serve

¹⁴"Now therefore, worship Yahweh with holy awe*g* and serve him in authentic love and loyalty. Remove *from*

---

a 24:4 Or "Seir."

b 24:5 In vv. 5–7 the author alternates between using "your forefathers [ancestors]" and "you [plural]" as a way of reminding the people of that generation that they were included in the redemptive history of their people.

c 24:10 Or "from his hand."

d 24:11 "The lords of Jericho" may be a reference to the spiritual powers (principalities) that held Jericho and the other city-states in their grip. Joshua battled not only against flesh and blood but also against principalities and powers (Eph. 6:10–18).

e 24:12 See Ex. 23:28; Deut. 7:20. The hornet is likely an idiomatic expression for being thrown into a panic. One can get a picture of a man thrashing at a swarm of hornets trying to sting him. That is the word picture here. As God's presence invaded the land, it brought panic into the hearts of God's enemies.

f 24:12 That is, Og and Sihon. See 12:2–13:11.

g 24:14 Or "fear" or "reverential honor."

your hearts every false god to whom your fathers bowed down beyond the Euphrates and in Egypt and serve Yahweh. [15]If it seems wrong in your eyes to serve Yahweh, then make your decision today which gods you will worship—the gods which your ancestors worshiped in Mesopotamia or the gods which the Amorites worship in the land where you are now living—but I and my family, we will *give our lives to* worship and serve Yahweh!"[a]

[16]The people responded *enthusiastically*: "Far be it from us to abandon Yahweh and serve other gods! [17]Our God, Yahweh, set us and our fathers free from *slavery in* the land of Egypt, the house of bondage. He performed these many great signs *and wonders* before our eyes. Yahweh *supernaturally* protected us throughout our entire journey as we passed through the territory of other nations. [18]And as we advanced, Yahweh powerfully drove out from before us all the people, including the Amorites who inhabited the country. *Yes, Joshua!* We, too, will worship and serve Yahweh, for he alone is our God."

[19]Joshua warned the people, "Don't be so quick to say, 'We will worship and serve Yahweh,'[b] for he is a holy God. And he will tolerate no rivals.[c] God will not forgive the sin of unfaithfulness to him.[d] [20]If after Yahweh has been gracious to you, you turn and forsake him to worship other gods, then he will turn and deal harshly with you and totally consume you!"

[21]"No, no!" the people responded. "We promise to worship and serve Yahweh!"

[22]Then Joshua said to them, "You are witnesses against yourselves that you have chosen to serve Yahweh."

"Yes, we are witnesses," they responded.

[23]"Now then," said Joshua, "throw away these foreign gods that are among you, and yield your hearts fully to Yahweh the God of Israel!"

[24]And the people promised Joshua, "We really will worship and serve our God, Yahweh, and listen to his voice."

[25]On that day when the people were gathered at Shechem, Joshua made a covenant between them and Yahweh, which contained laws the people were to obey. [26]Joshua recorded all this in a book of divine instruction.[e] Then he set up a large stone memorial at the tent pole[f] near the holy place of Yahweh. [27]Joshua said to all the people, "Look at this stone! It will serve as a witness, for it heard all the words that Yahweh spoke to us;[g] it will be a witness against you if you rebel against our God." [28]Joshua then dismissed the people, each to their own inheritance.

---

a 24:15 The Septuagint adds the clause "for he is holy!"

b 24:19 Or "You will not be able to serve Yahweh."

c 24:19 Or "He is El, the Jealous." See Ex. 20:5; Deut. 4:24; 5:9.

d 24:19 Or "He will not forgive your transgressions and your sins." Joshua possibly knew that they were secretly practicing idolatry.

e 24:26 Or "the book of the law of God." It is difficult to identify this as any particular book included in the Old Testament.

f 24:26 Or "oak tree [terebinth]." This is a hapax legomenon that Rabbinical Judaism interprets as "pole." (See A. Cohen, *American Journal of Semitic Languages*, xl, pp. 160ff).

g 24:27 The stones (inanimate objects) can hear our words.

Joshua and Eleazar Buried in the Promised Land

[29]Some time later, Joshua son of Nun, the servant of Yahweh,[a] died at the age of one hundred and ten. [30]They buried him on his own property, at Timnath Serah[b] in the hill country of Ephraim, north of Mount Gaash.[c] [31]Israel was faithful to serve Yahweh during the lifetime of Joshua and the lifetime of the elders who lived on after Joshua, those who had experienced all the miracles that Yahweh had done for Israel.[d]

[32]They buried Joseph's bones, which the Israelites had brought up from Egypt, at Shechem, in the tract of land that Jacob bought for a hundred pieces of silver[e] from the children of Hamor, Shechem's father.[f] So *the land* became the inheritance of Joseph's descendants. [33]The *chief priest*[g] Eleazar son of Aaron also died. They buried him on the hill[h] of his son Phineas, which had been assigned to him in Ephraim.[i]

---

a 24:29 Finally upon his death Joshua was called "the servant of Yahweh," a title that had been used exclusively for Moses up to this point in the book of Joshua.

b 24:30 Or "Timnath Heres." See Judg. 2:9 and first footnote.

c 24:30 *Gaash* means "shaking" or "commotion."

d 24:31 See Judg. 2:7, 10.

e 24:32 Or "for a hundred qesitah," an unknown unit of money.

f 24:32 See Gen. 50:24–25. The Septuagint adds "There they deposited in his grave the flint knives used to circumcise the children of Israel at Gilgal, as the Lord commanded them when he brought them out of Egypt."

g 24:33 The words "chief priest" are found in some Syriac manuscripts and the Septuagint.

h 24:33 Or "Gibeah." *Gibeah* is the common Hebrew word for "hill."

i 24:33 The Septuagint adds, "At that time, the children of Israel took up the ark of God and carried it about among them."

THE BOOK OF

JUDGES

champion-deliverers

BroadStreet
PUBLISHING

JUDGES

Introduction

AT A GLANCE

Author: Samuel the prophet
Audience: Originally Israel; however, this theological history speaks to everyone.
Date: 1200–970 BC
Type of Literature: Theological history, prophetic literature
Major Themes: Idolatry and apostasy, disobedience and deliverance, godly leadership, and revelations of Christ
Outline:

I. Disobedience: Israel Turns from God — 1:1–2:5
   A. Victory and Defeat — 1:1–36
   B. Divine Mercy — 2:1–5

II. Discipline: The Lord Chastens Israel — 2:6–16:31
   A. Israel's Disobedience and Defeat — 2:6–3:6
   B. Othniel, Ehud, and Shamgar — 3:7–31
   C. Deborah and Barak — 4:1–5:31
   D. Gideon — 6:1–8:32
   E. Abimelech — 8:33–9:57
   F. Tola and Jair — 10:1–5
   G. Jephthah — 10:6–12:7
   H. Ibzan, Elon, and Abdon — 12:8–15:20
   I. Samson — 13:1–16:31

III. Disgrace: Israel Sinks into Anarchy — 17:1–21:25
   A. Idolatry — 17:1–18:31
   B. Immorality — 19:1–30
   C. Civil War — 20:1–21:25

ABOUT JUDGES

The seventh book of the Bible in the Hebrew Scriptures is *Shophetim,*[a] or "Judges."
It describes the various men and women who distinguished themselves in Israel
during the time period between the book of Joshua and the establishment of a

---

a *Shophetim* could also be translated, "avengers," "punishers," "defenders," "deliverers," "saviors," or possibly "governors." In a sense, there is a dynamic at play in the Old Testament that mirrors the New Testament: Joshua parallels the book of Ephesians; Judges parallels the book of Galatians, for the message of Galatians leads the people of God out of error and bondage. The twelve judges have a parallel with the twelve apostles of Jesus. The book of Judges can be kingdom in 1 Samuel. For four hundred years, Israel had no king or prophet to guide them. Instead, twelve consecutive judges led them. But the Hebrew word for "judge" has little comparison to the western concept of a judge, one who sits on the bench judging court cases argued by trained lawyers.

No, the judges were not law-court justices. Instead, they were Israel's champion-deliverers. God chose them to deliver Israel from enemy oppression, lead the people of God into a revival, and restore their national identity. The role of these deliverers cannot be understated, for without their impact and deliverance, Israel's enemies may have entirely consumed them. Some of the deliverers are well-known biblical champions, and others are somewhat obscure.

Who were the judges? They were unique men and women who carried God's presence—his Spirit—and were commissioned to deliver the people of Israel from the oppression of their enemies. They were saviors and rescuers, whom God raised up at the right time to rally the nation and bring victory to Israel. They were twelve divinely appointed champions who brought the people out of the wilderness mentality and into divine order and breakthrough when no one else could. Here are the six major judges and six minor judges:

Major Judges	Minor Judges
Gideon	Shamgar
Jephthah	Elon
Deborah	Jair
Ehud	Tola
Samson	Abdon
Othniel	Ibzan

The world of the judges had many similarities to the modern times we are living in now, making this book even more relevant for readers today. Throughout Judges, "Israel had no king" (17:6); when Jesus is not our King, the opinions of man rule. Then, "people did whatever they wanted to do" (17:6); today, wrong is celebrated, and that which is right is ridiculed. God's people were divided and fighting among themselves; today, divisions are rampant in our culture and in the church. God's people were conquered by many evil enemies; today, spiritual strongholds of hatred, sexual confusion, pride, and prejudice need to be overcome.

But even in the midst of all this darkness, God's merciful and loving character and his heart to deliver his people despite their failures remains the same. In the former days of Israel, "Yahweh raised up deliverers from among them who rescued them from the marauding bands. . . . His presence and power were with that leader, and he would rescue the people from their enemies as long as that deliverer lived" (2:16, 18). Yahweh still raises up such people, filled with faith and courage. He's doing it today. These are God's deliverers.

---

viewed as an apostolic manual for "last days" ministries. The judges were forerunners of the kingdom. God has promised that he will restore the era of deliverers (judges) in the last days to bring the church into complete victory. See Isa. 1:26; Obad. 21.

PURPOSE

The book of Judges explores one of the most crucial periods in the history of Israel, one of transition from slaves of Egypt to citizens of a kingdom. It showcases how Israel failed to live up to the covenant that Yahweh lovingly entered into with them and the resulting disastrous downfall and near destruction. It serves to warn the mind of the ease with which our human frailty and wandering ways can turn us from Yahweh. Yet it also serves to warm the heart by shining a bright revelation-light on our Savior's unspeakable compassion and long-suffering in the face of apostasy and disobedience.

One of the reasons Judges is in our Bible is to show us that God uses imperfect people. He looks for those who are available, teachable, and obedient. Each of the judges had some form of weakness or handicap that would disqualify him or her in the eyes of some. But God looks on the heart and specifically chose each one to demonstrate his power flowing through human weakness.[a] Yet while there was little to inspire us about their moral character, we do find a font of faith flowing from their lives.

Although Judges exposes the many failures of God's people, it also reveals the faith of champions who chose to challenge the status quo, trusting in God's sovereign goodness and revealing his mighty power. The secret of their success was the anointing of the Holy Spirit (Judg. 6:34) combined with an active faith in Yahweh. In fact, four of the deliverers are mentioned in the "Hall of Faith" found in Hebrews 11:32. As the book reveals: "Through faith's power they conquered kingdoms and established true justice. . . . It was faith that shut the mouth of lions, put out the power of raging fire, and caused many to escape certain death by the sword. Although weak, their faith imparted power to make them strong!" (Heb. 11:33–34).

Judges is classified by our Jewish friends among the books of the Bible known as the "Former Prophets" (which also includes Joshua, Samuel, and Kings). This means that the content of Judges can be considered prophecy; this book prophesies to the church today (1 Cor. 10:11), instructing us of the ways of God through the voices of champion-deliverers who believed the Word of Yahweh, confronted enemies inside and outside his people, and fought for their deliverance.

AUTHOR AND AUDIENCE

Jewish tradition states that the prophet Samuel wrote the book of Judges.[b] Many modern scholars believe there were also editorial revisions either during the reign of King Josiah or during the Babylonian exile. Either way, the book was an important reminder for God's chosen people, the Israelites, of a dark period in their history when they "did what was evil in the sight of Yahweh" (Judg. 2:11), when they "deserted" and "completely abandoned Yahweh" (2:12, 13), and when "Israel had no king, and everyone did whatever they wanted to do" (21:25). But it wasn't just the people in general who behaved badly; neither the deliverers God sent nor the tribal leaders exhibited godly character and obedience. Yahweh ultimately used flawed individuals to rescue his disobedient people. He still does.

---

a See Zech. 4:6; 1 Cor. 1:18–31; 2 Cor. 12:9.

b Samuel is traditionally viewed as the author of 1 and 2 Samuel and Ruth in addition to Judges. (See Bava Batra 14.b.)

Although the book was originally written to Israel, this theological history speaks to everyone. Every subsequent generation of God's people, the church of Jesus Christ, is tempted to imitate Israel's actions: do what is evil, desert and abandon their first love, and do whatever they want to do. Part of this is related to the fact that, like Israel, we are "resident aliens and foreigners in this world" (1 Pet. 2:11), living in a culture that presses in against us and pulls us toward wickedness. It also illustrates the maxim "everything rises and falls on leadership,"[a] for flawed, wicked leaders quite often lead flawed, wicked people.

The book of Judges stands as a reminder, from the Israelites to the church, of the perennial challenge to live for God, obey his Word, and guard against the spiritual influence of the world we find ourselves in.

MAJOR THEMES

Idolatry and Apostasy on Trial. The book of Judges could be classified as a tragedy, for it recounts Israel's history after the death of Joshua and their downward spiral into idolatry and apostasy. Two verses bookend this account, explaining the entirety of this sordid history: "Eventually, after that entire generation died and was buried, the next generation forgot Yahweh and all that he had done for Israel. The Israelites did what was evil in the sight of Yahweh and worshiped the images of Baal" (Judg. 2:10, 11); "In those days, Israel had no king, and everyone did whatever they wanted to do" (21:25).

Every generation subsequent to the death of Joshua stood accused of two things: worshiping false gods and living however they pleased. They forgot the wonders in the wilderness, the manna, the split-open rock which gave them water. Then later, the miracle-parting of the Jordan, the walls of Jericho falling down, the sun standing still, the empowerment of God to conquer their foes, and the many miracles of Yahweh under Joshua's leadership. How easy it is for the second generation of any movement to forget the power of the first generation, the truths they held on to, and the way they lived. How often we enshrine the memories of the past but fail to believe and apply the power present today to advance in the ways of God. In the case of Israel, we know why: they bowed before the false gods of the nations Yahweh warned against, wrecking their faith and leading to their near destruction.

Not only did Israel settle among the Canaanites, Hittites, Amorites, Perizzites, Hivites, and Jebusites, taking their daughters in marriage and marrying their own daughters to the foreigners' sons—they also served their false gods. In the absence of leadership directing Israel's hearts toward God in worship, there was a void. They filled it with false gods and a rejection of Yahweh's truth, leading to a life far from the heart of God. The cycle led to a four-hundred-year pattern of disobedience and deliverance from which the "last days" church would do well to learn.

Disobedience and Deliverance Cycle. During these crucial centuries in the life of Israel recorded in the book of Judges, there is a curious cycle in which Israel's disobedience and wickedness leads to punishment, which then cycles into prayers for rescue and Yahweh answering them to bring about a mighty deliverance.

---

a   John C. Maxwell, *21 Indispensable Qualities of a Leader* (Thomas Nelson, 2007).

This pattern within the book of Judges is repeated seven times in this way: Israel does what is "evil in the sight of Yahweh" (Judg. 2:11), then the people are given over into the hands of their enemies; Israel cries out to Yahweh, then he answers their prayer; Yahweh raises up a leader, then the Spirit of Yahweh comes upon the leader; Yahweh gives Israel a mighty deliverance through God's grace imparted to his deliverers; the people return to the Lord, and peace is regained for a season.

Chapter 6 offers a clear illustration of this principle: "Once again the Israelites did evil in the sight of Yahweh, so Yahweh handed them over to the Midianites for seven years" (v. 1). In response to the Midianites' crushing power, "the Israelites, with shattered hearts, cried out to Yahweh" (v. 6). So Yahweh sent them Gideon, promising: "My presence and my power will be with you. Believe me, Gideon, you will crush the Midianites as easily as if they were only one man!" (v. 16). Through God's empowering of this champion-deliverer, "Israel defeated Midian, who never troubled them again. The land had peace for forty years until Gideon died" (8:28).

The commentator Matthew Henry offers an important observation about this cycle: "The nation made themselves as mean and miserable by forsaking God, as they would have been great and happy if they had continued faithful to him."[a] The book of Judges has served as a clarion call for generations of Yahweh's children, instructing them in his ways and truth and calling them to faithful obedience. It offers a warning for the kind of swift discipline that awaits disobedience. It also assures us of Yahweh's blessed deliverance for the repentant. Though Israel was faithless and disobedient, Yahweh was faithful with deliverance. He was then—and he is now—offering the same deliverance yesterday, today, and forever.

Spirit-Empowered Leadership. Everything rises and falls on leadership, they say. The book of Judges ends with a rather ominous warning illustrating this maxim—not only summarizing this period of the deliverers but also foreshadowing what was to come: "In those days, Israel had no king, and everyone did whatever they wanted to do" (Judg. 21:25).

The book begins with a look back at Joshua, the leader who "released the people to go take possession of their territorial inheritance" (2:6). Under Joshua, the people did what was right under such Spirit-empowered leadership. However, once he died and the entire generation under his leadership was buried, "the next generation forgot Yahweh and all that he had done for Israel" (2:10), leading to cycles of disobedience and punishment.

Yet the Lord didn't abandon his people; he raised up deliverers to rescue them. These champions were not left to their own devices either, as if Yahweh called them without empowering them. No, "whenever Yahweh raised up a hero for them, his presence and power were with that leader, and he would rescue the people from their enemies as long as that deliverer lived" (2:18). What a comfort to know that when the Lord calls us, he empowers us; he will be with us wherever we go.

---

a Matthew Henry and Thomas Scott, *Commentary on the Holy Bible, Genesis–Esther* (Thomas Nelson Publishers, 1979), 66.

However, this doesn't mean there is no room for our own participation in God's empowerment. For the book of Judges also illustrates the other side of Spirit-empowered leadership: failure. Perhaps the model of such failed leadership is Samson, the last of the major deliverers. Samson was a mighty deliverer but riddled with compromise. He could tear a lion apart but could not control his lust. He was one man in the Bible who had some of the greatest potential, but he proved to be one of the greatest disappointments. Samson was a leader, a "man's man," with God's Spirit to strengthen him, yet he left a legacy of compromise and moral weakness. In spite of all this, Samson is listed in Hebrews 11:32 as a man of great faith. He ultimately returned to the heart of God and asked to be used by him, delivering God's judgment upon the Philistines and leading Israel to deliverance.

We can expect the Lord to speak to his leaders and to his people today, but they must consult Yahweh in prayer and seek him with all their heart, soul, mind, and strength. May the lives of the champion-deliverers throughout the book of Judges compel us to offer Christ's church good and godly Spirit-empowered leadership during these last days.

Revelation of Christ in the Champion-Deliverers. Throughout the book of Judges we meet twelve champion-deliverers—six major, six minor—who brought Israel into divine breakthrough when no one else could. They reveal the heart of God through not only their character and devotion but also their availability and faithfulness to the mission of God. We also find another revelation-truth embedded within each of these twelve individuals: each of the champion-deliverers reveals Jesus Christ in some way.

We see Jesus Christ revealed in the book of Judges as:

Our true Savior and Judge who delivers his people (Luke 4:18–19)
Our heavenly Othniel who obtained his bride (Judg. 1:12–15; 3:7–11)
The angel of the Lord (Judg. 2:1–5)
The tent peg/nail in the head of Sisera (Judg. 4:21; 5:26; Isa. 22:23)
The torch within the clay jars (Judg. 7:16–20; 2 Cor. 4:7)
Honey in the carcass of the lion (Judg. 14:8–18)
The jawbone (power of his prophetic word) of the donkey (Judg. 15:15–20)
The King in Israel (Judg. 17:6; 21:25)

These glimpses of our ultimate Champion-Deliverer in the book of Judges mirror the Bible's overarching theme throughout the Hebrew Scriptures of God's self-initiative in redeeming sinful humanity—which finds its ultimate fulfillment in Jesus. We find embedded here at least a hint of Jesus' sacrifice on the cross, his resurrection, his ascension into heaven, and glimpses of all that the believer enjoys in following him. As the apostle Paul wrote to Timothy, "Remember what you were taught from your childhood from the Holy Scrolls [the Hebrew Scriptures], which can impart to you wisdom to experience everlasting life through the faith of Jesus, the Anointed One!" (2 Tim. 3:15). In the book of Judges, this everlasting-life wisdom streams forth.

JUDGES

Champion-Deliverers

Judah Leads

1 And[a] after Joshua died, *the twelve tribal leaders*[b] consulted Yahweh for a prophetic sign[c] and asked, "Which tribe do you choose to be the first to lead the attack against the Canaanites?"

[2]Yahweh answered them,[d] "Let Judah take the lead.[e] [3]I have delivered the land into their hands."

Judah then enlisted support from their brother-tribe Simeon,[f] saying, "Follow us into our territory and fight with us against the Canaanites; then we will do the same for you." So the Simeonites *agreed and* joined them.

[4]When Judah advanced, Yahweh gave them victory over the Canaanites and Perizzites, and they defeated ten thousand men at Bezek.[g] [5-6]They encountered *King* Adoni-Bezek[h] fleeing with his army on the battlefield. They pursued him, captured him, and defeated the Canaanites and

---

a 1:1 See first footnote on Josh. 1:1.

b 1:1 Or "the Israelites." Not the entire nation but the twelve representatives of the twelve tribes came before the high priest to present their request before God.

c 1:1 Although the Hebrew verb *sha'al* means, in its basic sense, "ask" or "inquire," one subset meaning is to "inquire of," "consult deity," or "ask for an oracle [a prophetic sign or message]." It's not explicitly stated, but it is likely Israel came before Yahweh at Shiloh (see Josh. 18:1). They presented themselves there to consult the Urim and Thummim worn on the breastplate of Phineas the high priest. *Urim* means "lights" and *Thummim* means "perfections." See Ex. 28:30; Num. 27:21. The Israelites showed their commitment to following Yahweh's plan by seeking a prophetic indication of which tribe should go first in the attack. It is always wise to seek the Lord before we step out into a new chapter of our lives. See Prov. 3:5–6.

d 1:2 Our God answers prayer. We can expect the Lord to speak to his leaders and to his people today. Twelve times in Judges Yahweh spoke to the Israelites. See 6:16, 23, 25; 7:2, 4–5, 7, 9; 10:11; 20:18, 23, 28.

e 1:2 *Judah* means "praise." Praise will lead the way before us. See 2 Chron. 20:21.

f 1:3 One (Judah) can chase a thousand, but two (Judah and Simeon) can chase ten thousand (see Deut. 32:30). In the next verse they did just that! Simeon's cities were within the territory of Judah (see Josh. 15:26–32, 42; 19:1–9). Both Judah and Simeon had the same mother (Leah) and saw themselves as true brothers. *Simeon* means "one who hears." When worship and the prophetic flow together, we will win our battles.

g 1:4 *Bezek* means "lightning." Bezek is identified by some with Khirbet Bezqa, a site near Gezer, or possibly Khirbet Ibzik, about fifteen miles northeast of Shechem.

h 1:5–6 *Adoni-Bezek* means "the lord of lightning."

Perizzites. Then they cut off Adoni-Bezek's thumbs and big toes.[a] [7]Adoni-Bezek confessed, "I once had seventy[b] kings picking up scraps under my table with their thumbs and big toes cut off. Now God has paid me back for what I did to them!" They took him captive to Jerusalem, where he died.[c]

Judah's Victories

[8]The men of Judah attacked Jerusalem and captured it. They killed *the inhabitants of* the city[d] and set it on fire.[e] [9]Afterward, the men of Judah continued their advance and attacked the Canaanites living in the hill country, the southern desert region, and the western lowlands. [10]*Under Caleb's leadership,*[f] they fought against the Canaanites living in Hebron, formerly known as Kiriath Arba, and killed the three *Canaanite families descended from* Sheshai, Ahiman, and Talmai.[g] [11]From there, they attacked the city of Debir, formerly known as Kiriath Sepher.[h] [12]Caleb announced, "I will give my daughter Achsah[i] in marriage to the man[j] who attacks and captures Kiriath Sepher."

---

a 1:5–6 They cut off the king's thumbs so he would never be able to hold a sword or scepter again. They cut off his big toes so that he would never be able to flee. He reaped what he had sown (see v. 7; cf. Gal. 6:7).

b 1:7 The number *seventy* is the biblical number of the nations (Gen. 10 mentions seventy nations). In contrast, Jesus sent out seventy to bring the kingdom feast to the hungry among the nations. As they were sent out in Christ's name, Jesus saw Satan fall from heaven like "lightning" (Luke 10:17–19). This was the ultimate victory over Adoni-Bezek, the lord of lightning. Adoni-Bezek is a picture of Satan.

c 1:7 Although Jesus died in Jerusalem, by virtue of his resurrection, he lives today (see Rom. 6:10). But Satan was defeated in Jerusalem and stripped of his ability to conquer us all because of the cross of Jesus Christ. (See Col. 2:14–15; cf. John 3:18.)

d 1:8 Or "they put the city to the mouth of the sword." The words of our mouth are like the edge of a sword to defeat our enemies. See Heb. 4:12.

e 1:8 Although they conquered Jerusalem, they did not fully occupy it until the time of King David, when he established Jerusalem as the nation's capital.

f 1:10 See Josh. 15:14.

g 1:10 These three descended from the giant Anak (see Num. 13:22, 33), and their names represent the three "giants" we must topple to advance into our inheritance. *Sheshai* is taken from a word that means "white-washed." He points to the hypocrisy of the Pharisees that were like "tombs painted over with white paint" (Matt. 23:27), consumed with how they appeared to others. *Ahiman* means "brother of a gift" or "like a gift." He represents pride over giftedness. We all have spiritual gifts, but they are gifts of grace, not trophies. And *Talmai* comes from a word that means "scholar." True scholarship will always acknowledge how little humans know and how great God truly is. According to the parallel passage in Joshua, it was the descendants of these three sons of Anak that were conquered (see Josh. 15:13–14).

h 1:11 *Kiriath Sepher* means "city of books," and *Debir* means "the word." God is still looking for people who will "conquer" the book (Bible), view it as the Word of God, and make it their own.

i 1:12 *Achsah* means "anklet [that which beautifies the feet]." A believer who brings the good news to others is said to have "beautiful feet." See Song. 7:1; Isa. 52:7; Rom. 10:15.

j 1:12 Caleb knew it would take a special man to conquer a city with giants and thereby be a worthy husband for his daughter. Caleb knew that it would require a man endued with God's power and favor to take the city of Debir.

Othniel

¹³Caleb's nephew Othniel*ᵃ* the Kenizzite captured Kiriath Sepher; and Caleb gave him his daughter Achsah in marriage.

¹⁴One day, Othniel nagged her to ask her father for a field *as a wedding gift, so she went to him.* When she got down from her donkey, Caleb said to her, "What can I do for you?"

¹⁵"Please, give me a blessing," she replied. "I know you've already given me some arid desert land, but please give me a field with springs of water." So Caleb blessed her with *a field that had* both upper and lower springs.*ᵇ*

Judah Advances

¹⁶The descendants of Moses' father-in-law, the Kenite, joined the people of Judah, and went with them from *Jericho,* the City of Date Palms, to the Judean wilderness. The Kenites had settled there among the *Amalekites* at Arad.*ᶜ*

¹⁷Judah and their brother-tribe Simeon advanced to the city of Zephath and wiped out the Canaanites living there. That's why they now call the city Hormah.*ᵈ* ¹⁸*The men of* Judah captured Gaza,*ᵉ* Ashkelon,*ᶠ* Ekron,*ᵍ* and the territories surrounding each of these cities.

Israel Fails to Conquer the Land

¹⁹Yahweh's presence *and power* were with *the men of* Judah and they were able to conquer the hill country, but because the people of the lowlands had war chariots,*ʰ* they failed to drive them out. ²⁰Because Caleb conquered the three *giants,* the sons of Anak,*ⁱ* he was given the city of Hebron.

²¹The tribe of Benjamin, however, failed to conquer the Jebusites living in Jerusalem. So to this day, the Jebusites live among the Benjamites in Jerusalem.*ʲ*

---

a 1:13 Othniel was the first champion-deliverer (judge). He lived in the shadow of his famous uncle, Caleb. No dragon slayer did more for his princess. Othniel prefigures our Lord Jesus, the Living Word who took the "city of books" for his bride. *Othniel* means "lion of God" or "strength of God." He lived up to his name! Scholars believe Othniel was about fifty-three years old at this time. Arguably, Othniel could be considered the "ideal judge," who married an Israelite, mobilized all the people, and was Spirit-endowed to lead to victory. (Rick Wadholm Jr., *A Theology of the Spirit in the Former Prophets: A Pentecostal Perspective* [Cleveland, TN: CPT Press, 2018] 121–124, 210.)

b 1:15 Or possibly the name of a specific field: "He gave her [a field called] Upper and Lower Gulloth-Mayim."

c 1:16 Or "among the people at Arad."

d 1:17 This is an example of a Hebraic pun, or play on words. The words for "Hormah" and for the phrase "wiped out" are similar. *Hormah* means "totally destroyed" or "under the ban."

e 1:18 *Gaza* means "strong" or "stronghold." Gaza is located on the Mediterranean, and scholars consider it to be the oldest city of the Philistines. It is mentioned eighteen times in the Old Testament and once in the New Testament (see Acts 8:26).

f 1:18 *Ashkelon* means "weight." The town is possibly named for the weights of the scales used for measuring products. It is a coastal city located about thirty miles south of modern Tel Aviv.

g 1:18 *Ekron* means "torn up by the roots." It is mentioned over twenty times in the Old Testament.

h 1:19 Or "chariots with iron-rimmed wheels."

i 1:20 Since *Anak* can mean "long-necked," it is presumed that the "sons of Anak" were men of great height.

j 1:21 The inability of Israel to dispossess their enemies in vv. 19–29 (see Josh. 15:63) becomes a picture for us today of not dealing with every issue (enemy) within our hearts that prevents us from possessing our full inheritance in Christ. We will repeat the same patterns of defeat if we are not thorough in eliminating every evil from our lives. See Col. 3:5–11.

22-23Yahweh's *presence and power* were with Joseph's descendants, so they advanced toward Bethel and sent men ahead to spy out the city that was formerly known as Luz. 24The spies confronted a man coming out of Bethel and they said to him, "Show us the way to enter the city and we will treat you well."*a* 25So he showed the spies a secret entrance into the city, and they killed everyone living in Bethel with the sword*b* except that man and his family. 26Later the man *and his family* moved to the land of the Hittites*c* and built a town. The *new* town has kept the name Luz to this day.

27The Canaanites were determined to stay in their land, so the men of Manasseh did not conquer *the cities of* Beth Shean, Taanach, Dor, Ibleam, Megiddo, and their surrounding villages.*d* 28And whenever Israel gained the upper hand, they subjected the Canaanites to forced labor;*e* but they did not completely drive them out.

29The tribe of Ephraim failed to drive out the Canaanites living in Gezer, so the Canaanites continue to live there among them.

30The tribe of Zebulun failed to drive out the Canaanites living in Kitron*f* or Nahalol, so the Canaanites continue to live there among them.

31The tribe of Asher failed to drive out the Canaanites living in Acco, Sidon, Ahlab, Achzib, Helbah, Aphik, and Rehob, 32so the people of Asher live among the Canaanites residing in the land because they did not conquer them.

33Likewise, the tribe of Naphtali failed to drive out the Canaanites living in Beth Shemesh or Beth Anath,*g* so they live among the Canaanites residing in the land. However, they forced the inhabitants of Beth Shemesh and Beth Anath to serve them.

34The tribe of Dan *was least successful*. The Amorites forced them back into the hills*h* and they could no longer live in the valley. 35The Amorites persisted in living on Mount Heres, in Aijalon, and in Shaalbim. But when the descendants of Joseph grew stronger, they overpowered the Amorites and ruled over them. 36The boundary of the Amorites ran from Scorpion Pass*i* to Sela and continued northward from there.

---

a 1:24 Or literally "we will do *chesed* [covenant loyalty] to you."

b 1:25 Or literally "with the mouth" (i.e., "edge") of the sword. See Heb. 4:12.

c 1:26 The region from northern Syria into Asia Minor was known in the days of Joshua and Judges as the kingdom of Hatti, or "the land of the Hittites." The Talmud describes this region as the place where Phoenicians produced blue dye that the Israelites used for the blue fringes (tassels) of their garments. (See Num. 15:38; *Sotah* [Talmud] 46b.) According to Egyptian inscriptions dated to 1500 BC, the Hittites were expelled from the land of Canaan.

d 1:27 Or "and their daughter towns."

e 1:28 Eventually, Solomon conscripted the Canaanites to build the temple (see 1 Kings 9:20–22; 2 Chron. 8:7–8).

f 1:30 Traditionally identified in Jewish writings as Sepphoris, about four miles north of Nazareth.

g 1:33 *Shemesh* means "sun" and *Anath* means "the war goddess." They were Canaanite deities. It is likely that temples to these pagan gods were located in their respective cities.

h 1:34 Although our enemies may push God's people into retreat for a season, in Christ, our ultimate victory over our foes is secure.

i 1:36 Or "Akrabbim," possibly modern Neqb es-Safa, which descends from Beersheba to the Wadi Murra. Scorpion Pass lies about twenty miles south of the Dead Sea.

The Angel of Yahweh Rebukes Israel

2 The Angel of Yahweh[a] went up from Gilgal to Bokim and said to the people: "I rescued you from Egypt and brought you into the land I had promised to your ancestors. I said, 'I will never, never break my covenant with you, [2]and you are never, never to make a covenant with the inhabitants of this land. You must tear down their altars *to their false gods!*' But you have not listened to my voice. See what you have done! [3]Therefore listen to what I'm telling you—I won't drive them out before you. Instead, they will be *thorns* in your sides,[b] and their gods will become a trap for you!"

[4]After the Angel of Yahweh had delivered his message to all the Israelites, the people burst out with loud, bitter weeping. [5]So they named that place Bokim,[c] and *in that place of tears* they offered sacrifices to Yahweh.[d] [6]Then Joshua released the people to go take possession of their territorial inheritance.[e]

The Death of Joshua

[7]The people *faithfully* worshiped Yahweh all the days of Joshua and through all the days of the elders who outlived him. They had all experienced the many astounding miracles Yahweh had done for Israel. [8]Yahweh's servant, Joshua[f] son of Nun, died at the age of one hundred and ten [9]and the people buried him on his own parcel of land in the hill country of Ephraim at Timnath Serah,[g] north of Mount Gaash.[h] [10]Eventually, after that entire generation died and was buried, the next generation forgot

---

a 2:1 This verse implies that the Angel of Yahweh had appeared to the people in Gilgal and now reappeared to them. Although the Hebrew word for "angel" can mean "messenger," the "Angel of Yahweh" was a term used to express the Lord appearing to his people in human form. In v. 1 he says, "I rescued you from Egypt," clearly showing that the Angel of Yahweh was the Lord himself appearing to his people. He came as a representative of the heavenly court with a message for Israel. God had told his people in advance that he was sending an Angel to go before them. See Ex. 14:19; 23:20–24.

b 2:3 Or "they will become adversaries to you." See Num. 33:55.

c 2:5 Or "Bochim." *Bokim* means "weepers." Some scholars believe that Bokim was another name for Bethel (see LXX). The Israelites may have known it as the place near Bethel where Deborah, Rebekah's nurse, died (see Gen. 35:8).

d 2:5 The fact that they offered sacrifices at Bokim indicates that the Israelites had moved the tabernacle there from Gilgal.

e 2:6 The rebuke of the Angel of Yahweh had pierced their hearts. They repented, offered sacrifices to demonstrate their longing for restoration, and went out to conquer again. This account echoes the life of Joshua, during which the people did what was right under such Spirit-empowered leadership.

f 2:8 God designated no successor to Joshua. Among all the judges, only Caleb was called Yahweh's servant (Num. 14:24).

g 2:9 Or "Timnath Heres." *Timnath Heres* means "the [sacred] territory of the sun." It is interesting that Joshua spoke to the sun to stand still (see Josh. 10:12). *Timnath Serah* means "an abundant inheritance."

h 2:9 The Hebrew root for "Gaash" means "to quake."

Yahweh and all that he had done for Israel.[a]

Israel's Cycle of Apostasy

[11]The Israelites did what was evil in the sight of Yahweh and worshiped the images of Baal. [12]Israel deserted Yahweh, the God of their ancestors, who had rescued them from Egypt. They found new gods to worship—the gods of the people around them. They bowed down to them and provoked Yahweh to anger. [13]They completely abandoned Yahweh to serve Baal[b] and the images of the goddess Astarte.[c] [14]They caused the anger of Yahweh to be kindled[d] against Israel, and he handed them over to invaders, who plundered them. He surrendered them to their enemies on all sides, and they could no longer defend themselves. [15]Every time they went into battle, Yahweh raised his hand against them to their undoing,[e] just as he had warned them, and they were in great distress.

[16]Nevertheless, Yahweh raised up deliverers[f] from among them who rescued them from the marauding bands. [17]Rather than listen to their deliverers, they prostituted themselves to other gods and bowed down to worship them. This new generation quickly turned from the good path and refused to be like their ancestors who actually listened to Yahweh's commands.

[18]Yet, whenever Yahweh raised up a hero[g] for them, his *presence and power* were with that leader, and he would rescue the people from their enemies as long as that deliverer lived. Yahweh had mercy and pitied them because of their cries of distress and groanings under the grip of their oppressors.

[19]But when their champion died, then the people would relapse into their former idolatry. They would

---

a 2:10 They forgot the wonders in the wilderness, the manna, the split-open rock that gave them water. Then later, they failed to remember the Jordan miraculously parting, the walls of Jericho falling down, the sun standing still, the empowerment of God conquering their foes, and the many miracles of Yahweh under Joshua's leadership. How easy it is for the second generation of any movement to forget the truth and power of the first generation. We enshrine the memories of the past but fail to apply the power present today to advance in the ways of God. See 2 Tim. 3:5.

b 2:13 *Baal* means "lord" or "master." He was the chief male Canaanite fertility god. The Canaanites worshiped him at altars on high places or mountain summits within the land.

c 2:13 Ishtar, or Astarte, was the moon goddess, the chief goddess of sexuality, fertility, and war. See 1 Sam. 31:10.

d 2:14 Or "caused his anger to burn hot [blaze up]." There are four things in the Bible that kindle God's anger: (1) The oppression of widows, orphans, and strangers—see Ex. 22:21–24; (2) rebellion and idolatry—see Ex. 32:8–11; Deut. 9:19–22; (3) abandoning God and forsaking him—see Judg. 2:12; 3:7; (4) sin and wickedness—see Pss. 6:8; 38:1–5.

e 2:15 Or "defeat."

f 2:16 Or "judges." *Shophetim* could also be translated "avengers," "punishers," "defenders," "deliverers," "saviors," or possibly "governors." In a sense, Judges parallels the New Testament book of Galatians, for the message of Galatians leads the people of God out of error and bondage. (Similarly, Joshua parallels the book of Ephesians.) The twelve champion-deliverers have a parallel with the twelve apostles of Jesus. The book of Judges can be viewed as an apostolic manual for "last days" ministries. The judges were forerunners of the kingdom. God has promised that he will restore the era of deliverers (judges) in the last days to bring the church into complete victory. See Isa. 1:26; Obad. 21.

g 2:18 Or "judge."

worship other gods, bow down to them, and refuse to give up their evil ways. And each generation behaved worse than the one before it. ²⁰Then Yahweh became furious with Israel, saying, "Because this nation has violated the covenant that I commanded their fathers to keep, and because they no longer listen to my voice, ²¹I will no longer drive out any of the nations that remained in the land after Joshua died."

²²Over and over Yahweh tested Israel to see if they would faithfully walk in his ways, as their ancestors had done.ᵃ ²³So Yahweh intentionally left *pagan* nations in the land instead of driving them all out at once, and he did not give Joshua the victory over them, *nor did he drive them out after Joshua's death.*

The Nations Remaining in the Land

3 Here is a list of the nations that Yahweh permitted to remain in the land so he could use them to test the Israelites who had not known what it was like during the Canaanite wars. ²He wanted the succeeding generations of Israel, who had not known war before, to learn the art of warfare. ³So he left in the land the five Philistine principalitiesᵇ and all the Canaanites, Sidonians,ᶜ and Hivites who lived on Mount Lebanon from Mount Baal Hermon as far as Lebo Hamath. ⁴They remained in the land to test Israel to see if they would obey Yahweh's commands that Moses had given to their ancestors.

⁵So the Israelites settled among the Canaanites, Hittites, Amorites, Perizzites, Hivites, and Jebusites. ⁶They took their daughters in marriage and gave their own daughters to their sons; and the Israelites served their false gods.ᵈ

Othniel, the Champion-Deliverer

⁷The Israelites did what was evil in Yahweh's sight. They ignored Yahweh their God, and they served the Baal gods and the Asherah goddesses. ⁸Therefore Yahweh's blazing anger rose up against them. He surrendered them to Cushan-Rishathaim,ᵉ the king of Mesopotamia.ᶠ He kept the Israelites in bondage to himᵍ for eight years. ⁹Then the Israelites, *with shattered hearts*, cried out to Yahweh *for mercy,*ʰ and *he answered them* by raising up a champion-deliverer to rescue them, Othniel. He was Caleb's nephew, the son of his younger brother Kenaz. ¹⁰And the Spirit of Yahweh was upon

---

a 2:22 The Hebrew text has an infinitive verb without a subject, leaving the text ambiguous. It is therefore possible that vv. 22–23 continue the direct speech of Yahweh.

b 3:3 Or "tyrants" or "lords."

c 3:3 Sidonians may be a collective term for the Phoenicians. See Josh. 13:4.

d 3:6 See Ex. 34:16; Deut. 7:3; Ezra 9:12.

e 3:8 *Cushan* possibly means "darkness" and *Rishathaim* possibly means "double wickedness." Cushan-Rishathaim was an oppressive ruler over Israel for eight years because of their rebellion against God.

f 3:8 Mesopotamia was all the land between the Tigris and Euphrates rivers. This would include parts of modern Syria and Iraq.

g 3:8 Or "they served the king."

h 3:9 This was probably in a public assembly at Shiloh. Their cries came from broken hearts, as they were devastated with nowhere else to turn. Yahweh heard their repentant cries and answered them by raising up a champion-deliverer.

him[a] *and empowered him to liberate Israel from bondage.*[b] He became Israel's champion and went out to war, and Yahweh delivered into his hands Cushan-Rishathaim, the king of Mesopotamia. Othniel overpowered him,[c] [11]and after the land had peace for forty years, Othniel the son of Kenaz died.

Ehud, the Champion-Deliverer

[12]The Israelites again did what was evil in Yahweh's sight, and because they did what was offensive to Yahweh, he gave King Eglon of Moab power over Israel.[d] [13]Eglon formed an alliance with the Ammonites and Amalekites, and they attacked and defeated Israel. Eglon captured *Jericho*, the City of Date Palms. [14]King Eglon of Moab kept the Israelites in bondage to him[e] for eighteen years.

[15]Then the Israelites, *with shattered hearts*, cried out to Yahweh for mercy, and Yahweh raised up a champion-deliverer to rescue them— Ehud,[f] who was left-handed.[g] He was the son of Gera from the tribe of Benjamin.

One day, the Israelites sent him to present tribute to King Eglon of Moab. [16]Ehud had made for himself a two-edged sword over a foot long,[h] which he strapped under his coat, to his right thigh. [17]He *and his entourage* came before King Eglon, who was a very fat man, to present the tribute.[i] [18]After the formal presentation of the tribute, he told the men who accompanied him to go back home. [19]Ehud went with them *part of the way*, but he turned back at the carved stones[j] near Gilgal. He returned to Eglon and said, "Your Majesty, I have a secret message for you."

The king said to his attendants, "Leave us!"[k]

After all the king's servants had left, [20]Ehud approached King Eglon while he was sitting alone in his

---

a 3:10 The Targum reads "the Spirit of Prophecy came upon him," signifying a sudden and pronounced power of God's Spirit coming upon Othniel that transcended human strength or ability. The supernatural strength, wisdom, boldness, valor, and ecstasy of a prophet would manifest when the Spirit of God came upon him (see 1 Sam. 10:10).

b 3:10 The Septuagint adds "and they obeyed him."

c 3:10 The Jewish historian Josephus states that Othniel won the victory with a small band of courageous men who surprised the king's bodyguards, overpowered them, and killed the king. (See Josephus, *Ant.* 5.3.3.)

d 3:12 Or "Yahweh strengthened King Eglon against Israel."

e 3:14 Or "Israel served King Eglon." *Eglon* means "fat bull."

f 3:15 *Ehud* means "union" or "strong."

g 3:15 The Hebrew literally reads "restricted [crippled] in his right hand." Left-handed Ehud was from the tribe of Benjamin. *Benjamin* means "son of my right hand." Some scholars believe Ehud may have been the great-grandson of Benjamin. See 20:16. God will use his deliverers no matter what handicap they may have. Ehud's weakness became his strength.

h 3:16 The length of Ehud's sword in Hebrew is a *gomed*, a term which only occurs here in the Old Testament. It is believed to be a short cubit, or about thirteen inches long.

i 3:17 The tribute was likely fruit and produce of the land, along with quantities of wool, which would have required a number of people to carry it and present it to the king. Ehud, like God's servants today, carried both a gift and a sword: a gift to bless the lives of God's people and a sword to render judgment on everything that hindered their advance in the ways of God.

j 3:19 Or "quarries" or "carved images." It may have been the boundary line of Eglon's territory.

k 3:19 Or "Silence!" The king commanded his servants to leave the room before Ehud shared his "secret message."

cool upper room and said to him, "I have a message from God for you." As the king rose from his throne, ²¹Ehud reached *beneath his robe* with his left hand for the sword strapped to his right thigh, and he plunged it deep into Eglon's belly! ²²And the hilt also went in after the blade, and the fat closed over the blade. Ehud was unable to pull out the sword, and the dung came out.*ᵃ*

²³Stepping out of the king's upper room into the portico,*ᵇ* Ehud shut and locked the doors behind him. ²⁴After he had slipped away, the king's servants came to the doors of the upper room and discovered they were locked. So they told themselves, "He must be on the toilet."*ᶜ* ²⁵They waited and waited, but still the king did not emerge. Embarrassed, they finally took their key and unlocked the doors. And when they opened the doors, there was their master sprawled out on the floor, dead! ²⁶But Ehud had escaped while they stood there wondering what to do. He fled beyond the carved stones and made it to Seirah.

²⁷When he arrived *back in the land*, he sounded the war trumpet *with a loud blast* and rallied the people in the hill country of Ephraim. The Israelites went down from the hills *to fight against the Moabites* with Ehud leading the charge. ²⁸"Follow me closely," he said, "and pursue them, for Yahweh has delivered your enemies, the Moabites, into your hands!" So they followed his lead and secured the fords of the Jordan opposite *the land of* Moab and did not let anyone cross. ²⁹In the battle that ensued, they killed nearly ten thousand able-bodied men—brave warriors of Moab, and not one escaped. ³⁰On that day, Moab surrendered to Israel, and the land had peace for eighty years.

Shamgar, the Surprise Deliverer

³¹After Ehud, *God raised up* Shamgar son of Anath,*ᵈ* who killed six hundred Philistines with *nothing but* an ox-goad,*ᵉ* and Shamgar *the deliverer* rescued Israel.

Deborah, the Champion-Deliverer

4 After Ehud died, the Israelites returned to doing evil before the eyes of Yahweh, ²so he surrendered them to King Jabin*ᶠ* of Canaan, who ruled from Hazor. His army commander Sisera established his base in Harosheth*ᵍ* of the Gentiles. ³Jabin had nine hundred chariots with iron-rimmed

---

a 3:22 According to the Latin Vulgate, Midrash Rabbah, and the *Targum of Jonathan on the Prophets.* The meaning of the Hebrew in this last clause is uncertain.

b 3:23 The meaning of the Hebrew of this clause is uncertain.

c 3:24 The Hebrew uses the euphemistic saying, "Perhaps he is covering his feet." Compare 1 Sam. 24:3.

d 3:31 Or "Shamgar the Beth Anathite." Shamgar is not a Hebrew name, and his father, Anath, (the name of a pagan god of war) was a Canaanite, not an Israelite. God raised up a foreigner to bring deliverance to the nation. A nobody with a stick is more than enough when God is with him. *Shamgar* means "surprised stranger."

e 3:31 The Word of God is like an ox-goad that disciplines the heart and moves us closer to righteousness. See Eccl. 12:11.

f 4:2 *Jabin* means "intelligent." He becomes a type of the mind of the flesh.

g 4:2 *Harosheth* means "workmanship," "workshop," or "smithy." Archaeologists have recently uncovered ruins at El Awhat, north of Lake Galilee, that they believe to be the site of Harosheth of the Gentiles. One of their finds was a linchpin of a chariot wheel.

wheels, and he ruthlessly oppressed Israel for twenty years. Then the Israelites, *with shattered hearts*, cried out to Yahweh for help.

⁴*God raised up* Deborah[a] to lead Israel as a champion-deliverer. She was a prophetess[b] and a fiery woman.[c] ⁵She presided as Israel's judge under the Palm of Deborah, a certain palm tree[d] between Ramah and Bethel in the hill country of Ephraim, and the people of Israel came to her for *wise* decisions. ⁶*One day* she sent for Barak[e] son of Abinoam from the city of Kedesh in Naphtali and said to him, "Yahweh, the God of Israel, commands you: 'Go, deploy ten thousand men from the tribes of Naphtali and Zebulun, and march to Mount Tabor. ⁷I will draw Sisera, the commander of Jabin's army, to fight against you at the Kishon River. He will have his many chariots and soldiers, but I will give you victory over him.' "

⁸Barak replied, "I will go if you go with me, but if you don't go with me, I won't go either."

⁹"Very well," she answered. "I will go with you, but you will receive no glory in the victory because Yahweh will hand over Sisera to a woman."[f] So Deborah set off for Kedesh with Barak. ¹⁰Barak summoned the tribes of Zebulun and Naphtali to Kedesh, and ten thousand warriors followed him and Deborah also.

¹¹Now Heber the Kenite migrated away from the other Kenites (the descendants of Hobab,[g] Moses' father-in-law) and was living[h] close to Kedesh near the oak tree at Zaanannim.

¹²When Sisera found out that Barak son of Abinoam was marching toward Mount Tabor, ¹³he gathered together his nine hundred iron-rimmed chariots and all his soldiers and sent them from Harosheth of the Gentiles to the Kishon River.

¹⁴Then Deborah *prophesied* to Barak, "Today, Yahweh has given you victory over Sisera! Go! Yahweh is marching out before you!" Immediately, Barak charged down from Mount Tabor with his ten thousand warriors.

---

a 4:4 *Deborah* means "orderly motion" or "bee [because of its systematic instincts]." The root word means "oracle," "word," or "to speak."

b 4:4 Or "a prophet-woman." See the first footnote on Judg. 6:8.

c 4:4 Or "a woman of many torches/lightning flashes" or "woman [wife] of Lappidoth." *Lappidoth* means "torches" or "flaming sword." It seems that male-driven readings of the text have given the preference to naming an otherwise unknown male, who never gets mentioned elsewhere in the text, as husband of Deborah. (See Rick Wadholm Jr., "'Until I, Deborah, Arose' [Judges 4–5]: A Pentecostal Reception History of Deborah toward Women in Ministry," in Rick Wadholm Jr., Daniel D. Isgrigg, Martin W. Mittelstadt, eds., *Receiving Scripture in the Pentecostal and Charismatic Tradition: A Reception History* [Cleveland, TN: CPT Press, 2020].)

d 4:5 The palm tree is a biblical symbol of joyful victory. When Jesus entered triumphantly into Jerusalem, the people waved palm branches (see John 12:13; cf. Song. 7:7–8; Rev. 7:9–17). Deborah ruled as a prophetess while sitting under the realm of victory and prophetic revelation. The Palm of Deborah was between Ramah and Bethel in Mount Ephraim; *Ramah* means "high place," *Bethel* means "house of God," and *Mount Ephraim* means "double fruitful."

e 4:6 *Barak* means "lightning bolt."

f 4:9 This was a prophecy with a double meaning. Deborah would get the credit for the victory, and Jael would be the one to kill Sisera.

g 4:11 Hobab was another name for Jethro, Moses' father-in-law.

h 4:11 Or "had set up his tent."

The Victory of Deborah and Barak

[15]And Yahweh threw Sisera and his army into confusion before the onslaught of Barak and his men. Sisera and all his chariots and men were overwhelmed.[a] He leaped from his chariot and fled on foot. [16]Barak pursued the other chariots and the army to Harosheth of the Gentiles until Sisera's whole army was killed by the sword, and only Sisera survived. [17]He ran for his life to the tent of Jael[b] wife of Heber the Kenite, for there was friendship between King Jabin of Hazor and the family of Heber[c] the Kenite.

[18]Jael came out of her tent to greet Sisera and said to him, "Come in, my lord, come in here. You have nothing to fear." As soon as he entered her tent, she hid him under a blanket.

[19]Sisera said to her, "I'm so thirsty. Please let me have some water." So she opened a skin of milk, gave him some to drink, and covered him again. [20]He said to her, "Stand at the entrance of your tent. If anybody comes and asks you if there is anybody here, tell them, 'No.' "

[21]Exhausted, he fell fast asleep under the blanket. While he slept, Jael wife of Heber took a tent peg in one hand and a hammer[d] in the other and tiptoed over to where he was lying. And *with a crushing blow*, she drove the tent peg through his temple until it went down into the ground—he was dead!

[22]Just then,[e] Barak arrived in pursuit of Sisera. Jael went out of her tent to greet him and said, "Come, let me show you the man you're looking for." He went inside with her, and there was Sisera lying dead with the tent peg through his temple.

[23]On that day God humiliated King Jabin of Canaan before the Israelites. [24]The hand of the Israelites pressed harder and harder against King Jabin of Canaan until there was nothing left of him *but a memory*!

The Victory Song of Deborah and Barak

5 Deborah and Barak son of Abinoam sang this *victory* song:[f]

---

a 4:15 The Jewish historian Josephus writes that a mighty wind blew on the backs of Barak's charging men, and rain and hail went before them, leaving the Canaanites helpless. The rain would have neutralized Sisera's nine hundred chariots. (See Ps. 83:9; Josephus, *Ant.* 5.5.4.)

b 4:17 *Jael* means "climbing" or "mountain goat." God used two wild women to win the victory, Deborah and Jael.

c 4:17 *Heber* means "not of this world" or "that which passes further."

d 4:21 Both the tent peg and the hammer are symbols for God's Word. See Ezra 9:8; Eccl. 12:11; Isa. 22:23–25; Jer. 23:29; Zech. 10:4. The symbolism suggests a picture of the woman (the church) taking the hammer and tent peg in her hand (see the five-fold ministry, Eph. 4:11), and driving the Word through the temple (mind of the flesh), bringing a victory to God's people. *Jabin* means "intelligent." See Judg. 4:2 and the first footnote there; Rom. 16:20; 1 Cor. 1:18–25.

e 4:22 The Hebrew uses the word for "Behold!"

f 5:1 Deborah likely composed this song, and both Deborah and Barak sang it. Utilizing brilliant imagery and forceful expression, this chapter is considered a literary masterpiece. It may also have been included in the Book of the Wars of the Lord (see Num. 21:14) or the Scroll of the Upright One (see Josh. 10:13; 2 Sam. 1:18).

²Blessings be to Yahweh,
who gave us victory today!
For the people answered the call,
 and Israel threw off what once
 held us back.ᵃ
³Listen, you kings!
Open your ears, you princes!
For I will sing a song to Yahweh.
 I will make music to Yahweh, the
 God of Israel.
⁴Yahweh, when you advanced from
 Seir,ᵇ
and when you marched from
 Edom's plains,
the earth trembled,
 the sky poured,
 the clouds burst,
 ⁵and the mountains melted,
in the presence of Yahweh, the
 Glorious One of Sinai,
in the presence of Yahweh, the
 God of Israel!
⁶In the days of Shamgar son of
 Anath,
and in the days of Jael, *no one felt
 safe*;
the roads were deserted,ᶜ
and those who *dared to* travel took
 back roads.

⁷Champions were hard to findᵈ—
 hard to find in Israel,
 until I, Deborah, took a stand!
I arose as a mother in Israel!ᵉ
⁸The Israelites chose new gods,ᶠ
 which brought war into the
 land.ᵍ
Of forty thousand men in Israel,
 not a shield or spear was seen.ʰ
⁹My heart is with Israel's princes,
 with the people who gladly
 volunteered.
Praise Yahweh!
¹⁰Declare it, you *rich*
 who ride on your white
 donkeys,
 sitting on your *fancy* saddles!
Declare it, you *poor*
 who must walk wherever you
 go!ⁱ
¹¹Listen to the sound of singers at
 the well,ʲ
as they proclaim the victoriesᵏ of
 Yahweh,
 the righteous triumph of his vil-
 lagers in Israel!
Then the people of Yahweh
 marched out from their city
 gates!

---

a 5:2 The Hebrew text is uncertain. One possible translation is "When long locks of hair were worn loose in Israel." This could be a poetic picture of warriors running to the battle with their hair blowing in the wind. Others translate this as "When the leaders led [cast off restraint] in Israel," "Revelation was revealed in Israel [LXX]," or "When the breakers broke forth."

b 5:4 Probably referring to a mountainous region in Edom. See Deut. 33:2.

c 5:6 Or "caravans ceased."

d 5:7 Or "Villages were deserted."

e 5:7 Would that there were "mothers" of God's people today to lead them in the power of the Spirit into God's victories!

f 5:8 Or "God chose a new thing [leaders]."

g 5:8 Or "there was war [warriors] in [over] the gates."

h 5:8 Or "Then there was not seen a shield for five cities, nor a spear among forty thousand in Israel." Scholars acknowledge this entire verse to be difficult to translate.

i 5:10 This verse is a merism encompassing the entire population of Israel (both rich and poor).

j 5:11 Some possible translations of this could include "Hear the sound of the archers," "Hear the sound of thunder," or "Hear the sound of those who divide the sheep." The Hebrew is uncertain. See Isa. 12.

k 5:11 Or "righteous acts."

¹²Lead on, O Deborah, lead on!
Awake, awake! Break out in a
song!
Arise, O Barak, arise!
Son of Abinoam, arise!
Carry off your captives
and lead them all away!
¹³The remaining nobles marched out,
Yahweh's people came to me to
fight against the mighty ones.
¹⁴You men of Ephraim came out to
the valley,*ᵃ*
your brother Benjamin joined
your ranks.
Leaders came from Manasseh,*ᵇ*
and from Zebulun, those who hold
the ruler's staff.*ᶜ*
¹⁵Issachar's princes rallied to
Deborah,
Issachar stood fast alongside
Barak,
rushing into the valley under
Barak's command,
while among Reuben's clans there
was great searching of heart.
¹⁶Reuben, why do you remain by
the sheepfolds,*ᵈ*
listening for the shepherds to
whistle for their flocks?*ᵉ*
Among Reuben's clans there was
great searching of heart.

¹⁷Gad*ᶠ played it safe and* stayed east
of the Jordan,
and Dan lingered near their ships,
while Asher kept their distance and
stayed by the coast,
safe and secure in their harbors.
¹⁸But Zebulun and Naphtali defied
death
and risked it all on the heights of
the battlefield.*ᵍ*
¹⁹At Taanach foreign kings came
and clashed;
they battled by the stream of
Megiddo.
The kings of Canaan fought,
but they took away no spoils of
silver.
²⁰Even the stars in the sky joined in
the fight,*ʰ*
moving across the sky,
shining as they fought against
Sisera.
²¹The flooding Kishon swept them
away—
the ancient Kishon River*ⁱ con-
tended with them.*
I shall march and keep marching on.
So be strong, O my soul!*ʲ*
²²Then thundered the horses'
hooves, *pulling the chariots of the
kings of Canaan.*

---

a 5:14 Or "From Ephraim their root in Amalek." The Hebrew meaning is uncertain.
b 5:14 Or "from Makir [the son of Manasseh]."
c 5:14 Or "the rod of the scribe."
d 5:16 Or "by the campfires."
e 5:16 The men of Reuben loved their flocks (possessions) more than fighting for their brothers.
f 5:17 Or "Gilead."
g 5:18 Zebulun and Naphtali "triumphed because they did not love and cling to their own lives, even when faced with death" (Rev. 12:11).
h 5:20 Metaphorically, the stars represent the mighty host of heaven's angels. Deborah declared that the angelic realm wheeled into formation and joined Israel in their fight. See Heb. 11:34.
i 5:21 Or "the stream that had flowed for ages." The Targums render this "the stream of the ancients."
j 5:21 Or "I will step on the necks of strength."

Here they come galloping on,
  steeds and stallions[a] stampeding on,
  but they all got stuck in the mud![b]
²³"Speak a curse over Meroz,"[c] says the angel of Yahweh,[d]
  "and speak a double curse over those who live there.
For they did not come to help Yahweh's cause
  nor rally to Yahweh's side to fight the mighty."
²⁴The most blessed of all women is Jael,
  wife of Heber the Kenite—
  the most fortunate of Bedouin women.
²⁵Sisera *came to Jael's tent and* asked for water,
  but she gave him milk;
  she brought him buttermilk in a beautiful bowl.
²⁶With a tent peg in one hand
  and a workman's hammer in the other,
  she struck Sisera and pierced his skull;
  she drove the peg through his temple.[e]
²⁷She shattered his skull,
  and he lay still before Jael.

Sprawled on the tent floor,
  he bit the dust at her feet—
  deader than a doornail!
²⁸Sisera's mother waited for him at her window;
  she gazed from behind the lattice and lamented:
"Why is the clatter of his chariot so late in coming?
  Why are his horses so slow to return?"
²⁹The wisest of her princesses replied;
  indeed, she even thought to herself:
³⁰"They must be gathering and dividing the spoils:
  a slave-girl or two for each man,
  colorful cloth and garments as plunder for Sisera,
  two colorful garments, embroidered, and richly embroidered garments for my neck."
³¹Yahweh, may all who hate you perish in the same way!
But may those who love you shine like the sun,
  bright in its strength as it crosses the sky!"[f]

Then the land had peace for forty years.

---

a 5:22 Or "their mighty ones," possibly referring to the captains and princes of the Canaanites who rode in their chariots.

b 5:22 Implied in the context and the Septuagint.

c 5:23 Although unidentified in the text, Meroz may have been a city in the region that Sisera conquered, whose inhabitants did not resist him.

d 5:23 This angel may have been a reference to Barak, who was warring for God's people. Or it could be the "angel of Yahweh" that Barak expected to go with him to battle (see Septuagint).

e 5:26 See 4:21 and footnote.

f 5:31 Those who love him become like him. See Dan. 12:3; Matt. 13:43; 17:2.

Midianite Oppression

6 Once again the Israelites did evil in the sight of Yahweh, so Yahweh handed them over to the Midianites[a] for seven years. [2]The crushing power of the Midianites overwhelmed Israel, forcing the Israelites to make hiding places for themselves in caves and mountain strongholds. [3]Whenever the Israelites planted any crops, *and before they could reap the harvest*, the Midianites would come with the Amalekites and other desert tribes[b] and invade the land. [4]They would camp in their fields and destroy their crops as far as Gaza. They would seize all their sheep, cattle, and donkeys. They left nothing for the Israelites to live on. [5]When they invaded the land with their livestock and camels and tents, they were as numerous as locusts,[c] leaving the land desolate. [6]Israel was impoverished and helpless against them. Then the Israelites, *with shattered hearts*, cried out to Yahweh *for mercy*.

A Prophet Rebukes Israel

[7]When the Israelites, *with shattered hearts*, cried out to Yahweh because of the Midianite oppression, [8]he sent them a prophet[d] with this message: "Listen to the words of Yahweh, the God of Israel: 'I delivered you from Egypt and from a life of slavery.[e] [9]I snatched you from the brutality of the Egyptians. I rescued you from the people who invaded this land and fought against you. I drove them out as you advanced, and I gave[f] their land to you. [10]I told you that I am Yahweh your God, and that you must not worship the *false* gods of the Amorites, in whose land you dwell. But you did not listen to my voice.' "

Gideon, the Champion-Deliverer

[11]The Angel of Yahweh came to the village of Ophrah[g] and sat down under the oak tree[h] that belonged to Joash,[i] a man of the clan of Abiezer.[j] His son

---

a 6:1 The nomadic Midianites were descendants of Abraham's concubine, Keturah (see Gen. 25:1). *Midian* means "strife" or "contending." Moses married the daughter of Jethro, a Midianite (see Ex. 2:15–21; 18:1–27). The Midianites lived in Arabia and eventually were incorporated into the Arabian tribes. Symbolically, Midian is an illustration of compromise with the world and the strife that results (see James 4:4; 1 John 2:15–17). Midian and Moab had attempted to persuade Balaam to curse Israel (see Num. 22:4; Rev. 2:14), and it was the Midianite and Moabite women who seduced Israel (see Num. 25:1–18; 31:15–16).

b 6:3 Or "sons of the east [desert tribes]."

c 6:5 The Hebrew word for "locusts" is taken from a root word meaning "to multiply" or "a multitude."

d 6:8 The Hebrew text utilizes an obscure title, literally "a prophet-man." Although unnamed, Jewish tradition states that the prophet was Phineas son of Eleazar. (See Seder Olam Rabba, ch. 20, p. 53.) God had fulfilled his ancient promises to them, but they had failed to keep their promises to God, so the prophet rebuked Israel.

e 6:8 Or literally "from the slave barracks."

f 6:9 The series of verbs in the Hebrew text more forcefully expresses the action than an English translation can. It is describing energetic acts, as the verbs are in the cohortative form. Perhaps the sense could be conveyed as "I handed this land over to you, so *now what are you going to do about all this?*"

g 6:11 *Ophrah* means "dusty." It was a city of Manasseh.

h 6:11 Apparently, the Angel of Yahweh was invisible to Gideon. He may have been sitting there watching Gideon for some time before he revealed himself.

i 6:11 *Joash* means "Yahweh is strong." It is a shortened version of Jehoash.

j 6:11 *Abiezer* means "my father of help."

Gideon[a] was secretly threshing some wheat in a winepress so that the Midianites would not see him.[b] [12]Yahweh's Angel suddenly appeared to Gideon and said, "Yahweh's presence goes with you, man of fearless courage!"[c]

[13]"Me?" Gideon replied. "But sir, if Yahweh is truly with us, why have all these troubles come to us? Where are all his miracle-wonders that our fathers told us about when they said, 'Did not Yahweh deliver us out of Egypt?' But now Yahweh has abandoned us and put us under the power of the Midianites."

[14]Then Yahweh[d] himself faced Gideon directly and said, "Am I not sending you? *With my presence you have all you need.* Go in the strength that you now have[e] and rescue Israel from Midian's power!"

[15]Gideon said to him, "But Lord, how could I ever rescue Israel? *Of all the thousands* in Manasseh, my clan is the weakest, and I'm the least qualified in my family."

[16]Yahweh replied, "*My presence and my power* will be with you.[f] *Believe me, Gideon,*[g] you will crush the Midianites as easily as if they were only one man!"

[17]Then Gideon said, "If it's really true *that you will go with me and* that I have found grace before your eyes, then show me a miracle-sign to prove that you are really Yahweh[h] speaking with me. [18]Don't leave until I return with my offering to you."

And he answered, "I'll wait until you return."

[19]So Gideon went and cooked a young goat and many loaves[i] of unleavened bread. He placed the meat in a basket and the broth in a pot and took his offering and presented it to him under the oak tree.

---

a 6:11 *Gideon* means "warrior," "one who cuts down [trees]," "to cut in two," or "destroyer." God embedded his destiny as a champion-deliverer within his name. He is named in Heb. 11, the faith chapter (see Heb. 11:32), and also referred to in Isa. 9:3–4. A variant form of his name is used repeatedly for cutting down idols (see Deut. 7:5; 2 Chron. 14:3; 31:1; 34:4, 7; Ezek. 6:6).

b 6:11 Wheat was not threshed in a winepress but on an open, elevated place where the wind could blow the chaff away. Jewish and Christian traditions hold that Gideon was a timid, somewhat cowardly man who made excuses concerning himself and his family (see v. 15). God was going to do in Gideon what Gideon was doing with wheat—thresh his heart, and remove the chaff of unbelief from his true identity. God called Gideon to be a hero who would deliver Israel. God rescued a nation by first rescuing a man from his unbelief. Many believers today can draw strength and revelation from the wonderful story of Gideon.

c 6:12 God prophesied destiny over Gideon. He would become a fearless warrior. God often speaks things that are not visible and brings them into reality (see Rom. 4:17; Heb. 11:1). God called Abraham a father of a multitude before he even had a child. God called Gideon a brave warrior before he even went into battle.

d 6:14 The Angel of Yahweh unveiled himself as Yahweh! This divine encounter empowered Gideon to face overwhelming odds and defeat the Midianite armies. He went out in the *strength* of this encounter, clothed with the power of the Holy Spirit (see v. 34). Gideon found the power that he needed in the commission and authority God imparted to him that day.

e 6:14 Perhaps at that moment God infused a surge of his mighty power into Gideon.

f 6:16 These are the same reassuring words God spoke to Moses when he sent him to deliver the Israelites from Egypt (see Ex. 3:12).

g 6:16 The Hebrew is emphatic: "I absolutely will be with you."

h 6:17 Or "you."

i 6:19 Or "with an ephah of flour he made bread." An ephah was about twenty liters or three-fifths of a bushel. Gideon presented a significant offering, for it was a time of scarcity.

[20]God's Angel said to Gideon, "Place the meat and the bread on that rock and pour the broth over them." And Gideon did so. [21]Then Yahweh's Angel reached out the staff he was holding and touched the meat and the bread. All at once, *supernatural* fire sprang up from the rock and burned up the meat and the bread.[a] Then the Angel of Yahweh vanished from his sight.

[22]Immediately, Gideon realized that he had seen the Angel of Yahweh! *Terror stricken*, he said, "Oh, Lord Yahweh![b] I have seen the Angel of Yahweh face-to-face!"

[23]But Yahweh spoke to him and said, "Be at peace. Don't be afraid. You will not die." [24]So Gideon built an altar to Yahweh there and named it "In Yahweh there is Peace."[c] (The altar is still standing at Ophrah, which belongs to the clan of Abiezer.)

[25]That night, Yahweh spoke[d] to Gideon and said, "Take your father's bull and the second bull that is seven years old,[e] and go and demolish your father's altar to Baal.[f] And cut down the tree of the goddess Asherah, which is beside it. [26]And in their place, on top of the stronghold,[g] build a well-constructed altar to Yahweh your God. Use the Asherah tree you have cut down for firewood. Then take the second bull and burn it whole as an offering."[h] [27]So Gideon took ten of his servants and did what Yahweh had told him. Because he feared both his family and the men of the town he did it at night rather than in the daytime.

[28]When the people of the town got up early the next morning, they found the altar to Baal and the symbol of Asherah cut down, and the second bull burned on the new altar that Gideon had built there. [29]They asked each other, "Who did this?" After investigating thoroughly, they concluded that it was the work of Gideon son of Joash. [30]Enraged, they demanded of Joash, "Bring your son out here and we will kill him![i] He tore down the altar to Baal and chopped down the Asherah tree beside it."

[31]But Joash said to all those who confronted him, "Does Baal need you to fight his battles? Are you really going to rescue him? I will kill anyone who stands up for Baal before morning. If Baal is a god, let him fight his own battles and defend his own altar!" [32]From then on, Gideon's nickname was "Jerubbaal,"[j] that is to say, "Let Baal contend against him," because he broke down his altar.

---

a 6:21 Gideon's offering prefigures the sacrifice of Christ, whose body was laid upon a rock.

b 6:22 Or "Adonai-Yahweh."

c 6:24 Or "Yahweh-Shalom." See Eph. 2:14.

d 6:25 God possibly spoke to Gideon in a dream. See Job 33:14–15.

e 6:25 The bull was seven years old, the same age as Israel's oppression (see v. 1). Some Jewish scholars believe that Gideon's father had raised the bull to be sacrificed to Baal.

f 6:25 Gideon's commission began at home. Gideon first tore down the altar to Baal. He broke the stronghold of his family before he could break the stronghold of his nation. The church must first tear down the false altars in our hearts before we can deliver a nation.

g 6:26 Some Jewish scholars (Rashi, Kimchi) believe this was the same place (rock) where Gideon placed his offering to Yahweh.

h 6:26 See Lev. 4:13–21.

i 6:30 The Hebrew is the jussive form: "and let him die."

j 6:32 Or "Baal-Fighter."

³³Now all the Midianites, the Amalekites, and the people of the East formed an army. They crossed the Jordan and camped in the Valley of Jezreel *to fight against Israel.* ³⁴Then the Spirit of Yahweh clothed himself in Gideon *and enveloped him!*^a Gideon sounded a blast of the shofar to call the men of the clan of Abiezer to follow him. ³⁵He sent messengers throughout the territory of both parts of Manasseh, and throughout the territory of Asher, Zebulun, and Naphtali—to call them to follow Gideon into battle. And they all came to join him.

Gideon at the Threshing Floor

³⁶Gideon said to God, "If you have really chosen me to rescue Israel, as you said, ³⁷*then give me proof.* Here—I am placing a wool fleece on the threshing floor. If in the morning the dew is only on the wool but not on the ground around it, then I will know for sure that I'm the one you have chosen to rescue Israel, as you said."^b ³⁸And that is exactly what happened. When Gideon got up early the next morning, he squeezed the fleece and wrung out enough dew to fill a bowl.^c

³⁹Then Gideon said to God, "Don't be angry with me; let me speak just once more. Please let me ask you for one more sign. This time let the fleece be dry, and the ground wet." ⁴⁰That night God did what Gideon had asked. The next morning the fleece was dry, but dew covered the ground around it.^d

Gideon's Shrinking Army

7 Now, the Baal-Fighter (that is, Gideon) and his men rose early^e and encamped by the Spring of Trembling.^f The Midianites had encamped in the valley to the north, below Moreh.^g ²Yahweh spoke to Gideon: "You have too many in your army. If I give them victory over the Midianites, they might claim credit for themselves at my expense, thinking that they had won the victory on their own."^h

---

a 6:34 Gideon became a powerful warrior, for the Holy Spirit wore Gideon like clothing! Compare 1 Chron. 12:17–18.

b 6:37 God had "sheared" both Israel and Gideon (Ezek. 44:17–18) on God's "threshing floor" of chastening. Dew is consistently a biblical symbol of God's favor and the anointing of the Holy Spirit (see Deut. 33:28; Pss. 110:3; 133:1–3; Prov. 19:12; Hos. 14:5).

c 6:38 We are common jars (bowls) of clay (see 2 Cor. 4:7). Gideon was a bowl full of God's favor.

d 6:40 Gideon wanted not only the assurance that God's favor was upon him but also the assurance that God's favor was on the men (ground) *around* him as well. God does often give a confirming sign that he is with those he calls. See Ex. 3:12; 4:1–9; 1 Sam. 10:7. The two signs Gideon asked for would demonstrate Yahweh as sovereign over the land instead of Baal, who was believed to be the father of morning rain and dew among the Canaanites (as found in the texts of The Baal Cycle at Ras Shamra). Yahweh showed his power over the things the people believed were under Baal's control.

e 7:1 Or, if the Hebrew verb *tsaphar* was taken from a similar Arabic verb, one could translate it "they ran quickly."

f 7:1 Or, in Hebrew, *En-Harod*, which means "spring of trembling." It is identified as modern Ain Jalut. *Ain Jalut* means "the spring of Goliath." From this vantage point, Gideon's men could see the vast tents of the Midianite army. "Trembling Spring" speaks of the vulnerability of Gideon's army before a superior fighting force. God will meet us in our place of trembling.

g 7:1 *Moreh* means "teacher." God was indeed the teacher who taught Gideon to trust in him and who taught the Midianites that Yahweh is the true God. See John 14:26; 1 John 2:27.

h 7:2 See Ps. 115:1; Isa. 42:8.

³Announce to your men, 'All who are trembling and afraid, hurry back home and leave Mount Gilead!' "ᵃ So twenty-two thousand went back home, and only ten thousand stayed with Gideon.

⁴Then Yahweh spoke to Gideon again, "You still have too many men. Take them down to the water, and I will test themᵇ for you there. If I tell you a man should go with you, he will go. If I tell you a man should not go with you, he will not go."

⁵So Gideon brought the soldiers down to the water, and Yahweh said to him, "Separate those who drink from their cupped hands and drink as a dog laps from those who kneel down to drink." ⁶Of the ten thousand men, only three hundred lapped water from their cupped hands;ᶜ all the others knelt to drink.

⁷Then Yahweh told Gideon, "I will give you victory over the Midianites with the three hundred men who cupped their hands and drank. Tell everyone else to go home." ⁸So Gideon sent all the Israelites home except the three hundred, who kept the supplies and shofars of those who had left. Now the Midianites were camped down below in the valley.

⁹That night Yahweh commanded Gideon, "Get up and attack the camp; I am giving you victory over the Midianites! ¹⁰But if you are afraid to engage them,ᵈ first go down to the camp with your servant Purah.ᵉ ¹¹Listen to what they are saying, and then you will be brave and have the courage to attack."ᶠ So Gideon and his servant Purah went down and approached the outposts of the enemy camp. ¹²The Midianites, the Amalekites, and the desert tribesmen were spread out in the valley like a swarm of locusts. They had as many camels as there were grains of sand on the seashore.

¹³As soon as Gideon arrived, he heard an enemy soldier telling a friend about a dream. He was saying, "Well, I had a dream of this huge commotion in our camp. I dreamed a round loaf of barley bread came whirling into our camp and leveled a tent. It hit the tent

---

a 7:3 Gideon likely struggled with fear. Gideon was in effect saying to the Israelites, "All of you with my problem, go home!" Fear neutralizes the power of God and causes us to focus on ourselves and our weakness. See Deut. 20:1–4, 8; 1 Sam. 14:6; 2 Cor. 3:5; 2 Tim. 1:7.

b 7:4 Or "purify them." See John 15:3; Eph. 5:25–27. The Hebrew verb implies removing dross from a precious metal. God applied two tests to Gideon's men. One was a test of their courage, and the other was a test of how they drank from the spring. Both tests revealed the qualities God is looking for in those he uses. We must be brave, and we must drink deeply from the "spring" of God's grace. Also, with these two "tests," we may reflect back on Gideon's two tests of Yahweh. Yahweh proved faithful twice, and now Gideon must prove faithful twice.

c 7:6 That is, they would scoop the water in their cupped hands first, then drink from their hands instead of putting their heads down into the water. This would have been in the sight of the enemy's camp. Those drinking from their hands (see the five-fold ministry, Eph. 4:11) showed discipline and readiness in case of a surprise attack. These three hundred alert warriors would be the ones in Gideon's army. The Midianites numbered Midianites numbered one hundred thirty-five thousand, which meant they outnumbered Gideon four hundred fifty to one.

d 7:10 God showed compassion for Gideon because Gideon had never led an army before nor attacked a fierce foe.

e 7:10 Purah can be seen as a type of the Holy Spirit, who accompanies us in all our ways. *Purah* means "he is fruitful" or "fruitful branch."

f 7:11 Or "your hands will be strengthened."

so hard it turned it upside down, and the tent collapsed on the ground."[a]

[14]His friend interpreted the dream and said, "Your dream symbolizes the sword of the Israelite, Gideon son of Joash![b] It can't mean anything else! God has given him victory over Midian and our whole army!"[c]

Gideon Defeats Midian

[15]When Gideon heard about the man's dream and what it meant, he fell to his knees and worshiped *Yahweh*. Then he went back to the Israelite camp and shouted, "Come on, it's time to strike! Yahweh is giving you victory over the Midianite army!" [16]He divided his three hundred men into three groups and gave each man a shofar and a *clay* jar hiding a torch inside it. [17]He told them, "Follow me! When I get to the edge of the camp, watch me closely and do exactly what I do. [18]When my group and I blow our shofars, then you blow yours all around the camp and shout, 'For Yahweh and for Gideon!' "

[19-20]Just before midnight,[d] after the changing of the *Midianite* guard, Gideon and his hundred men came to the outskirts of the camp. Then each of the three groups blew the shofars and broke the clay jars *that hid the torches inside.*[e] They held their torches in their left hands, the shofars in their right, and shouted *a thunderous battle cry*, "A sword[f] for Yahweh and for Gideon!" [21]Each man held his position surrounding the camp. And the entire enemy army was shocked awake by the thunderous noises of Gideon's army! They all panicked and fled, yelling as they ran away!

[22]When they sounded their three hundred shofars, Yahweh made the

---

a 7:13 The barley loaf symbolized Israel's army that would invade and conquer the Midianites. The body of Christ is also that one loaf (see 1 Cor. 10:17), rolling down Mount Zion to destroy the tents of wickedness (the kingdoms of this world). See Dan. 2; 7; Rev. 11:15. Elisha multiplied twenty barley loaves to feed one hundred people with bread left over (see 2 Kings 4:42–44). Jesus multiplied five barley loaves (see John 6:9–13) and fed more than five thousand! The whirling barley loaf is a picture of Christ in us, who multiplies his life and power in believers today.

b 7:14 It is fascinating that Gideon overheard the Midianite dream interpreter speaking his name and the name of his father. Not only does God know your name, but so does the enemy, for you are a son or daughter of God! Gideon used this fear tactic when he instructed his three hundred men to shout both the name of Yahweh and the name of Gideon. It was the Lord who gave this plan to Gideon.

c 7:14 God gave a heathen man a dream, and he gave the interpretation to his friend. God has a thousand ways to deliver us and bring us victory.

d 7:19–20 Or "In the beginning of the middle watch." This implied that the night was divided into three watches of about four hours each. The middle watch would have begun around 11:00 p.m. In the time of Jesus, the Jews apparently adopted the Roman system of four night watches.

e 7:19–20 The shofars represent our prophetic message of power and grace to conquer. We "sound the shofar" each time we proclaim the Word of the Lord. The clay jars (pitchers) represent us. We are but clay vessels, who must be broken open so that Christ, our burning torch inside, can display his light. See 2 Cor. 4:6–12.

f 7:19–20 In effect, the "sword" was their shout and the shining torch. Without even a sword, Israel won a great victory by trusting in God's power, not their own. Their shouting and shofars would have stampeded the camels of the Midianites and caused havoc in their camp. This is perhaps the first instance of psychological warfare in history. (See M.A. Linebarger, *Phycological Warfare* [New York: Duell, Sloan, and Pearce, 1954].)

enemy troops turn against each other with their own swords. The Midianites fled toward Zarerah as far as Beth Shittah,[a] as far as the outskirts of *the town of* Abel Meholah[b] near Tabbath.

[23]Gideon called to arms men from the tribes of Naphtali, Asher, and both parts of Manasseh, and they rallied and pursued the Midianites. [24]Then Gideon sent messengers through the entire hill country of Ephraim, saying, "Join us in the fight against the Midianites. Deny them access to the River Jordan and the streams as far as Beth Barah, *and prevent them from crossing over.*" The men of Ephraim came together, and they held the River Jordan and the streams as far as Beth Barah.[c] [25]They captured the two Midianite chiefs, Oreb and Zeeb. They executed Oreb at Oreb Rock and Zeeb at Zeeb Winepress.[d] While the Ephraimites continued to pursue the Midianites, they brought the heads of Oreb and Zeeb to Gideon, who was now east of the Jordan.

Two Kings, Zebah and Zalmunna

8 The men of Ephraim[e] got into a heated argument with Gideon and complained to him, "Why didn't you tell us you were going to fight the Midianites? Why did you do that to us?"

[2]Gideon replied, "What have I accomplished compared to you? What your tribe did is worth so much more than what my whole clan has done.[f] [3]After all, through the power of God, you killed both Midianite chiefs, Oreb and Zeeb. What have I done compared with you?" After he said this, they calmed down and were no longer so angry.[g]

[4]Totally exhausted, Gideon and his three hundred men crossed the river Jordan and continued to pursue the enemy.[h] [5]When they arrived at Succoth,[i] he said to the men of the town, "Please give my men some loaves of bread. They are exhausted, and I am still pursuing the two Midianite kings, Zebah and Zalmunna."[j]

[6]But the leaders of Succoth replied, "Why should we give any food to your

---

a 7:22 *Beth Shittah* means "house of the scourge" or "house of acacia trees."

b 7:22 *Abel Meholah* means "meadow of the dance." It is the birthplace of Elisha (see 1 Kings 19:16).

c 7:24 *Beth Barah* means "house of the crossing [ford]." John baptized the people at this location ("the place of the crossing of the Jordan River," John 1:28).

d 7:25 *Oreb* means "raven," and *Zeeb* means "wolf." The places where the Ephraimites killed the Midianite chiefs became landmarks. Oreb Rock reminds us of the rock where Gideon presented Yahweh his offering, which the fire consumed. Zeeb Winepress reminds us of where Gideon was threshing his wheat.

e 8:1 Ephraim, the strongest and largest of the northern tribes, resented that a smaller tribe near their territory went into battle without them. Their pride had been wounded, and now they were jealous.

f 8:2 Or "Is not the gleaning of Ephraim better than the vintage of Abiezer?" This is a figure of speech, or proverb, meant to assuage the anger of the Ephraimites. Gideon was telling them that their mop-up operation was more effective than what Gideon and his army did.

g 8:3 See Prov. 15:1.

h 8:4 Meditate on this sentence. You may be weary, but God chose you to be one of his servants. May we continue to pursue all that God has for us until we experience ultimate victory.

i 8:5 Succoth is identified with Tell Deir 'Allah in the Jordan Valley.

j 8:5 *Zebah* means "victim," and *Zalmunna* means "protection denied" or "shade denied."

army? You haven't even captured Zebah and Zalmunna yet."

[7]So Gideon said, "All right! Since you won't help me,[a] when Yahweh has handed them over to me, I'll whip you with thorns and briars from the desert!" [8]Gideon went on to Penuel and made the same request of the people there, but the men of Penuel gave him the same reply as the men of Succoth. [9]So he informed them, "I'll come back victoriously, and when I do, I will tear your tower down!"[b]

[10]Zebah and Zalmunna were at Karkor[c] with an army of fifteen thousand men who survived, for one hundred twenty thousand sword-wielding soldiers had already been killed. [11]Gideon followed the desert trail of the nomads east of Nobah[d] and Jogbehah,[e] surprised the enemy's army, and ambushed them. [12]The two Midianite kings, Zebah and Zalmunna, escaped, but Gideon pursued and captured them, and terrified what remained of the Midianite army.

[13]While Gideon son of Joash was returning from the battle by way of Heres Pass,[f] [14]he captured a young man from Succoth and interrogated him. The young man wrote down for Gideon the names of the seventy-seven leading men of Succoth. [15]Then Gideon went to the men of Succoth and said, "You mocked me, *refused to help me*, and said that you couldn't give any food to my exhausted army because I had not yet captured Zebah and Zalmunna. Well, here they are!" [16]*As he had promised*, Gideon took desert thorns and briars and whipped[g] the leaders of Succoth. [17]As for Penuel,[h] Gideon tore down its tower and killed the men of that city.

[18]Then Gideon asked the kings, Zebah and Zalmunna, "What can you tell me about the men you killed at Tabor?"[i]

They answered, "They looked just like you. Every one of them looked like the son of a king."

[19]Gideon said, "They were my brothers, my own mother's sons. I swear, as surely as Yahweh lives, that if you had let them live, I would let you live." [20]Then he turned to Jether,[j] his firstborn son, and said, "Go ahead, kill them now!" But the boy wouldn't do it. He didn't draw his sword because he was still only a timid boy.

[21]Then Zebah and Zalmunna taunted Gideon, "Come on, kill us yourself. It takes a man to do a man's job."[k] So Gideon executed them and plundered the crescent ornaments that hung on the necks of their camels.

---

a 8:7 See Deut. 23:3–4; cf. Matt. 25:34–40.

b 8:9 Penuel was a fortress city, and its citizens relied on their strong tower to protect them. See 1 Kings 12:25.

c 8:10 *Karkor* means "battering down." It was east of the Dead Sea.

d 8:11 The city of Nobah is also known as Kenath (see Num. 32:42). *Nobah* means "to bark." Scholars identify it as modern Qanawat, on the western slope of Jebel ed-Druze.

e 8:11 *Jogbehah* means "he will be exalted."

f 8:13 *Heres* means "sun."

g 8:16 Or "threshed."

h 8:17 *Penuel* (or Peniel) means "face of God." Jacob wrestled the Angel of Yahweh at Penuel (see Gen. 32:30–31 and first footnote on Gen. 32:30).

i 8:18 This is not Mount Tabor in the north, but perhaps the location unspecified in 6:2.

j 8:20 *Jether* (a variant form of Jethro) means "excellence."

k 8:21 Or "strength comes with manhood."

Gideon's Ephod

²²After that, the Israelites said to Gideon, "*You're our war hero!* You're the one who saved us from the Midianites. You be our ruler! Then your son will rule after you, and then your grandson."

²³Gideon answered, "No. Neither I nor my son will be your ruler. Yahweh is to be your only King. ²⁴However, I do have one request," Gideon added. "Give me all the gold earrings you took from the Midianites." (It was the custom of the Midianites to wear gold earrings, because they were Ishmaelites.)

²⁵The people answered, "Gladly. They're yours!" They spread out a cloth, and each one placed on it the earrings they had taken as plunder. ²⁶Gideon received gold earrings that weighed seventeen hundred shekels,ᵃ not including the crescent ornaments, necklaces, and fine purple robes of the kings of Midian, nor the ornamental collars taken from the necks of their camels. ²⁷Gideon used all this plunder to make a sacred golden ephod.ᵇ He put it on display in his hometown, Ophrah, and all Israel strayed *from Yahweh* and gave over their heartsᶜ to the golden ephod. It was a seducing snare for Gideon and his family.

²⁸So Israel defeated Midian, who never troubled them again.ᵈ The land had peace for forty years until Gideon died.

The Death of Gideon

²⁹*Gideon,* the Baal-Fighter, son of Joash, returned to his own home and lived there. ³⁰Because he had many wives, Gideon fathered seventy sons. ³¹In addition, he took a concubine in Shechem. She bore him a son, and he named him Abimelech.

³²Gideon son of Joash died at a ripe old age and was buried in the tomb of his father Joash, at Ophrah, a town of the clan of Abiezer. ³³No sooner had Gideon died than the Israelites again abandoned the true God and worshipedᵉ the images of Baal. They made Baal-Berithᶠ their god ³⁴and no longer remembered Yahweh their God, who had saved them from all their enemies on every side. ³⁵The Israelites failed to demonstrate loyal love to the family of Gideon, the Baal-Fighter, for all the good that he had done for them.

Abimelech's Conspiracy

9 Abimelechᵍ son of Baal-Fighter (*or Gideon*) went to his mother's

---

a 8:26 That is, about forty-three pounds of gold.

b 8:27 The ephod was a decorated priestly vestment, somewhat like a full-length apron (see Ex. 28:4, 6–8, 31–32). The ephod was a means of discerning God's will, but ephods are also mentioned as objects of idolatrous worship (see Judg. 17:5; 18:14; cf. Hos. 3:4). It is likely that Gideon's ephod became an idol to the people, and they would come to seek oracles before it (see 1 Sam. 2:28; 23:6, 9; 30:7). The ark of glory and the tabernacle stood at Shiloh at this time (see Josh. 18:1), the place Yahweh had chosen as the place of worship for Israel. Instead, Gideon's ephod turned their hearts away from the true worship of Yahweh. Gideon refused kingship because he wanted priesthood. Perhaps the ephod of Aaron was now worn out and needed to be replaced. Gideon may have meant well, but the ephod became a snare for him and all Israel. Good intentions must never be a substitute for obedience.

c 8:27 Or "prostituted themselves."

d 8:28 Or "they raised their heads no more."

e 8:33 Or "they prostituted themselves with the gods of Baal."

f 8:33 Or "Baal [lord]-of-the-covenant."

g 9:1 *Abimelech* means "my father is king."

brothers and to the rest of her clan in Shechem and said to them, ²"Ask all the leaders*a* of Shechem, 'Which do you prefer: to have just one man as your ruler or have seventy of Baal-Fighter's sons rule over you?' And don't forget, I'm your own flesh and blood."

³When the brothers repeated these words to the leaders of Shechem, their hearts were drawn to Abimelech, for they said, "He is *from our hometown and* from our own clan." ⁴They gave him seventy shekels of silver*b* from the temple of Baal-Berith,*c* and Abimelech used it to hire reckless scoundrels to follow him. ⁵He went to his father's home in Ophrah and on one stone executed his seventy brothers,*d* the sons of Baal-Fighter. Jotham, Baal-Fighter's youngest son, escaped and went into hiding. ⁶All the citizens of Shechem and Beth Millo*e* gathered beside the sacred tree at the pillar in Shechem and crowned Abimelech king.

Jotham's Fable: The Thornbush King

⁷When Jotham learned about this, he climbed up on the top of Mount Gerizim*f* and shouted: "Listen to me, citizens of Shechem, so that God may listen to you. ⁸All the trees one day determined to anoint a king for themselves. They said to the olive tree, 'Be our king.'

⁹"But the olive tree answered, 'What? Give up my rich oil that is used to honor both gods and men, to hold sway over the trees?'

¹⁰"Next, the trees said to the fig tree, 'Come and be our king.'

¹¹"But the fig tree replied, 'What? Give up my good, sweet fruit to hold sway over the trees?'

¹²"Then the trees said to the vine, 'Come and be our king.'

¹³"But the vine answered, 'What? Give up my wine, which cheers both gods and men, to hold sway over the trees?'*g*

¹⁴"Finally, all the trees said to the thornbush, 'Come and be our king.'

¹⁵"The thornbush replied, 'If you really want to anoint me your king, then come and put your trust in my shade.*h* If you don't, then let fire blaze out of my thorny branches and consume the cedars of Lebanon!'

---

a 9:2 Or "baals [lords]." In Judges, the word "baal" is found only in this chapter and is used thirteen times in reference to leaders.

b 9:4 That is, they gave one shekel for each of Abimelech's seventy brothers, essentially saying each one was worth only a shekel to them.

c 9:4 Or "Baal [lord]-of-the-covenant."

d 9:5 The majority of the seventy brothers whom Abimelech killed were his half brothers.

e 9:6 *Beth Millo* means "house of fullness." Beth Millo may have been the tower of Shechem (see v. 46).

f 9:7 This was the mountain where half of the tribes of Israel proclaimed the blessings over the people if they kept the covenant (see Deut. 27:12). It stood opposite Ebal where the other half of the tribes proclaimed curses on the disobedient. Further, Joshua renewed the covenant at Shechem where he wrote the words of the law on a plastered stone that stood between Ebal and Gerizim (see Josh. 24:1–28).

g 9:13 The three trees represent what believers enjoy in following Christ: (1) Olive tree—the oil of anointing of the Holy Spirit. (2) Fig tree—the goodness and sweetness of Christ's love. (3) Vine—the joy and cheer that Jesus brings to our lives.

h 9:15 A thornbush offers no shade, and Abimelech (the thornbush) offered neither shelter nor care to Israel.

¹⁶"Now then let me ask you this: Do you really think you did a right and honorable thing when you made Abimelech king? Do you think you treated Baal-Fighter and his family fairly? ¹⁷And to think that my father fought for you, and risked his life* to save you from the power of the Midianites! ¹⁸Today, you have revolted against my father's family, murdered his seventy sons on a single stone, and made Abimelech, the son of his slave girl, king over the citizens of Shechem because he's your close relative. ¹⁹*What were you thinking?* If you have acted honorably and done what is right by Baal-Fighter and his family today, then may you enjoy Abimelech, *this thornbush king of yours*, and may he enjoy you too! ²⁰But if not, let fire come out from Abimelech and consume you, citizens of Shechem and Beth Millo, and let fire come out from you, citizens of Shechem and Beth Millo, and consume Abimelech!"

²¹After shouting these words, Jotham ran away and went to live at the Well* because he was afraid of his brother Abimelech.

King Abimelech

²²After Abimelech had ruled Israel for three years,* ²³God sent a spirit to stir up hostility* between Abimelech and the citizens of Shechem, and they rebelled against him. ²⁴God *sent this judgment* in order to avenge the brutal murder of Baal-Fighter's seventy sons and the shedding of their blood. Righteous retribution caught up with both Abimelech, who had instigated the murder of his half brothers, and the citizens of Shechem, who had aided and abetted him. ²⁵In their uprising against Abimelech, the citizens of Shechem placed bandits on the hilltops to ambush and rob everyone who passed by, and Abimelech heard of their treachery.

²⁶One day, a man named Gaal son of Ebed* moved with his clan into Shechem,* and Gaal won the confidence of the people. ²⁷After the grape harvest, they trod the grapes and celebrated a festival* in the temple of *Baal*, their god. While they were drinking and feasting, they cursed Abimelech. ²⁸Gaal son of Ebed *rose and* said, "Who is this Abimelech? We are the Shechemites now! Why should we serve him? Isn't he Baal-Fighter's son, and isn't *the governor of our city* Zebul* his deputy? Why should we take orders from him; we are descendants of Hamor, Shechem's founder.* Why should we be slaves of Abimelech? ²⁹If only the people of Shechem were under my command, then I would get rid of him. I would say to Abimelech, 'Assemble your whole army! *We'll defeat them all!*' "

---

a 9:17 Or "cast away his soul to a distance."

b 9:21 Or "Beer." Some scholars have identified this place as Beeroth.

c 9:22 God did not hand over Israel to a foreign power but to an unscrupulous ruler, Abimelech.

d 9:23 Or "a hostile spirit" or "a spirit of dissension."

e 9:26 *Gaal* means "to loathe" or "hateful." It was possibly a nickname. A related Hebrew word means "dung beetle." *Ebed* means "servant." If Gaal is not his actual name, it could be translated "a loathsome [dung beetle]," "hateful man," or "a servant's son." This derisive name hints at his low social status. He was a troublemaker.

f 9:26 Or "went on the prowl into Shechem."

g 9:27 Or "a praise-festival."

h 9:28 *Zebul* means "big shot" or "lofty one."

i 9:28 See Gen. 33:19. *Hamor* means "an ass [donkey]."

³⁰Zebul, the governor of the city, was infuriated when he heard of the taunts of Gaal son of Ebed. ³¹He secretly sent messengers to Abimelech, saying, "Gaal son of Ebed and his clan have come to Shechem. They're inciting the entire city against you. ³²Now then, under the cover of darkness, you and your men should come and take up concealed positions in the fields. ³³At sunrise launch your surprise attack and advance against the city. When Gaal and his men come out to face you, fight them with all your might."ᵃ

³⁴So Abimelech and all his men set out by night and took up concealed positions near Shechem in four groups. ³⁵Gaal son of Ebed went out and stood in the entrance of the gate of the city just as Abimelech and his soldiers got up from their hiding places.

³⁶When Gaal saw them, he said to Zebul, "Look, an army is marching down from the hilltops!"

Zebul replied, "That's nothing but shadows in the hills; they only look like men."

³⁷Gaal spoke up again: "No, look! I see people coming down the center, and another group from the direction of Oracle Oak."

³⁸Then Zebul said to him, "Where is all your big talk now? Weren't you the loudmouth who said, 'Who is Abimelech that he could make us his slaves?' The men you ridiculed are now coming to fight you! Go ahead—go and fight them!"

³⁹So Gaal led the men of Shechem and went out to fight Abimelech.

⁴⁰Abimelech chased him, and many Shechemites fell wounded and died before they could retreat to the city gate. ⁴¹Abimelech returned to his headquarters at Arumah, while Zebul drove Gaal and his clan out of Shechem.

⁴²The next day Abimelech found out that the people of Shechem were planning to go out on a foray into the countryside. ⁴³So he divided his men into three groups, and they set out to ambush the Shechemites in the fields. As soon as Abimelech saw the people leaving the city, he sprang up and attacked them. ⁴⁴Abimelech and his men advanced rapidly and occupied the city gate. The other two companies chased them down out into the open fields and killed them. ⁴⁵Abimelech fought hard all day at the gate of Shechem until he had captured the city. He massacred all its people, leveled the city to rubble, and scattered salt over it.ᵇ

⁴⁶When they heard the news, the leading citizens living in the Shechem Tower ran into the stronghold of the temple of Baal-Berith. ⁴⁷When Abimelech heard that they had assembled there, ⁴⁸he and all his forces went up Mount Zalmon.ᶜ Taking an axe in his hand, he cut off some branches and hoisted the bundle onto his shoulders. He ordered the men with him, "Quick! Do the same!" ⁴⁹So each one cut a bundle of branches and followed Abimelech. They piled them against the walls of the temple and with the people inside they set it on fire. So everyone who fled into the tower of

---

a 9:33 Or "do whatever your hand finds to do." See Eccl. 9:10.

b 9:45 Abimelech may have scattered salt over the city as a sign that retribution had been served over the gross injustice of the people of Shechem. See Deut. 29:23; Jer. 17:6. Shechem was rebuilt 150 years later in the reign of Jeroboam (see 1 Kings 12:25).

c 9:48 *Zalmon* means "dark one"; it possibly refers to Mount Ebal.

Shechem died; nearly a thousand men and women perished.

⁵⁰Next, Abimelech attacked the city of Thebez*a* and captured it. ⁵¹All the people had fled to the Tower of Strength in the middle of the city. They locked themselves in and climbed up onto the tower roof. ⁵²Abimelech advanced as far as the tower, stormed it, and set it on fire. ⁵³But a woman dropped a millstone on his head and fractured his skull.

⁵⁴Abimelech cried out to his armor-bearer, "Kill me with your sword so no one can say I was killed by a woman."*b* So his servant ran him through, and he died. ⁵⁵ When the Israelites saw that Abimelech was dead, everyone went home.

⁵⁶God avenged the evil that Abimelech had done to his father by murdering his seventy brothers. ⁵⁷God also punished the Shechemites for all their wickedness. *That day*, the curse of Jotham son of Baal-Fighter was fulfilled.

Tola, the Champion-Deliverer

10 After Abimelech died, *Yahweh* raised up a man of Issachar's tribe to deliver Israel. His name was Tola*c* son of Puah*d* and grandson of Dodo.*e* He lived in the village of Shamir*f* in the highlands of Ephraim. ²He was Israel's champion-deliverer for twenty-three years; then he died and was buried at Shamir.

---

a 9:50 *Thebez* means "brightness." It possibly refers to Tirzah.

b 9:54 See 2 Sam. 11:21.

c 10:1 The Hebrew word *tola*, a homonym, can be translated "scarlet" or "worm." The dried body of the female worm *coccus ilicis* was crushed (see Isa. 53:5) and then used to dye clothing scarlet or crimson. In those days, scarlet cloth was highly valued (Lam. 4:5). Exodus mentions "scarlet" twenty-six times referring to materials of the tabernacle. In Ps. 22, the psalm of the cross, Jesus identified himself as *tola*, "a . . . worm" (v. 6). Although it can be translated "worm," Jesus was saying that he was like the worm that bleeds scarlet, changing the very substance of those his blood touches. "When the female of the scarlet ['tola'] worm species was ready to give birth to her young, she would attach her body to the trunk of a tree, fixing herself so firmly and permanently that she would never leave again. The eggs deposited beneath her body were thus protected until the larvae were hatched and able to enter their own life cycle. As the mother died, the crimson fluid stained her body and the surrounding wood. From the dead bodies of such female scarlet worms, the commercial scarlet dyes of antiquity were extracted" (Biblical Basis for Modern Science, p. 73, 1985, Henry Morris). The tola worm left a scarlet stain on the tree to which it attached itself, but after three days, the scarlet stain turned white. See Isa. 1:18. Tola is a preview of our splendid Jesus who was like a crushed worm that bled scarlet.

d 10:1 *Puah* means "splendid."

e 10:1 *Dodo* comes from the root word for "beloved" or "lover." In Tola we see Jesus, who is now the Lover of our soul.

f 10:1 *Shamir* means "sharp point [thorn]." Jewish tradition states that God created the shamir stone as the means by which Moses engraved the names of the twelve tribes onto the stones of the breastplate. (See Tosefta, Soṭah, xv. 1 [ed. Zuckermandel, p. 321]; Soṭah 48b; Yer. Soṭah 24b.) Other traditions hold that shamir was a very small worm that could bore into stone. (See Rashi, Pes. 54a, Grünbaum ["Gesammelte Aufsätze," p. 32]; Maimonides, commentary on Ab. 5, 6.)

Jair, the Champion-Deliverer

³After Tola, *Yahweh* raised up a man from Gilead whose name was Jair.ᵃ He was Israel's champion-deliverer for twenty-two years. ⁴He had thirty sons, who rode on thirty donkeys, and thirty villages belonged to them.ᵇ These villages are in the region of Gilead and are called Jair's Villages to this day. ⁵Jair died and was buried at Kamon.ᶜ

Oppression by the Ammonites

⁶The Israelites again did evil in the sight of Yahweh, worshiping the Baals and the Ashtaroths,ᵈ the gods of Aram,ᵉ Sidon,ᶠ Moab,ᵍ and Ammon,ʰ and the gods of the Philistines.ⁱ Because Israel entirely abandoned the worship of Yahweh, ⁷Yahweh became furious with Israel, and he handed them over to the oppression of the Philistinesʲ and the Ammonites. ⁸They crushed and oppressed all the Israelites for eighteen years. They ruled over all the Israelites living east of the Jordan in Gilead, in the land of the Amorites. ⁹The Ammonites also crossed the Jordan and fought against the tribes of Judah, Benjamin, and Ephraim, leaving Israel distressed.

¹⁰Then the Israelites desperately cried out to Yahweh, "We have sinned against you because we have abandoned our God and have worshiped the Baals."

¹¹Yahweh answered them,ᵏ "Did I not rescue you *in the past* from *the power of* the Egyptians, the Amorites, the Ammonites, the Philistines, ¹²the Sidonians, the Amalekites, and the Midianites?ˡ When they swept over you and oppressed you and when you cried out in desperation to me, did I not deliver you and set you free from their power? ¹³Because you have abandoned me to serve false gods, I am no longer coming to your rescue! ¹⁴Go ahead and pray all you want to these new gods you have chosen. Let's see if they will come and deliver you in your time of trouble!"

¹⁵But the Israelites continued to plead with Yahweh, "Rescue us! We know we are guilty. You can do to us whatever seems good to you,ᵐ but *please*, come to our rescue!" ¹⁶So

---

a 10:3 *Jair* means "he enlightens."

b 10:4 Jair's thirty sons riding on thirty donkeys and owning thirty cities is expressed poetically in the Hebrew. The rarely used word for "donkeys" (burros) is a homonym for the word for "villages." The information implies a somewhat princely authority given to his sons.

c 10:5 *Kamon* means "elevation." It is identified as modern Qamm, on the Jordan-Irbid road.

d 10:6 Or "Astartes." These idols were local manifestations of the goddess Ishtar, the fertility goddess of the ancient Near East.

e 10:6 The chief gods of Aram were Hadad and Rimmon.

f 10:6 Or "Phoenicia."

g 10:6 The chief god of Moab was Chemosh.

h 10:6 The chief god of Ammon was Molech.

i 10:6 The gods of the Philistines were Dagon and Baal-Zebub.

j 10:7 This introduces the oppression of the Philistines, which will not even begin to be resolved until ch. 13 with Samson and would not be finally resolved until the champion-deliverer David.

k 10:11 Jewish tradition states that a prophet delivered this word to Israel.

l 10:12 As translated from the Septuagint. The Hebrew is "Maonites."

m 10:15 It is always better to throw yourself upon the mercy of God than to be subject to the cruelty of men. See 2 Sam. 24:12–14.

they threw away the false gods from among them and returned to worshiping Yahweh. *At last*, Yahweh felt[a] Israel's misery and could bear it no longer.

[17]Then the Ammonites mustered an army *and* encamped in Gilead, while the Israelites rallied together, and they encamped at Mizpah. [18]The commanders of the people of Gilead said to one another, "Whoever starts the fight against the Ammonites, we'll make him our leader."

Jephthah, the Champion-Deliverer

11 *Yahweh raised up* a brave, fearless champion from Gilead to deliver Israel. His name was Jephthah, and he was the son of a prostitute. *His father* Gilead[b] [2]had other sons by his wife, and when they grew up, they forced Jephthah to leave home. They said to him, "You will inherit nothing of our father's wealth because you are the son of another woman."[c] [3]Jephthah fled from his half brothers and lived in the land of Tob.[d] There he recruited a gang of lawless mercenaries who traveled around with him.

[4]Sometime later, the Ammonites waged war against Israel. [5]When they attacked Israel, the leaders of Gilead went to the land of Tob to find Jephthah and to bring him back from exile. [6]*Swallowing their pride*, they said to him, "Come and lead us so that we can fight the Ammonites."

[7]Jephthah answered, "You're the very people who hated me so much that you kicked me out of my father's house. Why are you coming to me now that you're in trouble?"

[8]They said to Jephthah, "We're turning to you now because we want you to lead us in battle. Come and fight the Ammonites. *You're the one we need!*"

[9]Jephthah said to them, "*Very well.* If you take me back home to fight the Ammonites and Yahweh gives me victory, then you will make me your ruler. Agreed?"

[10]"That's right," they replied. "With Yahweh as our witness,[e] we pledge our loyalty to you." [11]So Jephthah returned home with the leaders of Gilead, and the people made him their commander and ruler. Jephthah stated his terms[f] *in a solemn ceremony* at Mizpah in the presence of Yahweh.

Jephthah's Diplomacy

[12]Then Jephthah sent messengers to the king of Ammon to ask, "What is your quarrel with us? Why have you invaded our country?"

[13]The king of Ammon answered Jephthah's messengers, "When the

---

a 10:16 Or "saw."

b 11:1 Gilead was both a person (Num. 26:29) and is also the eponymous territory in northern Transjordan. However, some scholars believe the Hebrew text is using something of a figure of speech, "[the region of] Gilead fathered Jephthah," meaning that no one knows who his father was since so many men had relations with the prostitute.

c 11:2 *Jephthah* means "he opens up." Jephthah, the eighth deliverer, had a questionable past, like many of God's champions today. God will include even a person with a social stigma in God's "honor roll" of faith (see Heb. 11:32). This is God's grace.

d 11:3 Jewish commentators state that Tob was the name of the ruler of that land. *Tob* means "good." Scholars believe that the land of Tob was southeast of Lake Galilee and could be another name for Hippos in the Decapolis.

e 11:10 Or "Yahweh will be listening between us." This implies that God would punish either party if they broke the covenant.

f 11:11 Or in modern terms, "his oath of office."

Israelites came out of Egypt, they seized my land from the River Arnon to the River Jabbok, as far as the River Jordan. Now give it all back, and we'll be at peace."

¹⁴Jephthah again sent messengers back to the king of Ammon ¹⁵with this answer: "Israel seized neither the land of Moab nor the land of Ammon. ¹⁶When the Israelites left Egypt, they passed through the desert to the Red Sea and came to Kadesh. ¹⁷They sent messengers to the king of Edom requesting permission to go through his land, but the king of Edom refused. They also asked the king of Moab, but he too would not cooperate. So the Israelites were forced to remain at Kadesh. ¹⁸Leaving from there, they traveled through the desert in order to bypass the land of Edom and the land of Moab. When they arrived at the east side of Moab, on the other side of the River Arnon, they made camp there, but they did not cross the Arnon because it was Moab's boundary. ¹⁹Then, the Israelites dispatched messengers to Sihon, the Amorite king of Heshbon, and requested his permission to go through his country to their own land. ²⁰Because Sihon did not trust Israel, he assembled his whole army, made camp at Jahaz, and attacked Israel. ²¹But Yahweh, the *mighty* God of Israel, gave the Israelites victory over Sihon and his army. So the Israelites took possession of all the territory of the Amorites who lived in that land. ²²Then they occupied all the Amorite territory from the Arnon in the south to the Jabbok in the north

and from the desert in the east to the Jordan in the west. ²³Since it was Yahweh the *mighty* God of Israel who drove out the Amorites for his people, the Israelites, ²⁴who do you think you are to try to take it back? You should be satisfied with whatever land your god Chemosh*ᵃ* has won for himself, but we are going to keep everything that Yahweh our *mighty* God has given us. ²⁵Do you think you're stronger than Moab's king Balak son of Zippor?*ᵇ* He never challenged Israel over disputed land, did he? Did he ever go to war against us? ²⁶For three hundred years, Israel has been living here and occupying Heshbon, Aroer, and the towns around them, and all the cities on the banks of the Arnon River. Why have you waited until now to try to take them back? ²⁷No, I have not wronged you; rather, you are doing me wrong by attacking me. Let Yahweh be the judge, and let him decide today which of us is right, Israel or Ammon."

²⁸But the king of Ammon ignored Jephthah's message.

Jephthah's Foolish Vow

²⁹Then the Spirit of Yahweh rushed upon Jephthah *and empowered him*. He *and his men* marched through Gilead and Manasseh and returned to Mizpah in Gilead, and from there, he stalked the Ammonites. ³⁰Jephthah promised Yahweh: "If you give me victory over the Ammonites, ³¹I will offer up to you as a burnt offering the first thing that comes out of my house to greet me when I return in victory. I will sacrifice that one as an offering to you."*ᶜ*

---

a 11:24 *Chemosh* means "swift subduer." A later king of Moab sacrificed his son as a burnt offering to the god Chemosh (see 2 Kings 3:27).

b 11:25 See Num. 22:2; Deut. 23:4; Josh. 24:9.

c 11:31 The custom of the day was to house both livestock and family together. No doubt, Jephthah assumed it would be an animal he would offer or perhaps a servant, but not his daughter.

³²So Jephthah crossed the river *with his men* to fight the Ammonites, and Yahweh gave him victory. ³³He struck at them from Aroer to the area near Minnith,ᵃ twenty villages in all, and as far as Abel Keramim.ᵇ The Israelites brought the Ammonites down to the dustᶜ in a great slaughter.

Jephthah's Daughter

³⁴When Jephthah arrived home at Mizpah, his daughter came hurrying out *of the house* to welcome her father home, dancing to the rhythm of tambourines. She was his only child—his one and only. ³⁵When he realized who had come out, he ripped his cloak and was overcome with grief. He exclaimed, "Oh no! My *dearest* daughter, you have torn my heart to shreds!ᵈ Must it be you I offer?ᵉ I have made a solemn promise to Yahweh, and I cannot retract it!"

³⁶She said to him, "My father, you have made a vow to Yahweh and he has delivered you from your enemies, the Ammonites. Do to me what you promised him you would do. ³⁷But please grant me one thing. Spare me for two months and let me go with my friends to grieve. Let me be free to wander on the hills and to lament my sad fate."ᶠ

³⁸"Go," he replied, and he sent her away for two months. She and her friends went into the mountains and grieved because she was going to die unmarried and childless. ³⁹After two

months, she returned to her father, and Jephthah fulfilled his vow to Yahweh. His daughter died still a virgin.

(This was the origin of the custom in Israel ⁴⁰that young women would go away each year to grieve and lament for the daughter of Jephthah of Gilead.)

Ephraim's Envy

12 *Jephthah's actions grievously offended* the men of Ephraim. They assembled their forces and crossed the Jordan River to Zaphonᵍ *to confront Jephthah*. They said to him, "Why did you cross the border to fight the Ammonites without inviting us to join you? We're going to burn your house down over your head!"

²Jephthah replied, "I and my people were in the middle of a serious conflict with the Ammonites. I summoned you, but you ignored me. ³When I realized that you were not coming to help us, I risked my own life to cross the border to fight them. Yahweh *empowered* me to be victorious over them. So why are you coming to fight with me now?" ⁴Then Jephthah gathered all the men of Gilead and fought the men of Ephraim. The men of Gilead defeated them, for the Ephraimites insulted them, saying, "You men of Gilead are nothing but renegades from Ephraim and Manasseh!"

⁵In order to keep the Ephraimites from escaping, the men of Gilead captured the places where they could

---

ᵃ 11:33 *Minnith* means "distribution." Minnith was a district east of the Jordan known for growing corn.

ᵇ 11:33 Or "meadow of the vineyards."

ᶜ 11:33 Or "he humbled [humiliated] the Ammonites."

ᵈ 11:35 Or "you have driven me to my knees."

ᵉ 11:35 Or "you have become a stumbling block to me."

ᶠ 11:37 Or "weep over my virginity."

ᵍ 12:1 *Zaphon* is the word for "north." A possible translation is that "[they] crossed the Jordan River and went north."

cross the Jordan. When any Ephraimite tried to escape and asked permission to cross the river, the men of Gilead would ask, "Are you an Ephraimite?" If he said, "No," [6]they would tell him to say "Shibboleth." But if he could not pronounce it correctly and said "Sibboleth,"[a] the men of Gilead would seize him and kill him there at the crossing place of the Jordan. At that time, they killed forty-two thousand[b] Ephraimites.

[7]Jephthah ruled Israel for six years. When he died, they buried him in his hometown in Gilead.

Champion-Deliverers: Ibzan, Elon, and Abdon

[8]After Jephthah, *Yahweh raised up* Ibzan,[c] *a champion-deliverer* from Bethlehem who ruled Israel. [9]He had thirty sons and thirty daughters. He gave his thirty daughters in marriage outside his tribe and brought thirty women from outside the tribe as wives for his sons. Ibzan ruled Israel for seven years. [10]When he died, they buried him at Bethlehem.

[11]After Ibzan, *Yahweh raised up* Elon,[d] *a champion-deliverer* from Zebulun, who ruled Israel for ten years. [12]When he died, they buried him at Aijalon in the territory of Zebulun.

[13]After Elon, *Yahweh raised up* Abdon[e] son of Hillel,[f] a champion-deliverer from Pirathon,[g] to rule Israel. [14]He had forty sons and thirty grandsons, who rode on seventy donkeys.[h] Abdon led Israel for eight years. [15]When he died, they buried him at

---

a 12:6 Because of their accent, the men of Ephraim were unable to pronounce Shibboleth; they pronounced it as "Sibboleth." It would be equal in English to the difference between "shin" and "sin." *Shibboleth* means "stream," "branch," or "torrent." *Sibboleth* means "ear of corn." The men of Ephraim were betrayed by their speech. Believers today can likewise reveal who we are by our words (see Matt. 12:36–37). Since our words have power to release life or death, we must use them wisely (see Eph. 4:29).

b 12:6 Or possibly "2,040."

c 12:8 Ibzan, the ninth champion-deliverer, was from the tribe of Zebulun (see Josh. 19:10, 15). *Ibzan* can be translated as "famous," "splendid," "brilliant," or "shining." Ibzan multiplied his family and influence by marrying his sons and daughters into the other tribes of Israel. Jewish tradition holds that Ibzan was another name for Boaz, the husband of Ruth and the ancestor of David. The Talmud asserts that Ibzan (Boaz) consummated his marriage with Ruth on the last night of his life. (See *Bava Batra* 91a.)

d 12:11 *Elon* can be translated as "strong tree," "oak," "pillar," "post," "[political] chief," "mighty man," "powerful," or "stability."

e 12:13 Abdon, of the tribe of Ephraim, was the eleventh champion-deliverer. *Abdon* can be translated "lowly servant," "worker," "laborer," "minister," or "service."

f 12:13 Abdon's father was Hillel. The name *Hillel* means "high praise," "rejoice," "celebrate," "shout," or "shine forth." One could say from the meanings of Abdon and Hillel: High praises produce a servant spirit (cf. Isa. 57:15).

g 12:13 *Pirathon* means "leader," "prince," "chief," "surpassing," "peak," or "highest."

h 12:14 Each one of Abdon's sons and grandsons owned his own donkey, a symbol of his prestige and prosperity. Today, we would say something like, "they each owned their own home," to denote their affluence. The number seventy is used sixty-one times in the Bible. It can represent God's people in motion, God's people expanding into their purpose, and perfect spiritual order carried out with power. During the wilderness journeys of Israel, they stopped at Elim, which had seventy palm trees (see Ex. 15:27). Jesus dispatched seventy apostles to heal, preach, and deliver (see Luke 10:1–12).

Pirathon in the territory of Ephraim in the hill country of the Amalekites.

The Birth of Samson, a Champion-Deliverer

13 Once again, the Israelites continued doing evil in the sight of Yahweh, so he subjected them to Philistine[a] rule for forty years.

[2]There was a certain man from the tribe of Dan, who lived in the city of Zorah,[b] named Manoah.[c] His wife was barren and childless, [3]but the Angel of Yahweh appeared to her and said, "Look here! You are no longer barren and childless, for you will conceive and give birth to a son. [4]Now be careful not to drink any wine or beer and to eat nothing considered unclean. [5]You will conceive and will give birth to a son. Raise the boy as one dedicated to God[d] from the womb and never cut his hair. He will begin to deliver Israel from Philistine power."

[6]So Manoah's wife went to her husband and said, "A man sent from God came to me! He looked like an angel of God—incredibly awesome.[e] I didn't ask where he came from, and he didn't tell me his name, [7]but he told me, 'You will become pregnant, and you will have a son. Make sure you don't drink any wine or beer, and eat nothing unclean, for the boy will be fully devoted to God from the womb to the day he dies!' "

[8]Manoah pleaded with Yahweh, "O my Lord, please send the man of God back to us. Have him come to instruct us how to raise the son who is to be born."

[9]God answered Manoah's prayer and sent the Angel of God to the woman again while she was sitting alone in the field. Her husband Manoah was not with her [10]so she ran at once to tell him the news: "Look! Come quickly! He reappeared—the same man who came to me that day!" [11]So Manoah got up, followed his wife, and went to the man. Manoah said to him, "Are you the man who appeared and spoke to my wife?"

"I am," he said.

[12]Manoah replied, "Well, when *Yahweh* fulfills your prophecy, how should we raise the boy, and what is his life mission?"

[13]The Angel of Yahweh answered, "Do everything that I instructed your wife. [14]She must abstain from anything that comes from the grapevine and drink no alcohol, nor should she eat anything unclean. She must do all that I have commanded her."

[15]Manoah said to the Angel of Yahweh, "Please stay here until we cook a young goat for you."

---

a 13:1 The word for "philistine" can be translated as "rolling," "migratory," "wallowing in the dust," "wandering," "deviating off course," or "rejected." The Philistines are mentioned thirty-four times in the book of Judges. The Philistines were Israel's constant foe until David defeated them. In the days of Samson, the Israelites had been content to have them as neighbors in the land.

b 13:2 *Zorah* means "hornet's nest." The birth of a champion-deliverer will always stir up a hornet's nest.

c 13:2 *Manoah* means "rest" or "restoring."

d 13:5 Or "he will be God's Nazarite." A Nazarite was a special class of Jewish men who were dedicated to God. They were forbidden to cut their hair, drink alcohol, or touch any dead thing. The word "Nazarite" is taken from the Hebrew word *nazar*, which means "dedicated to God," "set apart," "consecrated [as a prince]," or "an unpruned branch." See Num. 6.

e 13:6 Or "very frightening."

[16]The Angel of Yahweh said to Manoah, "Even if you detain me, I will not eat your food. But if you want to prepare a burnt offering, offer it up to Yahweh." Manoah did not realize that he was speaking with the Angel of Yahweh.

[17]*Stunned*, Manoah asked the Angel of Yahweh. "What is your name? When *Yahweh* fulfills your prophecy, we want to honor you!"

[18]The Angel of Yahweh replied, "Why ask for my name? It is 'Wonderfully Hidden!'"[a] [19]So Manoah prepared the young goat and his grain offering and took them to the rock to offer them up to Yahweh, the wonder-working *God*. While Manoah and his wife watched, [20]flames burst from the rock and ascended upward to heaven from the altar. The Angel of Yahweh, *wrapped* in the flames of fire, ascended into the sky.[b] Dazed, Manoah and his wife fell facedown to the ground *in worship*. [21-23]Only then did Manoah realize that he had met the Angel of Yahweh! He turned to his wife and said, "We're as good as dead! God has just visited us!"

But his wife said, "If Yahweh had planned to kill us, he wouldn't have accepted our burnt offering and our grain offering. He wouldn't have revealed all these things to us or have spoken to us as he did just now." And Manoah and his wife never encountered Yahweh's Angel again. [24]Manoah's wife gave birth to a son, and she named him Samson.[c] The boy grew up with Yahweh's blessing on his life.[d] [25]The Spirit of Yahweh began to stir his heart[e] while he was between Zorah and Eshtaol,[f] in the Camp of Dan.[g]

Samson Wants a Wife

14 One day Samson went down to Timnah where a Philistine girl caught his eye, [2]so he returned home and told his parents, "At Timnah I noticed a young woman among the daughters of the Philistines; get her for me now to be my wife."[h]

[3]His parents replied, "Why can't you find a woman from among our relatives, or at least from our tribe? You don't have to get a wife from the uncircumcised Philistines."

But Samson told his father, "Get her for me; I know she's the right one for me."

---

a 13:18 The Angel of Yahweh was God in a human form. His name can be translated "wonderful," "incomprehensible," "unknowable," "beyond understanding," or "transcendent."

b 13:20 There is at least a hint here of Jesus' sacrifice on the cross (burnt offering), his resurrection (grain offering), and ascension into heaven.

c 13:24 *Samson* means "sunbeam," "little sun," "sunny," or, if adjectival, "solar." He was the twelfth champion-deliverer. Samson is mentioned thirty-eight times in the Bible, including in Heb. 11:32 where he is noted for his faith.

d 13:24 Compare 1 Sam 2:26; Luke 2:52.

e 13:25 The Hebrew is literally "to strike as a bell." God's Spirit moved on Samson powerfully and empowered him.

f 13:25 *Eshtaol* means "a narrow pass." God's Spirit first gripped Samson when he was between a "hornet's nest" (Zorah) and a "narrow pass" (Eshtaol). We would say that he was between a rock and a hard place.

g 13:25 Or "Mahaneh Dan." This is possibly the place the tribe of Dan camped on their way to take Laish. See 18:11–12.

h 14:2 As in many other cultures, parents (especially the fathers) arranged marriages in the ancient Near East. See Gen. 21:21; 24:4; 34:8; Ex. 21:9.

⁴Now, his parents had no idea that Samson's passion for the girl was part of Yahweh's plan to create an opportunity to come against the Philistines who ruled over Israel at that time.

Samson and the Lion
⁵One day, Samson decided to go back to Timnah *to visit the Philistine woman*. As he was approaching the vineyards of Timnah, a full-grown lion suddenly came roaring toward him. ⁶The Spirit of Yahweh entered Samson*ᵃ* and empowered him to tear the lion to pieces with his bare hands as if it were a young goat! But he never disclosed to his father and mother what he had done. ⁷Afterward, he went into Timnah and talked with the Philistine woman, because Samson was convinced that she was the right one for him.

⁸Later, Samson returned to marry her. On his way there, he turned aside to look at the lion's remains, and to his surprise, there was a swarm of bees, honey, and honeycomb in the carcass of the lion! ⁹He scooped some of the honey*ᵇ* into his hands and continued on his way, eating as he went. When he rejoined his father and mother, he gave some to them, and they ate too. But he did not tell them he had scooped it from the lion's carcass. ¹⁰So Samson's father accompanied him to Timnah to *arrange* the marriage.

Samson's Wedding Feast
Following the custom for young men*ᶜ* about to marry, Samson threw a party*ᵈ* that lasted for seven days. ¹¹When the Philistines saw him, they arranged for thirty *Philistine* men to accompany him *as groomsmen.*ᵉ ¹²Samson challenged them with a riddle, "Hey, I have a riddle for you.*ᶠ* If you can solve my riddle within the seven days of our feast, then I will give each of you a linen garment and a set of fine clothing. ¹³But if you cannot solve it, then you must give me thirty linen garments and thirty sets of fine clothing."*ᵍ*

"Ask away," they said to him. "Let's hear your riddle."

¹⁴He said to them:

---

a 14:6 Or "The Spirit of Yahweh rushed upon him."

b 14:9 The Jewish historian Josephus writes that Samson took three honeycombs from the lion's carcass and gave them to a woman in Timnah (*Ant.* 1.5.c.8 sect. 6). Part of the Nazarite vow is a prohibition from touching anything dead or unclean (see Num. 6:6). By touching the carcass of the lion, Samson violated his vow to God.

c 14:10 The Hebrew word for "young men" can also mean "chosen men [warriors]." See 20:15–16.

d 14:10 This was a wedding feast with alcohol. Assuming Samson was drinking with the others, he again broke another part of his Nazarite vow not to drink alcohol. The only remaining part of his vow was not to cut his hair, but soon he would violate that too.

e 14:11 Many modern commentators surmise that the Philistines assigned thirty men to keep watch over Samson due to their concern over his unusual strength.

f 14:12 Or "Let me riddle you a riddle." The Hebrew word for "riddle" (*chidah*) can also mean "dark saying," "hard question," or "conundrum," and is taken from a root word meaning "to tie into a knot." Riddles were common as a source of entertainment in ancient times. The queen of Sheba tested Solomon's wisdom by presenting him with riddles (see 1 Kings 10:1). God instructed Ezekiel to present a riddle to the people of Israel (see Ezek. 17:2). The book of Proverbs was written, in part, to "unveil the deeper meaning of parables, poetic riddles, and epigrams" (Prov. 1:6).

g 14:13 That is, "costly festive garments," a cultural mark of favor.

"From the eater came something
   to eat,
From the strong came something
   sweet."

After three days, they were still stumped and could not figure it out. [15]On the fourth day,[a] they said to Samson's bride, "Have you invited us here to bankrupt us? Do whatever it takes to persuade your husband to tell you the answer to his riddle, or we will burn down your father's house with you and your family inside!"

[16]So Samson's bride went to him and turned on the tears and sobbed, "Honey, you don't really love me! You hate me! You've challenged my countrymen with a riddle, but you haven't told me *its meaning*!"

"Listen," he said to her. "I haven't even told my parents. So why should I tell you?" [17]She continued to cry on his shoulder for the remaining days of their feast, and on the seventh day, because she had so persistently nagged him, he finally *gave in and* divulged the secret. Then she went and explained the riddle to her countrymen.

[18]On the seventh day before the sun had set, the townsmen answered him:

"What could be sweeter than
   honey?
And what is stronger than a lion?"

And Samson angrily replied,

"If you hadn't used my cow for
   your plow
you wouldn't know my riddle now!"

[19]Then suddenly, the Spirit of Yahweh rushed upon Samson, infusing him with power! He went down to Ashkelon[b] and killed thirty of their men. He stripped them of their linen[c] tunics and their robes and gave them in payment to those who had explained the riddle. Then, in a blazing fury, he returned to his father's house. [20]Meanwhile, *unknown to* Samson, his bride married his best man.

Three Hundred Foxes

15 Later, during the wheat harvest, Samson went to visit his wife and took a young goat as a gift[d] for her. He said *to her father,* "I'm going into my wife's bedroom to sleep with her." But her father wouldn't let him enter. He said to Samson, [2]"I thought you really despised her and had divorced her,[e] so I gave her to your best man.

---

a 14:15 Or "seventh day" (Masoretic Text).

b 14:19 Ashkelon was a Philistine city on the Mediterranean Sea north of Gaza, about two days' journey from Timnah.

c 14:19 Linen was used for the garment of a priest. Thirty is the number of a mature priesthood, for men could only become priests at the age of thirty. Samson's riddle has revelation hidden within it for the church today. Seven days they feasted trying to solve the riddle. We are in the seventh day from Adam (see 2 Pet. 3:8), and we are about to unravel the riddle of life. The ones who solve the riddle receive new garments: costly festive wedding garments (i.e., are clothed with immortality).

d 15:1 Taking her a young goat as a gift, in that culture, would be the ancient counterpart to giving her chocolate and roses.

e 15:2 Or "in hating, you hated her," a figure of speech to say that he divorced her.

Look, her younger sister is even more beautiful than she. Take her instead."

³Samson said, "That does it! This time I'll settle my score with you Philistines for good!" ⁴Samson went out and caught three hundred foxes,ᵃ tied their tails together in pairs, and lashed a torch between each pair of tails. ⁵He lit the torches and set the foxes loose in the grain fields of the Philistines, burning all their grain to the ground, including the sheaves and the standing grain, as well as their vineyards and olive groves.

⁶"Who did this?" the Philistines demanded.

"Samson," someone told them, "because his father-in-law from Timnah gave Samson's bride to his best man." So the Philistines went and burned both the woman and her father to death.

⁷"Because you did this despicable act," Samson vowed, "I won't rest until I get even with you!" ⁸He was so furious that he launched a vicious attack on the Philistines and *single handedly* slaughtered many of them. Afterward, he went and hid in a cave in the cliff of Etam.ᵇ

Samson versus the Philistines

⁹The Philistines retaliated by setting up camp in Judah and deploying their men near the town of Lehi. ¹⁰The men of Judah asked the Philistines, "Why are you coming against us?"

The Philistines replied, "We've come to capture Samson and repay him for what he did to us."

¹¹So three thousand men of Judah went to Samson's cave in the cliff of Etam, and they said to him, "What are you trying to do to us? Don't you realize the Philistines rule over us?"

Samson replied, "I only did to them what they did to me."

¹²The men of Judah told him, "We've come to take you prisoner and hand you over to the Philistines."

"All right," Samson said, "but promise me that you won't kill me."

¹³"We promise not to kill you," they replied. "We'll only tie you up and hand you over to the Philistines." They bound him with two brand new ropes and led him from *the cave* near the cliff *of Etam to Lehi.*ᶜ

¹⁴When the Philistines saw Samson coming, they raised a shout of triumph. Immediately, *the mighty* Spirit of Yahweh came rushing upon Samson! He snapped the ropes off his arms as if they were strings catching fire, and they fell from his wrists. ¹⁵He spotted a raw jawbone of a donkey lying there on the ground and picked it up. He began to *swing it wildly* and used it to kill *a thousand Philistines* that day.

The Song of Samson

¹⁶Samson then said,

"With only a donkey's jawbone,
    I made heaps *of donkeys* out of
      them!ᵈ
With only a donkey's jawbone,
    a thousand men lie slain!"

---

a 15:4 Or "jackals."

b 15:8 *Etam* means "lair of ravenous beasts."

c 15:13 *Lehi* means "jawbone."

d 15:16 The Hebrew word for "donkey" and the word for "heaps" are homonyms. The wordplay is lost in English translations. If God can use the jawbone of a donkey, he can use you and your words (jawbone) to win a victory over the enemy.

[17]When he finished boasting, he threw the jawbone to the ground. That's how the place got its name—Jawbone Hill.[a]

[18]Afterward, Samson was terribly thirsty and cried out to Yahweh, "I was strengthened by your great power to win this awesome victory. Will you now leave me here dying of thirst—and let me fall into the hands of these pagans?"[b] [19]So God *answered Samson's prayer* and split open the rock basin *under Lehi*, and water gushed out! Samson drank and his spirit was revived. He named that place "The Spring for the One Who Cried,"[c] and it is still there in Lehi to this day.

[20]Samson led Israel as its champion-deliverer for twenty years during the period of Philistine oppression.

Samson in Gaza

16 One day, Samson went to Gaza, a Philistine town, and slept with a prostitute there.[d] [2]Word soon spread that Samson was in town, so the men of Gaza gathered and hid at the town gates, *cutting off his escape.* They made no move during the night, saying, "We'll kill him at dawn when he tries to leave."

[3]But in the middle of the night, Samson got up and left. On his way out of Gaza, he took hold of the doors of the town gate and ripped them off their hinges—two posts, the gates, and the locking bar. He hoisted them all on his shoulders and carried them off a great distance to the top of the hill across from Hebron.[e]

Delilah, a Double Agent

[4]Some time later Samson fell in love with a woman named Delilah[f] from the Sorek Valley.[g] [5]The rulers of the Philistines went to her *with a plan*: "Trick Samson into telling you the secret of his great strength. Find out how we can subdue him. We'll tie him up and

---

a 15:17 Or "Ramath Lehi."

b 15:18 Or "uncircumcised."

c 15:19 Or "En Hakkore [crier's fountain]." There is a hidden spring called En Hakkore. God has a hidden spring reserved for those who cry. If tears have streaked your face and grief has torn your heart, there is a spring of restoration that God has for you. Drink of this living spring of water and he will comfort you and restore you.

d 16:1 Samson's moral failures outweighed his physical strength. Samson was a mighty deliverer, but he was riddled with compromise. He was mighty in strength but weak in self-control. He was a man who had some of the greatest potential in the whole Bible, but he proved to be one of the greatest disappointments as well. Yahweh blessed his life from birth (see 13:24). Samson was a leader, a "man's man," with God's Spirit to strengthen him, yet he left a legacy of compromise and moral weakness. He could tear a lion apart, but he could not control his lust. In spite of all this, Samson is listed in Heb. 11:32 as a man of great faith.

e 16:3 This was a superhuman feat to say the least. Samson carried the heavy gates, which were most likely two stories high, and the heavy posts that secured them, uphill to a location nearly forty miles away. Samson's offering to God in the high place was not an animal but the gates of a city! A supernatural infusion of strength came upon Samson. In Christ, we can do all things, for he strengthens us with might (see Eph. 3:20; Phil. 4:12–13). Let everyone who is weak say they are strong (see Joel 3:10).

f 16:4 *Delilah*, a Philistine name, possibly means "enfeebling," "weakening," or "languishing."

g 16:4 Or "Valley of the Choice Vines." It is known today as Wadi-es-Sarar, which begins about thirteen miles southwest of Jerusalem.

make him helpless. Then each of us will give you eleven hundred pieces of silver."[a]

[6]So Delilah approached Samson and asked, "Please dear, won't you tell me the secret of your strength and how you could be tied up and made helpless?"

[7]Samson replied, "If someone bound me with seven new bowstrings that haven't been dried, I'll become as weak as an ordinary man."

[8]So the Philistine tyrants brought Delilah seven new bowstrings, and she tied Samson up with them. [9]With men waiting in ambush in one of the inner rooms of her house, she cried out, "Samson! The Philistines are here to capture you!" But Samson snapped the bowstrings like a piece of string snaps when it is burned by a fire. So no one discovered the secret of his strength.

[10]Afterward, Delilah said to him, "You've made fun of me and told me lies! Please tell me how you can be tied up securely."

[11]Samson replied, "If someone bound me with brand-new ropes that have never been used, I'll become as weak as anyone else."

[12]So Delilah took new ropes and tied him up with them, and the men were waiting in ambush in the inner room as before. Delilah cried out, "Samson! The Philistines are here to capture you!" Once again, Samson easily snapped the ropes from his arms like they were threads.

[13]Delilah reprimanded him, saying, "You've made a fool of me and lied to me again! Now tell me the truth—how can you be tied up?"

Samson replied, "If you weave the seven braids of my hair into the fabric on your loom and tighten it with the pin, I'll become as weak as anyone else."

So while he slept, Delilah wove the seven braids of his hair into the fabric [14]and pinned it with a peg. Again she cried out, "Samson! The Philistines are here to capture you!" But Samson woke up and yanked his hair from both the loom and the fabric.

[15]"How can you say, 'I love you,' " pouted Delilah, "and yet you don't tell me your secrets? You've tricked me three times now, and you still haven't told me what makes you so strong!" [16]She tormented him day after day until he was sick to death of her nagging.

[17]Finally, he confessed to her everything: "I've never had my hair cut, because my parents dedicated me to God from birth. If anyone cuts my hair, my power will leave me, and I'll become as weak as anyone else."

[18]When Delilah realized he had finally disclosed his secret, she sent for the Philistine rulers. "Come quickly!" she said. "He's finally told me his secret!" So the Philistine rulers returned with the bribe money in their hands.

[19]Delilah lulled Samson to sleep with his head in her lap. Then she called in a barber[b] to cut off the seven locks

---

a 16:5 Five Philistine tyrants (perhaps a picture of our five senses) ruled over five cities. This would mean Delilah was being bribed with fifty-five hundred pieces of silver, an exorbitant amount! This shows how the fear of Samson had gripped these rulers. They were eager to pay any price to capture him.

b 16:19 Or "the man."

of his hair.[a] In this way she weakened him,[b] and his strength drained from him.

²⁰Then she cried out, "Samson! The Philistines have come to capture you!"

He woke up and thought, "I'll do the same as before and shake myself free." But he didn't realize that Yahweh had turned away from him.

²¹So the Philistines captured him and gouged out his eyes.[c] They took him down to Gaza, where they bound him with bronze chains and forced him to grind *grain* in the prison. ²²*But before long,* his hair began to grow back.

Samson's Victory in Death

²³One day, the Philistine tyrants celebrated a great festival to offer extravagant sacrifices to their god, Dagon.[d] They praised Dagon, saying,

"Our god has given us victory!
Dagon has subdued our strong
    enemy Samson!"

²⁴When the people saw their idol,[e] they too joined in the praises, saying,

"Our god has delivered our enemy
    to us!
The one who devastated our
    country
    and piled our corpses high!"

²⁵By now, the people were getting drunk and demanded, "Bring out Samson and let him dance for us!" So he was brought from the prison to amuse them, and they displayed him between the main pillars *that supported their temple.*

²⁶*Blind* Samson said to the young servant who was leading him by the hand, "Let go of me and let me feel the pillars that hold up the temple. I want to lean against them." ²⁷The temple was completely packed with people. All the Philistine rulers were there, and there were some three thousand men and women in the balcony watching as Samson provided them some amusement.

²⁸Then Samson prayed to Yahweh, "Lord Yahweh, please remember me again. O God, impart *your* strength to me just one more time. With one blow let me take revenge on the Philistines for gouging out my eyes." ²⁹⁻³⁰Then Samson reached toward the two center pillars that held up the temple, his left hand on one and his right hand on the other, and he prayed, "Let me die with the Philistines." Then with *all his might*, with both hands he pushed against the pillars, and the temple came crashing down on the Philistine rulers and all the people. So Samson killed more enemies through his death than in his entire lifetime.

---

a 16:19 Samson's true strength was not from some magical power in his long hair but in his devotion to God and in his vow to be pure. The seven braids of hair remind us of the seven Spirits of God that are the true source of strength and anointing for God's servants. See Isa. 11:1–2; Rev. 1:4; 3:1; 4:5; 5:6.

b 16:19 Or "humiliated him."

c 16:21 The loss of anointing will always lead to spiritual blindness and bondage.

d 16:23 The word *Dagon* means "fish"; it has a homonym meaning "grain." The image of Dagon, the fish god, was a representation of a half man and half fish.

e 16:24 Or "saw him." This was not Samson, for he was still in the prison, and the Philistines had not yet brought him out to be mocked (which they do in v. 25). The "him" is the idol of their god, Dagon.

³¹Then his brothers and entire family went down *to Gaza* to get his body. They brought him back home and buried him between Zorah and Eshtaol, next to his father, Manoah. Samson had led Israel for twenty years.

Micah's Shrine

17 There was a man named Micah from the hill country of Ephraim.ᵃ ²He said to his mother, "When someone stole your eleven hundred shekels of silver,ᵇ I overheard you speak a curse over the thief. Well, *it turns out,* I have the money. I'm the one who took it. *Here—I'm bringing it back.*"

Immediately, his mother, *wanting to revoke her curse,* said: "O my son! May Yahweh bless you!"

³So he returned the eleven hundred shekels of silver to his mother, but she said to him, "I give it back to you, for I solemnly dedicate this silver to Yahweh for my son to make a carved image, an idol covered with silver." ⁴So from the silver he returned to his mother, she took two hundred shekels of silver and gave them to a silversmith, who molded them into an idol and overlaid the idol with silver. Micah kept the idol in his house.

⁵Now Micah had a shrine,ᶜ and he made some idols and a *counterfeit* ephod and ordainedᵈ one of his sons as his priest. ⁶In those days, Israel had no king. People did whatever they wanted to do.

Micah's Counterfeit Priest

⁷At the same time, there was a young manᵉ from the *priestly* tribe of Levi living in Bethlehem in Judah. ⁸He left there to search for another place to live. On his journey, he came to Micah's house in the hill country of Ephraim. ⁹Micah asked him, "Where are you from?"

"I'm a Levite from Bethlehem in Judah," he said, "and I'm looking for a place to live."

¹⁰"Live here with me," Micah said to him. "Be my father and priest, and I'll pay you ten shekels of silver a year and provide your clothes and your food." ¹¹So the Levite agreed to move in with him and the young man became like one of his sons. ¹²Then Micah ordained the young Levite as his priest, and he lived in his house. ¹³And Micah declared, "Now I know that Yahweh will bless me and prosper me, since a Levite now serves as my priest."ᶠ

The Migration of the Tribe of Dan

18 In those days there was no king in Israel, and the tribe of Dan sought a territory to settle in. They still had no place to call their own among the tribes of Israel. ²So the Danites sent out from Zorah and from

---

a 17:1 *Micah* means "Yahweh the Incomparable" or "Who is like Yahweh?" According to Jewish tradition, Micah's mother was Delilah. Most scholars believe that chs. 17–18 form an appendix to the book and that the events of these two chapters actually happened much earlier, possibly during the days of the champion-deliverer Othniel.

b 17:2 Eleven hundred shekels would amount to over one hundred pounds of silver ($30,000).

c 17:5 Or "house of God." Micah attempted to begin his own religious system of worship, complete with a priestly ephod (priestly vest). Compare 1 Kings 12:25–33.

d 17:5 Or "filled the hand of."

e 17:7 His name was Jonathan, son of Gershom. See 18:30.

f 17:13 He was Micah's priest, not God's.

Eshtaol five of their valiant men*a* to spy out the land, telling them, "Go, explore the land." When they advanced to the hill country of Ephraim, they got as far as Micah's house and camped near there. ³When they approached Micah's house, they recognized the voice*b* of the young Levite, so they went over to him and asked, "Why are you here? Who brought you here? What are you doing in this place?"

⁴He replied, "Micah helped me. He hired me, and I've become his priest."

⁵Then they said to him, "Good! Please pray to God for us and find out if our mission will succeed."

⁶The priest replied, "You have nothing to worry about. The eyes of Yahweh are watching over your mission.*c* *You will succeed.*"

⁷So the five spies went *northward* and came to Laish. They observed that the people were wealthy and living in security, after the manner of the Sidonians.*d* Their quiet and carefree community lacked nothing. Furthermore, they lived far from the Sidonians and had no dealings with anyone, leaving them defenseless.

⁸When the spies returned to Zorah and Eshtaol from their expedition, they were asked, "What's your report?"

⁹"Come on, let's do this!" they replied. "Listen, we've seen the land, and it's very good. Don't just sit here *wasting time*; let's go quickly and invade the land to conquer and possess it. ¹⁰When we arrive, we will encounter an unsuspecting people. The land is wide open and fruitful. God has indeed given it into your hand!"

¹¹So six hundred Danites, fully armed for war, set out from Zorah and Eshtaol. ¹²They went up and camped west of Kiriath Jearim in Judah. (To this day that place is called The Camp of Dan.) ¹³From there they passed through the hill country of Ephraim until they arrived at the house of Micah.

¹⁴Then the five men who had explored the region of Laish remarked to their comrades, "Did you know there's an ephod somewhere in these houses, and other idols and an idol overlaid with silver? So decide what you'll do about it."

¹⁵So they stopped there and came to Micah's house where the young Levite lived, and they greeted him. ¹⁶While the six hundred fully armed Danites stationed themselves by the entrance of the gate, ¹⁷the five spies proceeded to enter and take the idol overlaid with silver, the ephod, and the other idols. Now the priest was standing with the six hundred fully armed men at the entrance of the gate. ¹⁸When he saw the men going into Micah's house to take the idol overlaid with silver, the ephod, and the other idols, the priest said to them, "What are you doing?"

¹⁹They said to him, "Be quiet! Don't say a word, just come with us and be our priest and a father *to us all*. Isn't it better for you to be a priest representing an entire tribe of Israel rather than the house of only one man?" ²⁰The offer pleased the priest and he accepted. He took all the idols and the ephod and joined the Danites.

²¹They resumed their journey with their children, their livestock, and

---

a 18:2 Or "prosperous men."

b 18:3 That is, his dialect. From his accent, they recognized he was from their district in Judah.

c 18:6 Or "Yahweh's eyes [go] before you."

d 18:7 That is, the Phoenicians.

their possessions going in front of them.*ᵃ* ²²When they had traveled a considerable distance from Micah's home, Micah and his neighbors gathered and chased the Danites until they caught up with them. ²³They shouted at the Danites, who turned around and answered Micah, "What's your problem? Why have you come *against us* with such a company?"

²⁴He replied, "Why did you take the gods that I made, kidnap my priest, and march off? What's left for me now? How dare you ask me, 'What's my problem?'"

²⁵The Danites retorted, "We don't want to hear any more of your complaints lest some of our hot-tempered men here attack and kill you, *your friends*, and your household." ²⁶So the Danites went their way. When Micah realized that he was outnumbered, he turned around and went back home.

The Danites Conquer Laish

²⁷The Danites, Micah's priest, and all that Micah had made, came to Laish, a city of quiet and unsuspecting people. They slaughtered them and burned down their city. ²⁸No one came to their rescue, because Laish was far from Sidon and they had no dealings with Aram. Laish was in the valley that belonged to Beth Rehob. The Danites rebuilt the city and lived in it. ²⁹Although the city used to be called Laish, they named the city Dan after their ancestor Dan the Israelite.

³⁰The Danites erected their own idol *to worship*. Jonathan son of Gershom,

son of Moses, and his sons served as priests to the tribe of the Danites until the time the nation went into captivity.*ᵇ* ³¹So they enshrined the idol Micah had made, and they made it their own even though the *proper* house of God*ᶜ* stood at Shiloh.

The Outrage of Gibeah

19 These were the days when there was no king ruling in Israel.

Now there was a Levite who lived in the remote hill country of Ephraim. He took as his mistress*ᵈ* a woman from Bethlehem in Judah, ²but she eventually was unfaithful. She deserted him and returned to her father's house in Bethlehem where she stayed for four months.

³The Levite*ᵉ* set out with his servant and a pair of donkeys to find her, win back her heart, and try to persuade her to return home with him. She received him into her father's house, and when the girl's father saw him, he received him warmly. ⁴His father-in-law, the girl's father, pressed him to stay, so the Levite stayed with him three days, and they ate and drank together.

⁵On the fourth day, early in the morning, he started to leave, but his father-in-law, the girl's father, insisted, "Eat something first to give you strength *for your journey*; then you can leave." ⁶After the two of them sat down and had breakfast together, the girl's father said to the Levite, "You might as well stay overnight and enjoy

---

a 18:21 They did this to defend themselves from an attack from the rear.
b 18:30 Either the captivity of Israel under Tiglath-pileser in 734 BC (see 2 Kings 15:29), or the exile after the fall of Samaria in 722 BC (see 2 Kings 17:6).
c 18:31 That is, the tabernacle Moses had made during their days in the wilderness.
d 19:1 Or "concubine."
e 19:3 Or "Her husband." However, the English terminology for marriage does not fit the cultural relationship presented in chs. 19–20.

yourself." ⁷The Levite started to leave, but his mistress' father kept urging him to stay until he turned back and spent another night there.

⁸Early in the morning of the fifth day, he was about to leave when the girl's father said, "Come, have breakfast." They ate together and lingered there until past noon. ⁹Then the Levite, his mistress, and his attendant started to leave. But his mistress' father said to him, "Look, the day is almost gone; stay another night here and enjoy yourself. Tomorrow, you can start early on your journey and head for home."

¹⁰But the Levite refused; he and his two donkeys, his servant, and his mistress set out and traveled as far as the vicinity of Jebus—that is, Jerusalem. ¹¹Late in the day, they were near Jebus, and the servant said to his master, "Let's go into this town of the Jebusites and spend the night there."

¹²His master said to him, "*No.* They are not of Israel. We will not enter a town of foreigners. We will go on to Gibeah. ¹³Come," he said to his attendant, "we'll go to another town and spend the night either in Gibeah or in Ramah." ¹⁴So they traveled on, and as the sun set, they were near Gibeah in the territory of Benjamin.

¹⁵They turned off there and entered Gibeah to spend the night. The Levite, *his servant, and his mistress* sat down in the town square, but nobody invited them indoors to spend the night. ¹⁶In the evening, an old man came into town from working in his field. This man was from the hill country of Ephraim and resided at Gibeah, where the townspeople were of the tribe of Benjamin. ¹⁷He happened to see the travelers sitting in the town square. The old man inquired, "Where do you come from? And where are you headed?"

¹⁸The Levite replied, "We're just passing through. We're traveling from Bethlehem in Judah to the other end of the hill country of Ephraim, where I live. I just made a journey to Bethlehem of Judah, and now we're on our way to the House of Yahweh,ᵃ but nobody has offered us hospitality. ¹⁹We have plenty of straw and feed for our donkeys, and bread and wine for me and the woman and for the attendant with us. *All we need is a roof over our heads*; we lack nothing."

²⁰"Rest easy," said the old man. "I'll take care of all your needs. You won't need to spend the night in the square." ²¹So the old man took them into his house. He prepared fodder for the donkeys; then they washed their feet, and they ate and drank together.

The Depraved Men of Gibeah

²²They were enjoying themselves when suddenly some perverted and depraved menᵇ of the town surrounded the house and pounded on the door. They called to the aged owner of the house, "Bring out the man you invited into your house so that we can have sex with him." ²³The owner of the house went out to reason with them. "Please, my friends," he said. "Don't commit such a wicked act. This man is my guest! Do not perpetrate this outrage. ²⁴Look, here are the man's mistress and my virgin daughter—let me bring them out to you. Do what you wish with them. Have your pleasure with them, but

---

a 19:18 Or "on our way to my house" (LXX). If the Hebrew is to be preferred, "the House of Yahweh" stood at Shiloh.

b 19:22 Or "sons of Belial," an evil spirit that dwelt in the underworld.

don't do such an outrageous thing to this man." ²⁵But the men refused to listen to him, so the Levite seized his mistress and pushed her out to them. They raped her repeatedly all night until morning and finally let her go when dawn broke.

²⁶At sunrise the woman staggered back to the house where her master had spent the night and collapsed at the entrance of the man's house. ²⁷When the Levite arose in the morning, he opened the doors of the house to start on his journey, and he saw his mistress lying at the entrance of the house with her hands on the threshold. ²⁸"Get up," he said to her, "it's time to go." But there was no response, for she was dead.ᵃ The man placed her body on the donkey and set out for home. ²⁹When he arrived home, he took a sword, cut the corpse of his mistress limb by limb into twelve pieces, and sent them, *one for each tribe*, throughout Israel. ³⁰And everyone who saw this horrible display, cried out, "Never have we seen such brutality take place from the day we came up from the land of Egypt to this day. We need to decide what we should do about this!"

Israel's Civil War

20 The Israelites were united as one man from Dan in the north to Beershebaᵇ in the south, including those living in Gilead on the other side of the Jordan. Everyone assembled together before Yahweh at Mizpah. ²All the leadersᶜ of all the people from the tribes of Israel presented themselves in the assembly of God's people, four hundred thousand fighting men armed with swords. ³The Benjamites heard that the Israelites had assembled at Mizpah. The Israelites said to them, "Tell us, how did this evil rape and murder happen?"

⁴The Levite, whose mistress had been murdered, replied, "My mistress and I stopped in Gibeah in *the territory of* Benjamin to spend the night. ⁵That night, the *depraved* men of Gibeah came after me to harm me, gathering around the house in the night where I was staying. They intended to kill me, but instead, they raped my mistress, and she died. ⁶This deliberate, outrageous act of depravity was committed in Israel! Therefore, I took her body and cut it in pieces and sent the pieces throughout every part of Israel. ⁷Now you Israelites must decide on a response! Let's do something about it here and now!"

Attempt at Extradition

⁸Then all the people stood in unison and declared, "None of us will go back to our cities or return to our homes. ⁹This is what we're going to do to Gibeah: We'll cast lots to *choose who will* fight against it. ¹⁰And we'll take a tenthᵈ of the men of our tribes of Israel to carry supplies for our forces. When our army arrives at Gibeah in the territory of Benjamin, we'll give them what they deserve for the outrageous,

---

a 19:28 The last clause, implied in the Hebrew, is taken from the Septuagint.

b 20:1 "From Dan . . . to Beersheba" is a merism, meaning every Israelite, for Dan was the northernmost city in Israel and Beersheba was in the far south.

c 20:2 The Hebrew reads "All the corners." This is a figure of speech for the tribal leaders.

d 20:10 Or "ten men of a hundred throughout all the tribes of Israel, and a hundred of a thousand, and a thousand of ten thousand."

disgraceful act they committed in Israel." ¹¹So all the men of Israel united as one man to come against Gibeah.ᵃ

¹²The Israelite tribes sent couriers throughout the tribe of Benjamin, saying, "What is this brutal crime that you have done? ¹³We demand that you surrender the depraved perverts from Gibeah *who took part in this evil act.* We'll put them to death and purge the evil out of Israel."

But the Benjamites refused to yield to the demands of their brothers the Israelites. ¹⁴Instead, the Benjamites gathered warriors from all their towns to come to Gibeah and fight *their brothers*, the Israelites. ¹⁵On that day, the Benjamites gathered a force from their towns of twenty-six thousand armed men, not including the seven hundred elite soldiers of Gibeah. ¹⁶Among Benjamin's elite troops, seven hundred were left-handed, and each of them could sling a rock and hit a target within a hairbreadth without missing. ¹⁷The tribes of Israel had four hundred thousand experienced soldiers armed with swords, not counting Benjamin's warriors.

The Israelites Inquire of God at Bethel
¹⁸*Before the battle*, the armies of Israel went to the house of Godᵇ to seek counsel from God. The Israelites inquired, "Which tribe gets to go first to battle the Benjamites?"

Yahweh answered, "Judah will go first."

¹⁹The Israelites got up the next morning and encamped near Gibeah. ²⁰The men of Israel took up battle positions against the Benjamites at Gibeah, ²¹but the Benjamites rushed out of the city, and slaughtered twenty-two thousand Israelites.

²²The men of Israel encouraged one another and resumed their battle positions where they had lined up the first day. ²³The Israelites wept before Yahweh until evening, and they inquired of Yahweh, "Should we go out again to battle with our brothers the Benjamites?" And Yahweh answered, "Yes, go back into the battle!"

²⁴The next day, the Israelites advanced toward the Benjamites. ²⁵When Benjamin marched out from Gibeah to engage them, they struck down another eighteen thousand Israelite swordsmen.

²⁶After losing again, the entire Israelite army went up to the house of God,ᶜ and they sat there fasting and weeping before Yahweh all day until evening and presented burnt offerings and peace offerings before Yahweh. ²⁷The Israelites inquired of Yahweh *at Shiloh*, for the ark of God's covenantᵈ was there in those days. ²⁸Phineas son of Eleazer, son of Aaron, ministered there before *the ark.*ᵉ He inquired *of Yahweh*, saying, "Should we resume our battle with our brothers, the Benjamites? Or should we quit?"

Yahweh answered, "Attack! For tomorrow I will give you the victory!"

---

a 20:11 It is striking that the tribes refused to come together to help one another throughout most of the book of Judges until this clear moment of uniting to destroy one of their own tribes.

b 20:18 Or "to Bethel."

c 20:26 The Latin Vulgate reads "the house of God at Shiloh." The Hebrew is *Bethel*, which means "the house of God."

d 20:27 This is the only mention of the ark in the book of Judges.

e 20:28 Or "it."

Victory

²⁹So Israel set ambushes all around Gibeah. ³⁰On the third day, one company of Israelites advanced against the Benjamites, deploying against Gibeah as they had before. ³¹This tactic drew the Benjamites out of the city to attack the advancing Israelite army, leaving the city unguarded. They began to inflict casualties on the Israelites as before. There they killed about thirty men of Israel.

³²The Benjamites boasted, "We are defeating them just as we did before!"

But *when the Benjamites had taken the bait*, the Israelites said, "Retreat, and draw them away from the city to the main roads." ³³Every Israelite rose from his position and took their assumed positions at Baal-Tamar. Then the Israelites who were hiding in ambush jumped up from their positions west of Gibeah.ᵃ ³⁴Ten thousand elite soldiers from all over Israel made their direct assault on Gibeah.

The fighting was fierce. And the Benjamites had no clue that disaster was at their doorstep. ³⁵On that day, Yahweh struck down the Benjamites before Israel. The Israelites slaughtered 25,100 swordsmen of Benjamin. ³⁶Then the Benjamites realized that they were defeated. The Israelites had moved back because they were depending on the surprise attack they had set up near Gibeah.

³⁷The men of Israel who had been waiting in ambush made a mad dash for Gibeah, attacked the city, and killed its inhabitants. ³⁸The Israelites' strategy was to send up a smoke signal from the city once they had sacked it, ³⁹and when the men of Israel saw the smoke signal, they would turn and rejoin the battle.

When the Benjamites had inflicted about thirty casualties on the men of Israel, they said, "Look, we are defeating them as we did in the first battle!"

⁴⁰But when the smoke signal began to go up from the city, the Benjamites looked behind them and saw the whole city going up in smoke!

⁴¹When the men of Israel turned back, the men of Benjamin saw that disaster had come upon them, and they panicked. ⁴²So they fled toward the wilderness, retreating from the Israelites, but the Israelites overtook them and killed them there. ⁴³Surrounding the Benjamites, the Israelites chased them and easily overran them in the area east of Gibeah.

Survivors

⁴⁴Eighteen thousand Benjamites died, all of them valiant fighters. ⁴⁵As they turned and fled in the wilderness to Rimmon Rock, the Israelites picked off another five thousand Benjamites on the main roads. They chased them as far as Gidom, killing two thousand more there. ⁴⁶That day, a total of twenty-five thousand sword-bearing Benjamites fell, all of them valiant fighters. ⁴⁷But six hundred men who had fled to the wilderness camped at Rimmon Rock and remained there for four months. ⁴⁸The men of Israel went back to the Benjamites and slaughtered every living thing in every town—men and beasts and all that were found, and they burned down every town they came across.

Israel's Compassion for the Tribe of Benjamin

21 The men of Israel had bound themselves by an oath at Mizpah: "Not one of us will give his

---

ᵃ 20:33 As translated from the Septuagint. The Hebrew is *Maareh-Geba*.

daughter in marriage to a Benjamite." ²And then the people came to Bethel and sat until evening before God, and they raised their voice with groaning and great weeping. ³They said, "Yahweh, the *true* God of Israel, we have lost one of our own tribes today. Why has this happened to Israel?"

⁴When the next day dawned, the people got up early, built an altar there, and offered burnt offerings and peace offerings. ⁵Then the Israelites asked one another, "Which tribe of Israel failed to appear in our assembly before Yahweh?" Under the terms of their solemn oath, whoever did not come before Yahweh at Mizpah should be put to death. ⁵Even so, the Israelites had compassion for their brothers of the tribe of Benjamin and were grieved deeply *over their loss.* They lamented, "One of our tribes has been eliminated from Israel this day. ⁷How can we provide wives for the few survivors since we have sworn by Yahweh that we will not give any of our daughters as wives for them?"

⁸Then they inquired, "Were there any from the tribes of Israel who did not come up before Yahweh at Mizpah?" They found out that no one from Jabesh-Gilead had come to the assembly. ⁹When the roll was called among the people, not one of the inhabitants of Jabesh-Gilead was there. ¹⁰So the people sent twelve thousand soldiers with the command: "Go to the inhabitants of Jabesh-Gilead and kill them with the sword, including the women and children. ¹¹This is what you are to do: exterminate every man and every woman who is not a virgin." ¹²And they found four hundred unmarried young virgins among those living in Jabesh-Gilead. They seized them and brought them to the camp at Shiloh in the land of Canaan.

¹³Then the whole congregation sent word to the Benjamites at Rimmon Rock and offered them peace.ᵃ ¹⁴The Benjamites returned, and the Israelites presented the young women they had spared at Jabesh-Gilead. But they were not a sufficient number of wives for them all.ᵇ

¹⁵The people were remorseful and had compassion on the tribe of Benjamin because Yahweh had taken out a tribe of Israel. ¹⁶The elders of the tribes said, "Where are we to find wives for the survivors of Benjamin since there are no more women left in their tribe?" ¹⁷And they said, "There must be heirs for the survivors of Benjamin to prevent the tribe from being wiped out from Israel. ¹⁸Yet we cannot give them any of our daughters as wives." For the Israelites had sworn, "A curse will rest on anyone who gives a wife to a Benjamite."

The Festival at Shiloh

¹⁹So they said, "Look, Yahweh's yearly festival is taking place at Shiloh, just north of Bethel, and east of the main road that goes up from Bethel to Shechem, and a little south of Lebonah."ᶜ ²⁰And they instructed the Benjamites, "Go and hide in the vineyards. ²¹Watch for the young women of Shiloh to come out for their dances. When they come out of the vineyards, grab

---

a 21:13 Or "proclaimed peace to them."

b 21:14 Apparently, there were only four hundred wives for six hundred men (20:47).

c 21:19 Some Jewish scholars believe the location described here was not Shiloh, but where the vineyards were. Lebonah is recognized as modern el-Lubban, about three miles northwest of Shiloh.

one of the young women of Shiloh to be your wife. Then go and live in your tribal land of Benjamin. ²²If their fathers or their brothers come to complain to us, we'll tell them, 'Do us this favor, please. Grant us permission for the Benjamites to keep them as wives because in battle we didn't seize them from you. And since you didn't give them to us, you're not guilty of breaking your oath.' "

²³So the Benjamites took as many wives as there were men from among the dancers, and they carried them away. Then they returned to their own territory and rebuilt towns to live in. ²⁴The Israelites dispersed by tribes and families, and they went out from there to their own territories.

²⁵In those days, Israel had no king, and everyone did whatever they wanted to do.

THE
PASSION
TRANSLATION

THE BOOK OF
RUTH

courageous love

BroadStreet
P U B L I S H I N G

RUTH

Introduction

AT A GLANCE

Author: Traditionally Samuel the prophet
Audience: Originally Israel, but this theological history speaks to everyone
Date: Difficult to determine with any accuracy, but likely sometime during the early monarchy (1030–970 BC) and about eighty to one hundred years before David
Type of Literature: Theological history
Major Themes: Outsiders and insiders, God's faithfulness, and God as Kinsman-Redeemer
Outline:
Love's Resolve: Ruth's Noble Choice — 1:1–22
Love's Response: Ruth's Lowly Service — 2:1–23
Love's Request: Ruth's Tender Appeal — 3:1–18
Love's Reward: Ruth's Forever Joy — 4:1–22

ABOUT RUTH

Behold the book of courageous love, which the German writer Goethe described as "the most charming whole"—and what a charming book it is! The book of Ruth may be delightfully short in length, yet it is grand and sweeping and universal in its literary narrative and revelation-insight into the heart of God.

Set in the time of the book of Judges, this popular Old Testament story has fascinated readers for thousands of years. Inspired by God and esteemed by Jews and Christians alike, Ruth is one of the loveliest epics of all time. It deserves to be honored as an enchanting and beautiful love story between Ruth and Boaz, an intermarriage of Jew and gentile. Its literary style is simple, fresh, and graceful. You will notice a stark contrast between reading the rough stories of conquest in the book of Judges and the subtlety and emotion of Ruth. It is a pastoral poem of only eighty-five verses, a sermon that preaches not mighty deeds but acts of supernatural love.

Ruth's undying devotion to her mother-in-law Naomi has gone down in Israel's history as an example of courage and selflessness. Ruth, the gentile from Moab, became a direct ancestor of David and of our Lord Jesus Christ. As we read the book of Ruth, we see that mercy triumphs over judgment, the least become the greatest, famine leads to harvest time, and despair turns into delight. In Judges we meet a woman who was as strong as a man (Deborah), and in Ruth we meet a man who was as tender as a woman (Boaz). Think of the four chapters of Ruth as the four acts of a play:

Act One: Naomi and Ruth
Act Two: Ruth Meets Boaz in the Harvest Fields
Act Three: Naomi Sends Ruth to the Threshing Floor
Act Four: Ruth and Boaz—Life Lived to the Full

All of these acts work together to paint a glorious whole that (1) emphasizes the faithfulness of one woman to another, mirroring the faithful heart of God himself; (2) reveals the sovereignty of God during desperate times; and (3) establishes the chain of genealogy leading to Israel's Messiah, who redeems not only Jews but gentiles as well.

There are two books in the Bible that are named after a woman: Ruth and Esther. Ruth was a gentile who married a Jew and became an ancestor of our Lord Jesus. Esther was a Jew who married a gentile and ended up saving the Jewish people. Ruth was also the great-grandmother of King David, who was Israel's greatest king and in the lineage of Jesus the Messiah. The story of Ruth begins with a famine and ends with the birth of a baby—the ultimate reversal that anticipates the Christ child who would be born into a spiritually impoverished world in order to rescue it from sinful ruin and redeem it unto the richness of God's everlasting life!

PURPOSE

Narratively, the book of Ruth takes place during the middle year in the book of Judges. This is important because the book is a microcosm of faithfulness to both God and neighbors during a period when "the Israelites did what was evil in the sight of Yahweh" (Judg. 2:11) and "everyone did whatever they wanted to do" (Judg. 21:25). Ruth is a stark contrast to Judges, showing that even as the nation rejected and abandoned Yahweh, a remnant of faithful individuals still existed—and one was a non-Jewish Moabite, no less!

Another purpose of the book of Ruth is to showcase the faithfulness of God. God is named twenty-five times in the four short chapters of Ruth, and time and time again those chapters reveal God's grace and faithfulness to Israelites in the midst of the chaotic period of the Judges. Part of this faithfulness is the establishment of the genealogy of David and Jesus, reminding the reader that Yahweh's sovereign hand was still firmly at the helm of his salvation plan, which is for all people—gentiles included. This sovereignty extends today over all our personal circumstances as well (even our failures) for his good purposes.

AUTHOR AND AUDIENCE

Although the book of Ruth doesn't claim a particular author, scholars have traditionally identified Samuel as the writer of this account of Naomi and Ruth, Ruth and Boaz. The book follows Judges in the canon of Scripture for a reason: it was written to offer a stark contrast to the disobedience and disastrous destruction of Israel's unfaithfulness. The author's moving narrative is a powerful illustration of common-folk faithfulness to Yahweh that has resonated with the people of God through the centuries.

For generations, Jews have read Ruth publicly in their congregations during the Feast of Pentecost following Passover. And Christians have looked to its pages for reminders of God's special care over our lives, his acceptance of outsiders into his family, and his redeeming love that was ultimately fulfilled in Ruth's very own descendent, Jesus Christ. In the end, the book of Ruth paints a beautiful picture of the church of Jesus Christ, reminding us that it is made up of gentiles who are brought into God's covenant of grace through the ultimate Kinsman-Redeemer.

MAJOR THEMES

Outsiders Become Insiders. The book of Ruth presents to the world a moving picture of God as the God of the outsider as much as the insider. For Ruth, a Moabite from a gentile nation, is not only a positive example of faithfulness to the law in contrast to Israel's idolatry and faithless living but also the model convert, pledging to Naomi that her mother-in-law's "God will now be my God" (Ruth 1:16) at a time when Israel had abandoned Yahweh. As a result, Yahweh's favor was clearly upon her. He turned his face toward her in faithfulness even though she had been outside his covenant people.

This portrait of God is made complete by the church of Jesus Christ. His desire is that all people—Jews and gentiles alike—would be part of one family: his family! Made up of gentiles who are brought into God's covenant of grace through Boaz, the kinsman-redeemer, the church offers the radical invitation to people from every tribe and nation, language and background to join God's family, with Christ as the head.

Consider this: a non-Jewish outsider played a pivotal role in God's promise of salvation, standing in the long line of women leading to the birth of the Redeemer, Jesus Christ. This paints in bright, bold, beautiful colors the revelation-truth that God not only invites outsiders into his work, beckoning them into his covenant of grace, but uses outsiders to do his work, unfolding his heart along the way.

Our Circumstances, God's Faithfulness. After beginning the story that unfolds in the book of Ruth, one could understandably mistake it for a book of abandonment. In the opening verses we find severe famine, the death of husbands, childlessness and barrenness, and familial abandonment. One of the main characters even changed her name to Bitter, for she believed God had dealt her "a bitter blow," bringing her back to her homeland "empty and destitute" (Ruth 1:20, 21). However, the reader would be mistaken to assume this is the crux of the matter.

Instead, this is a love story as much between God and man as it is between man and woman. For the same opening words of this matchless narrative direct the reader's attention to the divine sovereignty orchestrating the events that follow: *Elimelech* means "my God is King," immediately introducing the God who rules over our circumstances with care. God himself is even identified as *Shaddai,* which can mean "God of the holy mountain," "God of the wilderness," "God the destroyer of enemies," "God the all-sufficient One," "God the nurturer of babies [the breasted One]," "God the almighty," "the sovereign God," or "the God who is more than enough."

Some have understood the key verse to be 2:12, where, in talking with Ruth about her sacrifice for Naomi, Boaz says, "Because of what you've done, may you have a full and rich reward from Yahweh, the God of Israel, under whose wings you have come to find shelter!" Ruth found herself under the sheltering wings of God, and so do we! Although our circumstances may seem hopeless, God is the all-sufficient One who is more than enough, faithfully nurturing us as needy infants, fighting our enemies standing in our paths, and walking with us through whatever wilderness in which we find ourselves.

The book of Ruth reveals the sovereignty of God in a special way, bringing the lens of revelation-insight to bear on the singular circumstances of a pair of women and showcasing how he overrules all circumstances (even our failures) for his good purposes. Nothing just happens; God is in control of your life! God's plans and purposes take us from emptiness to fullness, poverty to riches. You can find hope in the detours of life, no matter how dire. The most painful time of Ruth's life became her most pivotal, propelling her to a destiny she never would have imagined.

We find that God's ultimate faithfulness, grace, and loyalty often unfold in relationships between people. Ruth is the epitome of this grace-gift offered to each and every one of us, for her name includes the meanings "close friend," "neighbor," and "shepherdess." In Hebrew, Ruth sounds like "refreshing"— which she was for her mother-in-law Naomi. God continues to unfold his faithfulness to the world using people to refresh the weary, extend neighbor-love to the downtrodden, and befriend those who feel abandoned.

God's Kinsman-Redeeming Love. There is a special Hebrew word that sits at the center of this matchless story, one that also sits at the center of the heart of God. The word is *ga'al*, which means "kinsman-redeemer." This term is used eleven times throughout Ruth and signifies a legal function of a near relative. If a widow was childless, under the law, a close male relative could "redeem" her through marriage and buy back her property. This kinsman-redeemer ensured that the widow's inheritance rights were not lost, and he provided for her off-spring. Naomi is a prime example, for when her husband and sons died, she was destitute. Yet she had near relatives living in Bethlehem who would qualify to be her kinsman-redeemers, one of whom was Boaz.

Naomi isn't the only example of destitution. Every person on the planet is in need of a redeemer to save them. Boaz is a picture of our Lord Jesus Christ. Jesus is our Kinsman-Redeemer! He is a kinsman, for he took upon himself our nature of flesh and blood to take away our curse (see Gal. 3:13; Heb. 2:11) and our slavery to sin. He is the appointed heir of all things (see Heb. 1:1–3). He has perpetuated the nature, character, and kingdom of God upon the earth. He has perpetuated God's name (see Eph. 1:20–23; Phil. 2:6–11). Jesus Christ is seen in the book of Ruth as:

The Bread of Abundance — Ruth 1:6; John 6:48
The Mighty Man of Wealth — Ruth 2:1; Phil. 4:19
The One from Bethlehem — Ruth 2:4; Mic. 5:2; Matt. 2:5–6
The Lord of the Harvest — Ruth 2:4–17; James 5:7
The Full Reward — Ruth 2:12; Rev. 22:12

The Kinsman-Redeemer — Ruth 2:20; Gal. 3:13
The One whose Name is Famous — Ruth 4:14; Eph. 1:20–23; Phil. 2:1–11
The Restorer and Sustainer of Life — Ruth 4:15; John 11:25; Heb. 1:3

Undoubtedly, the book of Ruth contains one of the most delightful love stories of the Old Testament. It is offered up from God's heart to yours as a matchless picture of redeeming love. Ruth's love for Naomi manifested itself in her faithfulness, care, and protection, standing by her mother-in-law's side when Naomi was left abandoned. Boaz (the son of Rahab, see Matt. 1:5) is a key figure in the story of Ruth because he acted as a kinsman-redeemer, protecting Elimelech's family inheritance by marrying Ruth. These actions illustrate the redeeming love not only between two women and between a man and a woman but also between humanity and Yahweh—the *ga'al* of the world.

RUTH

Courageous Love

Tragedy Comes to a Family

1 [1-2] During the era when champion-deliverers ruled in Israel,[a] a severe famine overtook the land. Elimelech,[b] a man of importance,[c] left Bethlehem and immigrated to the country[d] of Moab. He took with him his wife Naomi[e] and their two sons, Mahlon[f] and Chilion.[g] They belonged to the clan of Ephrath from Bethlehem in Judah. While residing in Moab, [3] Elimelech died and left his widow Naomi alone with her two sons. [4] The two sons both married Moabite[h] women, Orpah[i] and Ruth.[j] About ten years later, [5] Mahlon and Chilion also died and left Naomi all alone without husband or sons.

---

a 1:1–2 The period of the champion-deliverers, or judges, covered about three hundred years (1400–1100 BC).

b 1:1–2 *Elimelech* means "my God is King." He was a descendant of Nahshon, a prince of the tribe of Judah (see Num. 1:7), and an ancestor of David. Elimelech takes his family and leaves the "house of bread" (Bethlehem).

c 1:1–2 The Hebrew word *ish* means "a certain man." In Rabbinic literature, *ish* refers to a man of importance either in learning or in social status (i.e., a wealthy man).

d 1:1–2 Or "fields of Moab." Moab was the son of Lot's incestuous relationship with his daughter (see Gen. 19:30–37). Moab and his tribe lived east of the Dead Sea.

e 1:1–2 *Naomi* means "pleasant," "gracious," "sweet," "agreeable," "delightful," and "unsurpassed in beauty."

f 1:1–2 *Mahlon* means "ill [sickly]," "worn out," "afflicted," or "wounded." Ruth was married to Mahlon, a picture of the law that is unable to save us (see Acts 13:39; Rom. 3:20; 7:9–11; 8:3; Heb. 7:19). But Ruth (and we) will find another spouse (Boaz/Jesus).

g 1:1–2 *Chilion* means "destruction" or "consumption."

h 1:4 According to Deuteronomy 23:3–6, the Israelites were not to marry with the Moabites, and the people of God were never to welcome the Moabites' descendants into their families. However, it is the graciousness of Yahweh, who excludes such persons through sin, that will welcome through his abounding love and kindness the very ones he excluded. And Yahweh would go further in that this family line would include David, Solomon, and Jesus, and thus establish an eternal throne and home by turning the cursed into the blessed.

i 1:4 *Orpah*, a homonym, can mean either "fawn" or "[back of the] neck." The proper name Orpah sounds like the Hebrew word for "rebellious." Orpah turned her back on Naomi and returned to her home. Orpah was a good woman but not as faithful and resolute as Ruth.

j 1:4 The Hebrew name *Ruth* has many possible meanings, including "close friend," "neighbor," "shepherdess," "beautiful," "delightful," "pleasing," and "satisfied." *Ruth* also sounds like the Hebrew word for "refreshing." The name Ruth occurs 12 times in this book. However, the Hebrew word *ruth* (or a variant form) is used 187 times in the Old Testament. See also Matt. 1:5.

Naomi and Ruth Return to Bethlehem

[6]Sometime later, Naomi heard that Yahweh had visited his people and blessed them with an abundant harvest;[a] so she decided to leave Moab with her daughters-in-law. [7]With Orpah and Ruth at her side, Naomi began her journey to return to the land of Judah. [8]*But soon* Naomi said to them, "Each of you, go back to your mother's home. May Yahweh show his loyal love and kindness to you—the same loyal love and kindness you've shown to me and to those who have died. [9]And may Yahweh give you another husband and cause you to find rest in a *happy* home."

Then Naomi *tenderly embraced* Orpah and Ruth and kissed them goodbye, but they wailed and sobbed. [10]*Through their tears,* they said to her, "No! We want to be with you and go with you to your people."

[11]"My daughters, you must go back," Naomi answered. "Why do you want to come with me? Do you think I could have sons again to give you new husbands?[b] [12]Turn around my daughters and go back home, for I'm too old to marry again. Even if I thought there was still hope for me, and married today and gave birth to sons, [13]would you wait until they had grown up? Should you live for so many years without husbands? No, my daughters, *you must not return with me.* My life is too bitter for you to share it with me because Yahweh has brought calamity to my life!"[c]

[14]When they heard Naomi's words, Orpah and Ruth wailed and sobbed again. Then Orpah embraced and kissed her mother-in-law goodbye *and went back home,*[d] but Ruth clung tightly to Naomi and refused to let go of her.[e] [15]Naomi said, "Ruth, listen. Your sister-in-law is going back *to Moab* to her people and to her gods.[f] Now go with her."

---

a 1:6 Or "Yahweh had visited [observed, taken note of] his people and given them food." It is notable that, while in the law, famine is attributed to unfaithfulness and fruitfulness to faithfulness, here Yahweh simply blessed the people in the days of the judges when everyone did whatever they wanted to do. This reveals the mercies of Yahweh, who still brings sunrise and rainfall to all, whether they do good or evil (see Matt. 5:45). The theme of the goodness and faithfulness of Yahweh runs throughout this book.

b 1:11 Naomi was referring to the law of levirate marriage, where the next closest relative marries a widow to produce a child and heir for the deceased husband so that their inheritance will not be lost.

c 1:13 Or "the hand of Yahweh has gone out against me."

d 1:14 Orpah never saw the face of her kinsman-redeemer. She died as she lived—in Moab. See Luke 9:62; John 6:63–69.

e 1:14 The Hebrew verb for "cling tightly" is *davqah.* It carries the sense of permanent bonding (as with adhesive). The term is used in the Bible for covenantal devotion and clinging to God or a person. Loaded with spiritual meaning to a Hebrew speaker, this is the major term for spiritual cleaving to God in Rabbinic literature. In a sense, Ruth was entering into a covenant with Naomi. The Targum states, using several sources, that Ruth truly desired to be a proselyte to the Jewish faith. (See *Ruth R. 2.20; B. Yev. 47b;* and *Rashi* on 1:16–17.) The Jewess Naomi is a type of Israel, and the gentile Ruth is a type of the church. As Ruth stayed connected to Naomi (Israel), Naomi would lead her to Boaz (a type of our Kinsman-Redeemer, Jesus).

f 1:15 One of the gods of the Moabites was Chemosh (see Num. 21:29; 1 Kings 11:33). On our road to full restoration, we all face a choice either to return to Judah (the land of praise) and to Boaz (Jesus) or to turn back to other gods and the old order.

[16]*But tearfully,* Ruth insisted, "Please don't ask me *again* to leave you! I want to go with you and stay with you. Wherever you go, I will go; wherever you live, I will live. Your people will now be my people, and your God will now be my God.*a* [17]Wherever you die, I will die there, too;*b* that's where your people will bury me—*next to you.* Nothing but death itself will separate me from you, so help me God!"

[18]When Naomi realized that Ruth's heart was set on going with her, she said nothing more.

Naomi Returns to Bethlehem with Ruth

[19]Naomi and Ruth traveled together *from Moab* until they came to Bethlehem. The entire town was buzzing*c* when they heard they had arrived! Astounded, the women of the town said to one another, "Is this really Naomi, *who left us so long ago?*"

[20]"Please don't call me Naomi anymore," she insisted. "Instead, call me Marah,*d* because Almighty God*e* has dealt me a bitter blow. [21]When I left here, my heart was full*f* and content *with my family,* but Yahweh has brought me back empty and destitute. Why call me by my name, 'Pleasant,' when Yahweh has opposed me, and Almighty God has brought me so much trouble?"

[22]So Naomi returned to her village with Ruth, her Moabite daughter-in-law.*g* They arrived in Bethlehem just as the barley harvest had begun.*h*

Ruth Gathers Grain in the Field of Boaz

2 Naomi's *deceased* husband, Elimelech, had a very wealthy relative, an honorable and prominent man*i* in

---

a 1:16 See 1 Kings 22:4; 2 Kings 3:7; 2 Chron. 18:3; Jer. 31:33; 32:38. Ruth uses the name "Shaddai" (the Almighty) for God.

b 1:17 The old Ruth died. We, too, have been crucified with Christ. His cross was our cross (see Rom. 6:1–23; Gal. 2:20).

c 1:19 Or "they were beside themselves."

d 1:20 Or "Mara [a form of Miriam]." *Mara* means "bitter." *Naomi* means "pleasant." Life sometimes takes us from seasons of great pleasure into a wilderness where we drink "bitter waters." Yet in the wilderness, God will meet us and turn our bitterness into something sweet. See Ex. 15:22–27; Judg. 14:8; Rom. 8:28.

e 1:20 Or "Shaddai." This name of God is found forty-eight times in the Bible, with thirty-one of them in Job and six in Genesis. It is the most frequently used name for God prior to Moses' reception of the law at Sinai. *Shaddai* is taken from a Hebrew root word that carries multiple expressive meanings. It can mean "God of the holy mountain," "God of the wilderness," "God the destroyer of enemies," "God the all-sufficient One," "God the nurturer of babies [the breasted One]," "God the almighty," "the sovereign God," or "the God who is more than enough."

f 1:21 That is, blessed with husband and sons.

g 1:22 Naomi's sojourn in Moab lasted about ten years.

h 1:22 The season of famine had ended, and the season of harvest had begun. In Israel, the harvest season for barley is from mid-March through mid-April, the time of the Feast of Passover.

i 2:1 The description "honorable and prominent" comes from the Hebrew word *chayil.* *Chayil* can also mean "victorious," "powerful," "like an army," or "full of substance." Thus Boaz was a "mighty man of valor" or "valiant warrior." (We might say, "a knight in shining armor.")

Bethlehem named Boaz.*a* *2*One day Ruth the Moabite said to Naomi, "Let me go to the fields and pick up the leftover grain. Maybe someone will be kind enough*b* to let me gather the grain he leaves behind."

Naomi said to her, "Go, my daughter." *3*So Ruth went to the fields to gather the grain the reapers left behind.*c* It just so happened*d* that she found herself working at the edges of a field belonging to Boaz*e* of the family of Elimelech. *4*At that moment, Boaz came from Bethlehem *to survey his harvest.* He greeted the harvesters, "May Yahweh be with you."*f* They replied, "May Yahweh bless you." *5*Noticing Ruth, Boaz asked his foreman in charge of the harvesters,*g* "Who is that young woman over there?"*h*

*6*The foreman answered, "She's a Moabite girl who came back with Naomi from the country of Moab. *7*She asked for permission to gather the grain left behind by the reapers. Except for one short break, she's been on her feet working in the field since early this morning."

*8*Boaz walked over to Ruth and said, "Listen, my daughter, don't leave this field to glean somewhere else. Stay here in my field and follow the young women who work for me. *9*Watch my harvesters to see into which fields they go to cut grain, and follow them. When you're thirsty, go and drink from the water jugs that the young men have filled. I've warned the young men not to bother you."

*10*Astounded, Ruth bowed low with her face to the ground, and said to him, "I'm a foreigner. Why have you been so kind and taken notice of me?"

*11*Boaz answered, "I've heard all about what you've done for your mother-in-law since the death of your husband. I know your story—how you left your father and mother and your native land and came to a people and a culture that must seem strange to you. *12*May Yahweh reward you for your sacrifices, and because of what you've done, may you have a full and rich reward

---

a 2:1 *Boaz* means "strength." He is a prophetic figure of Jesus Christ, our older Brother (see Rom. 8:29; Heb. 2:6–13) and Kinsman-Redeemer (see 1 Pet. 1:18–19). "Boaz" was also the name of the left pillar of Solomon's Temple (2 Chron. 3:17). Boaz was a wealthy nobleman. Similarly, Jesus Christ is indeed the One who has made us "rich beyond measure" (2 Cor. 8:9; see Eph. 1:3).

b 2:2 Or "Maybe I will find grace with someone." See Gen. 6:8.

c 2:3 That there was grain left behind for the poor to pick up speaks to the covenant faithfulness of Boaz, who had instructed his workers to keep the commandment to care for the poor according to Deut. 24:19–22. God commanded this also to remind Israel that they were once slaves in Egypt who depended upon the generosity of Yahweh to feed them.

d 2:3 The Hebrew reads "her chance" or "chanced."

e 2:3 The fields of Boaz may have included the shepherd's field where the angels of glory announced Jesus' birth. See Luke 2:8–14.

f 2:4 Jesus, too, came from Bethlehem to bless his harvesters. Today's "harvesters" are the evangelists who go to the nations of the earth to preach the gospel of Jesus Christ. May Yahweh's blessing indeed be upon them as they seek a global harvest of souls.

g 2:5 The Holy Spirit is the Lord of the Harvest who equips and places each believer in the harvest fields where we will be the most effective. See Matt. 9:38.

h 2:5 Or "To whom does that young woman belong?" Ruth could have been between twenty-four and twenty-nine years old at this time. Boaz may have been in his forties.

from Yahweh, the God of Israel, under whose wings you have come to find shelter!"

[13]Ruth replied, "May I continue to find favor in your sight, kind sir. You have spoken to my heart kind and reassuring words that comfort me, even though I am not *as worthy as* one of your servant girls."

[14]At mealtime, Boaz said to her, "Come here[a] and eat with us. Here is bread, and wine to dip it in."[b] Ruth immediately sat down with the workers. Boaz handed her some roasted grain, and she ate all she wanted until she was satisfied—she even had some left over.

[15]After she had returned to gather grain, Boaz instructed his young men, "Let her glean even among the standing sheaves, and don't disgrace her. [16]Pull out from the bundles some handfuls of grain and drop them on purpose[c] for her to gather, and don't bother her."

[17]So Ruth gathered grain in Boaz's field until evening. When she threshed out what she had gathered, it came to more than half a bushel of barley.[d]

[18]She carried it back to town and showed her mother-in-law how much she had gleaned. Then Ruth also took out the roasted grain she had saved from mealtime and shared it with Naomi.

[19]Her mother-in-law asked Ruth, "Where did you gather *all this from*? In whose field did you work? May Yahweh bless the man who showed you special attention."

She told her mother-in-law about all that happened that day, and said, "The man in whose field I gathered grain today is Boaz."

[20]Naomi said to Ruth, "Yahweh's loving-kindness has not left us either through life or through death! Boaz is closely related to us. He is a kinsman-redeemer[e] of our family. May Yahweh *greatly* bless *Boaz!*"[f]

[21]Ruth the Moabite responded, "He even said to me, 'Stay close by my servants until they have finished all my harvest.' "

[22]Naomi replied, "It is best, my daughter, that you stay near his young women, otherwise you'll *be alone* and might be bothered in someone else's

---

a 2:14 Or "draw near."

b 2:14 Read this sentence again and picture Jesus, your heavenly Boaz, inviting you to have communion (bread and wine) with him.

c 2:16 These "handfuls of grain" dropped "on purpose" can signify the many extra blessings that fall upon us each day. We gather truths from Scripture for our needs each day, like Ruth gathered grain (see Matt. 13:1–23). Jesus, our heavenly Boaz, drops handfuls of revelation on purpose for us to gather an abundant supply. He wants us to know that he will provide all we need to meet the challenges of life. See 1 Kings 8:56; Ps. 103:5; Eph. 1:3; 3:20–21; Phil. 4:19.

d 2:17 Or "an ephah of barley." An ephah would weigh about thirty pounds.

e 2:20 The Hebrew term *ga'al* means "kinsman-redeemer." This term is used in various forms ten times throughout chs. 3–4. *Ga'al* signifies a legal function performed by a near relative. If a widow was childless, a close male relative was empowered to "redeem" her through marriage and buy back her property (see Lev. 25:25). This kinsman-redeemer ensured that the widow would not lose her inheritance rights and provided her with offspring. In the case of Naomi, she had other near relatives living in Bethlehem who would qualify to be her kinsman-redeemers, meaning that Boaz was perhaps one of several candidates.

f 2:20 The Hebrew is somewhat ambiguous: "May he [Boaz] be blessed by Yahweh, whose loyal love has not forsaken the living or the dead."

field." ²³So Ruth worked alongside the young women who served Boaz. She lived with her mother-in-law and gleaned in Boaz's fields until the end of the barley and wheat harvests.

Ruth and Boaz at the Threshing Floor

3 One day, Naomi said to Ruth: "I want to see you marry so that you'll be happy and secure.ᵃ ²Now listen, a man named Boaz is our relative.ᵇ You worked with his servant girls in his fields. This evening, he'll be winnowing barley on the threshing floor.ᶜ ³Now, take a bath and put on some nice perfume.ᵈ Dress in your best clothesᵉ and go to the threshing floor, but don't let him know you're there until he's had

plenty to eat and drink. ⁴Watch closely to see where he lies down.ᶠ Then go, uncover his feet, and lie down there.ᵍ He will tell you what to do."

⁵Ruth answered, "I'll do everything you've told me."ʰ

⁶That evening, Ruth went down to the threshing floor and did all her mother-in-law had told her to do. ⁷After his evening meal, Boaz was in a good mood. He went to lie down at the far end of the grain pileⁱ and fell fast asleep. Ruth quietly tiptoed over to him, uncovered his feet, and lay down.

⁸Around midnight, Boaz was startled, and he awoke. He was surprised to find a woman lying at his feet. ⁹"Who are you?" Boaz asked.

---

a 3:1 The Hebrew text is literally "Should I not seek rest [a home] for you so it may go well with you?"

b 3:2 Boaz is a picture of our Lord Jesus Christ. Jesus is our Kinsman-Redeemer. He is a kinsman, for he took upon himself flesh and blood to take away our curse (see Gal. 3:13; Heb. 2:11) and our slavery to sin. He is the appointed heir of all things (see Heb. 1:1–3). He has perpetuated the nature, character, and kingdom of God upon the earth. He has perpetuated God's name (see Eph. 1:20–23; Phil. 2:6–11).

c 3:2 Likewise, in the "evening" of this age, our heavenly Boaz is at his threshing floor separating the chaff from the grain (see Amos 9:9; Mal. 3:1–3; Matt. 13:1–58; Luke 3:16–17).

d 3:3 Or "anoint yourself." In this final season of harvest, we too are to wash ourselves by the Word of God (see John 15:3; Eph. 5:25–27), and we also will receive the anointing of the Holy Spirit through prayer and devotion before the Lord.

e 3:3 The believer today wears their "best clothes" when putting on Christ (cf. Rom. 13:11–14). We are clothed in his perfect righteousness. Then we go down humbly to meet our Beloved at his threshing floor.

f 3:4 We need to note the place where our Boaz lay down (the cross and empty tomb). He lay down to rest in his finished work (see John 19:30; Heb. 4:10).

g 3:4 Symbolically, we too uncover (reveal) his feet, his walk of holiness and love. We appropriate his grace to walk in his ways when we take our place resting with him in his finished work. We are a company of lovers resting at his feet—"a feet company" who will walk like him. All we have to do is listen and obey him, for he will tell us what to do (see John 7:17). Jesus will have a loving bride worshiping at his feet at midnight.

h 3:5 Like Mary, the mother of Jesus, Ruth accepted what the Lord had for her. "May everything you have told me come to pass" (Luke 1:38).

i 3:7 At the end of this age there will be a great harvest, a "pile of grain" brought to our Lord Jesus Christ.

"I am Ruth, your servant girl," she answered. "Spread the corner[a] of your garment over me[b] because you are a close relative by marriage, one who is my kinsman-redeemer."[c]

[10]Boaz said: "Dear woman, may Yahweh bless you, for this act of kindness you are showing me exceeds the kindness you have shown *to Naomi.* You didn't search for a young man to marry, either rich or poor. [11]My daughter, don't worry. I promise to do everything you ask, because everyone knows[d] you're a brave woman of noble character.[e] [12]It's true that I am a kinsman-redeemer, but you have a closer kinsman-redeemer than I. [13]Stay here tonight,[f] *and I will protect you.* In the morning, we'll see if he's willing to redeem you.[g] If he does, good;

let him. But if he refuses to redeem you, then I promise, as surely as Yahweh lives, I will. So sleep here until morning."

[14]So Ruth stayed near Boaz's feet that night. She awoke before it was light enough for anyone to recognize her. Boaz thought, "No one must know that a woman visited me at the threshing floor." [15]*As Ruth was about to leave,* Boaz said to her, "Here, bring me the cloak you're wearing and hold it open."

As she held it open, Boaz poured six measures[h] of barley into it. He then helped place it on her head to carry, and she went back to Bethlehem.

[16]When Ruth returned to her mother-in-law, Naomi asked her, "How did it go, my dear daughter? *How did Boaz receive you?*"

---

a 3:9 The garments of faithful Israelites included a tassel at each of the four corners according to Num. 15:38; Deut. 22:12. This was an outward sign of covenant faithfulness, which Ruth seemed to acknowledge when she asked Boaz to cover her with the "corner" of his garment. She knew him to be faithful to Yahweh in other ways, and in this fashion, she trusted he would be faithful to the covenant toward her and Naomi. Boaz would redeem what Yahweh sought to be redeemed, and Ruth was seeking the fulfillment of the promise to be "under the wing" of Yahweh's faithfulness. This same "corner" is the one that the woman with the issue of blood took hold of on Jesus' garment in Matt. 9:20. While the teachers of the law in Jesus' day wore their tassels extra long, as if they were extra faithful to Yahweh, the tassels at the edge of Jesus' garments conveyed the blessing of healing, in testimony to the faithfulness of Yahweh himself.

b 3:9 Or "spread your wing [or wings] over me." This was likely a figure of speech for "Please marry me." Ruth's actions were symbolic of a marriage proposal. Jesus spreads his wings over us and heals us (see Mal. 4:2; Luke 8:44). His mantle (cloak) of anointing covers us.

c 3:9 That is, "one who has the right to marry me." Ruth knew who she was. She boldly requested grace from Boaz. We too come boldly to the throne of grace. Ruth had no false humility; she was sincere and confident as she spoke to Boaz. She called herself his "servant." For the word "servant," the Greek Septuagint uses the word *doulos,* which means "a bondservant unto death."

d 3:11 Ruth, the bride, could not hide her true character. See Matt. 5:13–16; cf. Acts 26:26.

e 3:11 Or "virtuous woman." This is the Hebrew word *chayil,* which is often used in connection with military prowess and moral excellence. See the first footnote on 2:1. We can see Ruth as a metaphor for the "last-days" church, the virtuous, overcoming bride of Jesus Christ. See Eph. 5:25–27.

f 3:13 Ruth rested at Boaz's feet through the dark night until morning. See Ps. 23:2; Song. 1:16; Matt. 11:28; Heb. 4:1; 6:13–20.

g 3:13 That is, "we will see if he chooses to marry you."

h 3:15 The Hebrew text does not state what measure is involved, but it had to be an amount that a woman could carry on her head or shoulder. The majority of modern scholars conclude that the amount of barley could have exceeded fifty pounds. If so, this impressive amount of barley was designed to impress both Ruth and Naomi with Boaz's generosity and his determination to help them.

Ruth told Naomi everything that he did for her. ¹⁷She added, "Boaz gave me all this barley, saying, 'You must not go home empty-handed without a gift for your mother in law.' "

¹⁸Naomi answered, "My daughter, wait here until you see what happens. Boaz will not rest until he has finished*ᵃ* doing what he promised he would do today."

Boaz the Kinsman-Redeemer

4 No sooner had Boaz gone up to the city gate and sat down*ᵇ* when the kinsman-redeemer*ᶜ* of whom Boaz had spoken came passing by. Boaz called to him, "Come over here, friend; sit down with me. *We have some business to attend to.*" So the man went over and sat down.

²Then Boaz invited ten*ᵈ* men of the city council and said, "*Please,* sit down here with us." After they were seated, ³Boaz turned to the kinsman-redeemer and said, "*Sir,* Naomi has returned from the country of Moab, and she's selling the piece of property that belonged to our relative Elimelech. ⁴So I thought you ought to know about it.*ᵉ* Buy it if you want. We can make it official in the presence of those here and in the presence of the elders of our people. As the kinsman-redeemer, you have the first right of refusal. So redeem it if you choose to, but if not, tell me so I will know, *as I am next in line.*"

The man replied, "I'll redeem it."

⁵Then Boaz added, "The day you buy the field from the hand of Naomi, you also acquire Ruth the Moabite,*ᶠ* the widow of the dead.*ᵍ* Therefore, it will be your responsibility *to father a child* in order to maintain the dead man's name on his inheritance."

⁶At this, the kinsman-redeemer balked and said, "In that case, I'm not able to redeem it for myself without risking my own inheritance. Take my purchase option of redemption yourself, for I can't do it."*ʰ*

---

a 3:18 Jesus has "finished" all he needed to do to redeem us fully. We rest from our own labors in his finished work. The Hebrew word for "finished" is *kallah,* which is a homonym of the word for "bride." See John 19:30.

b 4:1 Jesus, our heavenly Boaz, went "up" in his ascension and "sat down" at the right hand of God in glory.

c 4:1 This man was in the position to be a redeemer; however, in the context of the business at the gate, he had not yet exercised his right to redeem and thus had not yet become the kinsman-redeemer in fact. See vv. 3, 4, 6.

d 4:2 The number ten is recognized biblically as the number of human responsibility (Ten Commandments). The law kept Ruth out (see Deut. 23:3). The law serves to add guilt to the human condition. Boaz prefigured Jesus, our gracious Kinsman-Redeemer, who has done for us what the law cannot (see John 1:17; Rom. 8:3–5; 2 Cor. 3:6).

e 4:4 See Jer. 32:6–12.

f 4:5 Boaz mentioned the land (field) before he mentioned Ruth (the treasure). Boaz was not afraid to pay the price to acquire both the field and the treasure. See Matt. 13:44.

g 4:5 The law is weak and sickly, like Ruth's deceased husband, Mahlon (see 1:1–2; Rom. 7:1–4).

h 4:6 The summary statement of the law is "I can't do it." Grace, not law-keeping, is our only hope of salvation (see Eph. 2:7–8; Titus 3:5). This man desired to preserve his name in Israel by not marrying the Moabite woman. However, his name has been lost. Boaz, on the other hand, not only preserved his name in this story that is read every year in the Jewish celebrations, but he also had his name inscribed upon the pillar in the temple of Yahweh built by Solomon. It is not in seeking to preserve our own name but seeking Yahweh's faithfulness that we receive an eternal name and are placed as pillars in the temple of our God.

[7](At that time in Israel, in order to finalize a transaction concerning redeeming and transferring property, a man would customarily remove a sandal[a] and give it to the other party, making the contract legally binding.) [8]So when the kinsman-redeemer said to Boaz, "Take my purchase option of redemption for yourself," he took off his sandal *and gave it to Boaz.*[b] [9]Then Boaz turned to the elders and announced publicly, "Today, you are witnesses that I have purchased from the hand of Naomi all that belonged to Elimelech and all that belonged to Chilion and Mahlon. [10]I have also acquired Ruth the Moabite, Mahlon's widow, to be my wife. I *will raise children with her* who will maintain the dead man's name on his inheritance so that the name of the dead may not be cut off from his village and from his family line. Today, you are witnesses of this transaction."

[11]Then all the elders and all the people who were at the gate said: "We are witnesses. May Yahweh make the woman who is coming into your house like Rachel and Leah, both of whom built up the house of Israel. May you become famous in Bethlehem! May you become very prosperous! [12]And may Yahweh give you children by this young woman, and through them, may your family be like the family of Perez, whom Tamar bore to Judah!"[c]

Boaz and Ruth Marry

[13]So Boaz and Ruth married, and they became one as husband and wife. Yahweh opened Ruth's womb, and she bore a son. [14]Then the women of Bethlehem blessed Naomi: "Praise Yahweh, who never abandoned you nor withheld from you a kinsman-redeemer! And may his name be famous in Israel![d] [15]May this child renew your life and sustain you in your old age! May your daughter-in-law, who loves you dearly, be more to you than seven sons could ever be, for she has given you a wonderful grandchild!"

[16]Then Naomi took her grandson and cuddled him in her arms and cared for him[e] as if he were her own. [17]The women of the neighborhood gave him a name, saying, "At last, Naomi has a son!" They named him Obed,[f] and he became the father of Jesse, the father of David.

---

a 4:7 The sandal symbolized the man's property rights. To give up the sandal meant he would no longer walk on that property and claim it as his; he had transferred the rights to another. This custom had become obsolete by the time of writing, which shows that the book of Ruth was written well after the events of Ruth had transpired.

b 4:8 Jesus received the rights (the sandal) to supersede the law and obtained the promise of a more excellent ministry than the law (see Heb. 8:1–6). We are his "seed" and joint heirs of his ministry.

c 4:12 The people of Bethlehem were recalling the story of Judah's sinning sons who did not have sons of their own through disobedience in Gen. 38. Judah himself sinfully slept with his Canaanite daughter-in-law (thinking she was a prostitute). But what was sinful, Yahweh turned to goodness through redemption.

d 4:14 Or "May his name be declared in Israel."

e 4:16 That is, Naomi became like a foster mother to Obed.

f 4:17 The name *Obed* means "worshiper" or "servant [of Yahweh]." It is possibly a shortened form of Obadiah, which has the same meaning.

The Genealogy of David

18Now these are the descendants of Perez:*a*

Perez became the father of Hezron,
19Hezron the father of Ram,
Ram the father of Amminadab,
20Amminadab the father of Nahshon,
Nahshon the father of Salmon,
21Salmon the father of Boaz,
Boaz the father of Obed,
22Obed the father of Jesse,
who had a *famous* son, *King* David.*b*

---

a 4:18 See Matt. 1:2–6.

b 4:22 The story of Ruth shows that the family of David was in reality from Bethlehem and that David's great-grandmother was Ruth, a gentile from Moab.

YOUR PERSONAL INVITATION

TO FOLLOW JESUS

We all find ourselves in dark places needing some light—light that brings direction, healing, vision, warmth, and hope. Jesus said, "I am light to the world, and those who embrace me will experience life-giving light, and they will never walk in darkness" (John 8:12). Without the light and love of Jesus, this world is truly a dark place and we are lost forever.

Love unlocks mysteries. As we love Jesus, our hearts are unlocked to see more of his beauty and glory. When we stop defining ourselves by our failures and start seeing ourselves as the ones whom Jesus loves, our hearts begin to open to the breathtaking discovery of the wonder of Jesus Christ.

All that is recorded in the Scriptures is there so that you will fully believe that Jesus is the Son of God, and that through your faith in him you will experience eternal life by the power of his name (see John 20:31).

If you want this light and love in your life, say a prayer like this—whether for the first time or to express again your passionate desire to follow Jesus:

Jesus, you are the Light of the World. I want to follow you passionately and wholeheartedly, but my sins have separated me from you. Thank you for your love for me. Thank you for paying the price for my sins. I trust your finished work on the cross for my rescue. I turn away from the thoughts and deeds that have separated me from you. Forgive me and awaken me to love you with all my heart, mind, soul, and strength. I believe God raised you from the dead, and I want that new life to flow through me each day and for eternity. God, I give you my life. Fill me with your Spirit so that my life will honor you and I can fulfill your purpose for me. Amen.

You can be assured that what Jesus said about those who choose to follow him is true: "If you embrace my message and believe in the One who sent me, you will never face condemnation, for in me, you have already passed from the realm of death into the realm of eternal life!" (John 5:24). But there's more! Not only are you declared "not guilty" by God because of Jesus, you are also considered his most intimate friend (see John 15:15).

As you grow in your relationship with Jesus, continue to read the Bible, communicate with God through prayer, spend time with others who follow Jesus, and live out your faith daily and passionately. God bless you!